STUDIES IN MODERN CAPITALISM / ETUDES SUR LE CAPITALISME MODERNE

THE CAPITALIST WORLD-ECONOMY

Essays by Immanuel Wallerstein

Cambridge University Press
Editions de la Maison des Sciences de l'Homme

Studies in modern capitalism · Etudes sur le capitalisme moderne

The capitalist world-economy

Studies in modern capitalism · Etudes sur le capitalisme moderne

This series is devoted to an attempt to comprehend capitalism as a world-system. It will include monographs, collections of essays and colloquia around specific themes, written by historians and social scientists united by a common concern for the study of large-scale long-term social structure and social change.

The series is a joint enterprise of the Maison des Sciences de l'Homme in Paris and the Fernand Braudel Center for the Study of Economies, Historical Systems, and Civilizations at the State University of New York at Binghamton.

Other books in the series

Pierre Bourdieu: *Algeria 1960*
Andre Gunder Frank: *Mexican agriculture 1521–1630: transformation of the mode of production*

This book is published as part of the joint publishing agreement established in 1977 between the Fondation de la Maison des Sciences de l'Homme and the Syndics of the Cambridge University Press. Titles published under this arrangement may appear in any European language or, in the case of volumes of collected essays, in several languages.

New books will appear either as individual titles or in one of the series which the Maison des Sciences de l'Homme and the Cambridge University Press have jointly agreed to publish. All books published jointly by the Maison des Sciences de l'Homme and the Cambridge University Press will be distributed by the Press throughout the world.

The capitalist world-economy

Essays by
IMMANUEL WALLERSTEIN

Director, Fernand Braudel Center for the Study of
Economies, Historical Systems, and Civilizations
at the State University of New York at Binghamton

Cambridge University Press

Cambridge
London New York New Rochelle Melbourne Sydney

& Editions de la Maison des Sciences de l'Homme
Paris

Published by the Press Syndicate of the University of Cambridge
The Pitt Building, Trumpington Street, Cambridge CB2 1RP
32 East 57th Street, New York, NY 10022, USA
296 Beaconsfield Parade, Middle Park, Melbourne 3206, Australia
and
Editions de la Maison des Sciences de l'Homme
54 Boulevard Raspail, 75270 Paris Cedex 06

First published 1979
Reprinted 1979, 1980

Printed in Great Britain at the
University Press, Cambridge

Library of Congress Cataloguing in Publication Data

Wallerstein, Immanuel Maurice, 1930–

The capitalist world-economy.

(Studies in modern capitalism)

1. Economic history – Addresses, essays, lectures.
2. Capitalism – Addresses, essays, lectures.
3. Social conflict – Addresses, essays, lectures.
4. Social sciences – Addresses, essays, lectures.
I. Title. II. Series.
HC51.W27   1978   330.9   78-2955
ISBN 0 521 22085 8 hard cover
ISBN 0 521 29358 8 paperback

Contents

v

Some reflections on history, the social sciences, and politics

I have been trained as a social scientist, have a PhD in sociology, and am at present a professor of sociology. My recent book, *The Modern World-System*, is nonetheless regarded by some people as a work of history, more specifically of economic history. I am politically committed and active, and regard open polemics as a necessary part of my *scholarly* activity. Some might feel that I am caught in a set of contradictions. I myself feel that I am being thoroughly consistent and that my concern with history, with social science, and with politics is not a matter of engaging in three separate, even if related, activities, but is a *single* concern, informed by the belief that the strands cannot be separated, nor should they if they could.

Since I am aware that this is very much a minority viewpoint in world scholarship, let me first state, quite briefly and schematically, my view of how it came to be that there were thought to be many social sciences and not one, that history and social science were distinct activities, and that scholarship and politics were not to be mixed. It was after all not always so. As late as the Enlightenment, these three cleavages – within the social sciences, between social science and history, between scholarship and politics – would have seemed bizarre to many, if not all, social thinkers, and to social thinkers of radically different persuasions.

It is only in the nineteenth century that the very words we use to describe the cleavages – economics, sociology, anthropology, political science, geography, history, and indeed politics (as quite distinct from political science) – came to be invented, or at least to be used in their current, relatively narrow sense, and more importantly came to be incarnated in segregated institutional structures – departments within universities, distinct scholarly associations within national boundaries, political parties and other structures within the 'political arenas' of the various nation-states.

The period from 1815 to 1873 was the period of relatively undisputed British hegemony in the capitalist world-economy. Great Britain was the 'workshop of the world', meaning that its manufactured goods were produced so efficiently and cheaply that they could, by and large, undersell similar goods produced in other countries in the market of those other countries. In such a situation, freedom of the world market from political constraints would benefit British producers primarily, affording them maximum profit. Britain became the leading proponent of free trade and allied 'freedoms' such as the abolition of the slave trade. And the British Navy enforced British ideology against dissenters. Adam Smith's doctrines on the desirability of segregating the market from the polity and 'society' grew to be *a priori* assumptions not only in Britain but more widely.

It was in such an atmosphere that the social sciences were born and differentiated themselves one from the other. It was in such an atmosphere that the distinction between the nomothetic and the idiographic became central to discourse about the social world. It was in such an atmosphere that positivism swept the intellectual world – combining as it did the facile presumption that there were universal laws about man accessible through induction from individual observations about social reality, with the hopeful parallel to a presumably irresistible drive to technical progress incarnated in the new certainties of the physical sciences. It was an era of easy self-confidence for the masters of the world.

After 1873 came the doubts bred by the Great Depression and the growing strength of political resistance to world capitalism. But, despite the emergence of counterideologies to the 'British hegemonic' world-view, the latter dominated world social science, especially inside academia. It is only in the late 1960s, when Britain's successor, the United States, had reached the same point that Britain had in 1873, the end of the crest of hegemony, that we began to see a *widespread* fundamental assault on the nineteenth-century world-view within and without the academy.

Let me therefore do no more than assert my version of the epistemological premises of an alternative world-view, as it affects my choices as a scholar.

I do not believe that the various recognized social sciences – in alphabetical order, anthropology, economics, geography, political science, and sociology – are separate disciplines, that is, coherent bodies of subject matter organized around separate levels of generalization or separate meaningful units of analysis. I believe instead they are a single subject matter. Like biology or psychology, this subject matter is very vast, and it might be convenient to subdivide it for heuristic or organizational purposes, though not for epistemological or theoretical purposes. If we wish to subdivide it, I do not believe the present divisions are the rational subdivisions of a unified social science, since I believe the differences *within* any of the five so-called fields are as great as the differences *between* them, a sure sign of illogical organization.

Let me be clear. Disciplines do exist. I believe psychology is different from social science or biology. But not all historically established divisions make sense. In the period since the Second World War, 'botany' and 'zoology' have disappeared from the face of the world of knowledge, to be fused (which is more than merely being grouped together) in 'biology'. Biology now has many subfields but none to my knowledge is called 'botany' or 'zoology'. A similar fusion and redivision would be salutary in the social sciences. The resistance to it, however, is still great.

I go still further. Many who would agree with my views about a single social science nonetheless see a distinction between social science as generalizing and 'model-building' and history as concrete and particularistic. Even those who advocate close interaction between social science and history still talk in terms of two separate disciplines, two 'methods' which should inform and instruct each other.

I believe, however, that history and social science are one subject matter, which I shall call (inelegantly, but in order to avoid confusion) historical social science. The premises are simple. One cannot talk about (analyze) any particular set of occurrences without using concepts that imply theorems or generalizations about recurrent phenomena. Thus all 'history' is based on 'social science'. However, conversely, not only is all 'social science' a set of inductions from 'history', but there are *no* generalizations which are ahistorical, that is, universal. Concepts and theorems are historically rooted and valid only within certain parameters of time and space, however broad. Nor do I regard this as simply the consequence of scholarly fallibility, one day to be overcome by greater knowledge. I regard this as inherent in the assumption of a permanently evolving social world. (Whether this last premise is equally applicable to the physical world is not a matter on which I am competent to have a judgment, although my initial prejudice would be to suspect it is so.)

Let me once again be clear. I do not deny that in a piece of research one might not be more immediately concerned with explaining why a certain sequence of events occurred and that, in another piece of work, one might be more immediately concerned with identifying the patterns that are similar in several sets of events. But to reify the motives of scholars in doing particular research into two disciplines – the first history, the second social science – is to give misleading substance to the accidental and passing, and to miss the intellectual unity of the two enterprises. It is also to miss the fact that most competent scholars spend most of their time moving back and forth between the two emphases, rather than 'specializing' in one of them.

Finally, and no doubt most controversially, I would drastically narrow, if not abolish, the gap between historical social science and politics. I do not believe there is or could be such a thing as value-free historical social science. Every choice of conceptual framework is a political option. Every assertion of 'truth', even if one qualifies it as transitory truth, or heuristic theory, is an assertion of value. All good scholarship is polemic (but not all polemic is good scholarship).

I believe that our concepts reflect the evolving social situations in which we live. I have earlier argued that this precisely explains some assumptions about epistemology which have been prevalent and are presently being challenged. To take another very obvious current example, the 'Third World' exists as a concept which organizes some analyses because (I simplify) there was a Bandung Conference in 1955. The 'Third World' as a concept is now disappearing in the 1970s because (again I simplify) of Nixon's visit to Mao and the OPEC price rise. The emergence and decline of a concept does not mean it did not have 'truth value' *for* a certain historical period and *about* a certain historical period.

Not all concepts originate with self-proclaimed scholars, that is, with specialists in the manipulation of ideas and large bodies of data. Many, indeed perhaps most, concepts originate among participants in the 'real world'. And scholars are sometimes among the last, rather than the first, to perceive the utility of these concepts. In fact, I believe that when one talks of the merits of the unity of theory and praxis, one is referring precisely to the fact that the scholar who is not personally involved is the weaker for it as a scholar. The medievalist who is not immersed in some archives may never do very useful analysis. But it may equally be true that the medievalist who is not immersed in the political environment of today may not be able to perceive very obvious 'truths' about the medieval world.

Let me once again be clear. I am not merely perorating against the 'ivory tower'. I am arguing for an integral connection between historical social science and politics which is avowed and unashamed. I do not believe this detracts from 'objectivity'. Quite the contrary, I believe this is the *only possible* road to objectivity. The so-called disengaged scholar has merely erected some barriers to the observation of his premises. Objectivity can only be the vector of work representing fairly the totality of social forces in the social world. This is not truth as the result of Mills' 'marketplace of ideas', but truth as the composite statement of existent social reality.[1]

The implications of my premises for the methodology of historical social science are the following. In the nineteenth-century world-view history was the reconstruction of the particular by its isolation from more general trends, and the social sciences attempted to discover universal laws by assembling the particular data of either 'historians' or the drones of the profession, the empirical researchers. The name of the first game was to identify uniqueness; the name of the second was to establish abstract propositions, the more abstract the better.

However, if there is but a single historical social science integrally linked to politics, then perhaps we should invert our methodology. We may still specify; we may still abstract. But now we would neither specify in order to isolate the unique, nor accumulate specifications in order to abstract. Perhaps our new motto should

---

1. I developed this argument earlier in 'L'organisation sociale des sciences humaines et l'objectivité', *Cahiers internationaux de sociologie*, 50 (1971), 41–78.

be: the purpose of abstractions is to arrive at specificity. In trying to *interpret* the real world, which is perhaps the only thing we can do, we must apply to it successive abstractions, each capturing a part of the global reality (whatever this be, for the purposes of a specific piece of work) until, by adding abstraction to abstraction, we have arrived at a comprehensible picture of what has existed over time and space (and how that relates to the social time and space in which we live and work).

What is so different about this approach from that of the other world-view is what lies at the end of the tunnel. Truth is no longer defined as 'wie es eigentlich gewesen ist', a theoretically unrealizable objective (even if it were a desirable one, which I very much doubt). Nor is truth seen to be a set of theorems, ultimately sparse and mathematical. Truth becomes an interpretation, meaningful for our times, of the social world as it was, as it is, as it will be.

Acknowledgments

The majority of articles in this volume of collected essays has already appeared separately. We are grateful to the editors of these publications for their kind cooperation in granting permission to publish here. The following chapters originally appeared in:

1   *Comparative Studies in Society and History*, 16:4 (September 1974), 387–415
2   *Studies in Comparative International Development*, 7 (Summer 1972), 95–101.
3   I. Wallerstein (ed.), *World Inequality* (Montreal: Black Rose Books, 1975), pp. 12–28
4   *African Studies Review*, 17 (April 1974), 1–26
5   *Theory and Society*, 3 (Winter 1976), 461–83
6   *Studies in Comparative International Development*, 12 (Spring 1977), 29–40
7   L. Coser and O. Larsen (eds.), *The Uses and Controversy of Sociology* (New York: Free Press, 1976), pp. 131–5
8   *Social Forces*, 55:2 (December 1976), 273–83
9   *British Journal of Sociology*, 27:3 (September 1976), 345–54
10   Ernest Q. Campbell (ed.), *Racial Tensions and National Identity* (Nashville: Vanderbilt University Press, 1972), pp. 206–26
11   Edward Allworth (ed.), *The Nationality Question in Soviet Central Asia* (New York: Praeger, 1973), pp. 168–75
12   *Canadian Journal of African Studies*, 7:3 (1973), 375–80
13   *American Journal of Sociology*, 81:5 (March 1976), 1199–213
14   *Politics and Society*, 5:3 (1975), 367–75
15   Sixth Sorokin Lecture (Saskatoon: University of Saskatchewan, 1975)

16 Originally prepared for a volume of essays on Fanon to be edited by Emmanuel Hansen and Adele Jinadu
17 Originally prepared for seminar on the 'Nuevo Orden Internacional' sponsored by the Centro de Estudios de Desarrollo (CENDES) of the Universidad Central de Venezuela, 17–21 October 1977

Part I

The inequalities of core and periphery

---

1 ✦ The rise and future demise of the world capitalist system: concepts for comparative analysis

The growth within the capitalist world-economy of the industrial sector of production, the so-called 'industrial revolution', was accompanied by a very strong current of thought which defined this change as both a process of organic development and of progress. There were those who considered these economic developments and the concomitant changes in social organization to be some penultimate stage of world development whose final working out was but a matter of time. These included such diverse thinkers as Saint-Simon, Comte, Hegel, Weber, Durkheim. And then there were the critics, most notably Marx, who argued, if you will, that the nineteenth-century present was only an antepenultimate stage of development, that the capitalist world was to know a cataclysmic political revolution which would then lead in the fullness of time to a final societal form, in this case the classless society.

One of the great strengths of Marxism was that, being an oppositional and hence critical doctrine, it called attention not merely to the contradictions of the system but to those of its ideologists, by appealing to the empirical evidence of historical reality which unmasked the irrelevancy of the models proposed for the explanation of the social world. The Marxist critics saw in abstracted models concrete rationalization, and they argued their case fundamentally by pointing to the failure of their

1

opponents to analyze the social whole. As Lukacs put it, 'it is not the primacy of economic motives in historical explanation that constitutes the decisive difference between Marxism and bourgeois thought, but the point of view of totality'.[1]

In the mid twentieth century, the dominant theory of development in the core countries of the capitalist world-economy has added little to the theorizing of the nineteenth-century progenitors of this mode of analysis, except to quantify the models and to abstract them still further, by adding on epicyclical codas to the models in order to account for ever further deviations from empirical expectations.

What is wrong with such models has been shown many times over, and from many standpoints. I cite only one critic, a non-Marxist, Robert Nisbet, whose very cogent reflections on what he calls the 'Western theory of development' concludes with this summary:

[We] turn to history and only to history if what we are seeking are the actual causes, sources, and conditions of overt changes of patterns and structures in society. Conventional wisdom to the contrary in modern social theory, we shall not find the explanation of change in those studies which are abstracted from history; whether these be studies of small groups in the social laboratory, group dynamics generally, staged experiments in social interaction, or mathematical analyses of so-called social systems. Nor will we find the sources of change in contemporary revivals of the comparative method with its ascending staircase of cultural similarities and differences plucked from all space and time.[2]

Shall we then turn to the critical schools, in particular Marxism, to give us a better account of social reality? In principle yes; in practice there are many different, often contradictory, versions extant of 'Marxism'. But what is more fundamental is the fact that in many countries Marxism is now the official state doctrine. Marxism is no longer exclusively an oppositional doctrine as it was in the nineteenth century.

The social fate of official doctrines is that they suffer a constant social pressure towards dogmatism and apologia, difficult although by no means impossible to counteract, and that they thereby often fall into the same intellectual dead end of ahistorical model building. Here the critique of Fernand Braudel is most pertinent:

1. George Lukacs, 'The Marxism of Rosa Luxemburg', in *History and Class Consciousness* (London: Merlin Press, 1968), p. 27.
2. Robert A. Nisbet, *Social Change and History* (New York: Oxford University Press, 1969), pp. 302–3. I myself would exempt from this criticism the economic history literature.

Marxism is a whole collection of models...I shall protest..., more or less, not against the model, but rather against the use to which people have thought themselves entitled to put it. The genius of Marx, the secret of his enduring power, lies in his having been the first to construct true social models, starting out from the long term (*la longue durée*). These models have been fixed permanently in their simplicity; they have been given the force of law and they have been treated as ready-made, automatic explanations, applicable in all places to all societies...In this way has the creative power of the most powerful social analysis of the last century been shackled. It will be able to regain its strength and vitality only in the long term.[3]

Nothing illustrates the distortions of ahistorical models of social change better than the dilemmas to which the concept of stages gives rise. If we are to deal with social transformations over long historical time (Braudel's 'the long term'), and if we are to give an explanation of both continuity and transformation, then we must logically divide the long term into segments in order to observe the structural changes from time A to time B. These segments are however not discrete but continuous in reality; *ergo* they are 'stages' in the 'development' of a social structure, a development which we determine however not *a priori* but *a posteriori*. That is, we cannot predict the future concretely, but we can predict the past.

The crucial issue when comparing 'stages' is to determine the units of which the 'stages' are synchronic portraits (or 'ideal types', if you will). And the fundamental error of ahistorical social science (including ahistorical versions of Marxism) is to reify parts of the totality into such units and then to compare these reified structures.

For example, we may take modes of disposition of agricultural production, and term them subsistence cropping and cash cropping. We may then see these as entities which are 'stages' of a development. We may talk about decisions of groups of peasants to shift from one to the other. We may describe other partial entities, such as states, as having within them two separate 'economies', each based on a different mode of disposition of agricultural production. If we take each of these successive steps, all of which are false steps, we will end up with the misleading concept of the 'dual economy' as have many liberal economists dealing with the so-called underdeveloped countries of the world.

3. Fernand Braudel, 'History and the Social Sciences', in Peter Burke (ed.), *Economy and Society in Early Modern Europe* (London: Routledge and Kegan Paul, 1972), pp. 38–9.

Still worse, we may reify a misreading of British history into a set of universal 'stages' as Rostow does.

Marxist scholars have often fallen into exactly the same trap. If we take modes of payment of agricultural labor and contrast a 'feudal' mode wherein the laborer is permitted to retain for subsistence a part of his agricultural production with a 'capitalist' mode wherein the same laborer turns over the totality of his production to the landowner, receiving part of it back in the form of wages, we may then see these two modes as 'stages' of a development. We may talk of the interests of 'feudal' landowners in preventing the conversion of their mode of payment to a system of wages. We may then explain the fact that in the twentieth century a partial entity, say a state in Latin America, has not yet industrialized as the consequence of its being dominated by such landlords. if we take each of these successive steps, all of which are false steps, we will end up with the misleading concept of a 'state dominated by feudal elements', as though such a thing could possibly exist in a capitalist world-economy. But, as André Gunder Frank has clearly spelled out, such a myth dominated for a long time 'traditional Marxist' thought in Latin America.[4]

Not only does the misidentification of the entities to be compared lead us into false concepts, but it creates a non-problem: can stages be skipped? This question is only logically meaningful if we have 'stages' that 'coexist' within a single empirical framework. If within a capitalist world-economy, we define one state as feudal, a second as capitalist, and a third as socialist, then and only then can we pose the question: can a country 'skip' from the feudal stage to the socialist stage of national development without 'passing through capitalism'?

But if there is no such thing as 'national development' (if by that we mean a natural history), and if the proper entity of comparison is the world system, then the problem of stage skipping is nonsense. If a stage can be skipped, it isn't a stage. And we know this a posteriori.

If we are to talk of stages, then – and we should talk of stages – it must be stages of social systems, that is, of totalities. And the only totalities that exist or have historically existed are minisystems

4. See André Gunder Frank, 'The Myth of Feudalism', in *Capitalism and Under-development in Latin America* (New York: Monthly Review Press, 1967), pp. 221–42.

and world-systems, and in the nineteenth and twentieth centuries there has been only one world-system in existence, the capitalist world-economy.

We take the defining characteristic of a social system to be the existence within it of a division of labor, such that the various sectors or areas within are dependent upon economic exchange with others for the smooth and continuous provisioning of the needs of the area. Such economic exchange can clearly exist without a common political structure and even more obviously without sharing the same culture.

A minisystem is an entity that has within it a complete division of labor, and a single cultural framework. Such systems are found only in very simple agricultural or hunting and gathering societies. Such minisystems no longer exist in the world. Furthermore, there were fewer in the past than is often asserted, since any such system that became tied to an empire by the payment of tribute as 'protection costs'[5] ceased by that fact to be a 'system', no longer having a self-contained division of labor. For such an area, the payment of tribute marked a shift, in Polanyi's language, from being a reciprocal economy to participating in a larger redistributive economy.[6]

Leaving aside the now defunct minisystems, the only kind of social system is a world-system, which we define quite simply as a unit with a single division of labor and multiple cultural systems. It follows logically that there can, however, be two varieties of such world-systems, one with a common political system and one without. We shall designate these respectively as world-empires and world-economies.

It turns out empirically that world-economies have historically been unstable structures leading either towards disintegration or conquest by one group and hence transformation into a world-empire. Examples of such world-empires emerging from world-economies are all the so-called great civilizations of premodern times, such as China, Egypt, Rome (each at appropriate periods

---

5. See Frederic Lane's discussion of 'protein costs' which is reprinted in part 3 of *Venice and History* (Baltimore: Johns Hopkins Press, 1966). For the specific discussion of tribute, see pp. 389–90, 416–20.
6. See Karl Polanyi, 'The Economy as Instituted Process', in Karl Polanyi, Conrad M. Arsenberg and Harry W. Pearson (eds.), *Trade and Market in the Early Empire* (Glencoe: Free Press, 1957), pp. 243–70.

of its history). On the other hand, the so-called nineteenth-century empires, such as Great Britain or France, were not world-empires at all, but nation-states with colonial appendages operating within the framework of a world-economy.

World-empires were basically redistributive in economic form. No doubt they bred clusters of merchants who engaged in economic exchange (primarily long distance trade), but such clusters, however large, were a minor part of the total economy and not fundamentally determinative of its fate. Such long-distance trade tended to be, as Polanyi argues, 'administered trade' and not market trade, utilizing 'ports of trade'.

It was only with the emergence of the modern world-economy in sixteenth-century Europe that we saw the full development and economic predominance of market trade. This was the system called capitalism. Capitalism and a world-economy (that is, a single division of labor but multiple polities and cultures) are obverse sides of the same coin. One does not cause the other. We are merely defining the same indivisible phenomenon by different characteristics.

How and why it came about that this particular European world-economy of the sixteenth century did not become transformed into a redistributive world-empire but developed definitively as a capitalist world-economy I have explained elsewhere.[7] The genesis of this world-historical turning point is marginal to the issues under discussion in this paper, which is rather what conceptual apparatus one brings to bear on the analysis of developments within the framework of precisely such a capitalist world-economy.

Let us therefore turn to the capitalist world-economy. We shall seek to deal with two pseudoproblems, created by the trap of not analyzing totalities: the so-called persistence of feudal forms, and the so-called creation of socialist systems. In doing this, we shall offer an alternative model with which to engage in comparative analysis, one rooted in the historically specific totality which is the world capitalist economy. We hope to demonstrate thereby that to be historically specific is not to fail to be analytically universal. On the contrary, the only road to nomothetic propositions is

7. See my *The Modern World-System: Capitalist Agriculture and the Origins of the European World-Economy in the Sixteenth Century* (New York: Academic Press, 1974).

through the historically concrete, just as in cosmology the only road to a theory of the laws governing the universe is through the concrete analysis of the historical evolution of this same universe.[8] On the 'feudalism' debate, we take as a starting point Frank's concept of 'the development of underdevelopment', that is, the view that the economic structures of contemporary under-developed countries is not the form which a 'traditional' society takes upon contact with 'developed' societies, not an earlier stage in the 'transition' to industrialization. It is rather the result of being involved in the world-economy as a peripheral, raw material producing area, or as Frank puts it for Chile, 'underdevelop-ment...is the necessary product of four centuries of capitalism itself'.[9]

This formulation runs counter to a large body of writing concerning the underdeveloped countries that was produced in the period 1950–70, a literature which sought the factors that explained 'development' within non-systems such as 'states' or 'cultures' and, once having presumably discovered these factors, urged their reproduction in underdeveloped areas as the road to salvation.[10]

Frank's theory also runs counter, as we have already noted, to the received orthodox version of Marxism that had long domin-ated Marxist parties and intellectual circles, for example in Latin America. This older 'Marxist' view of Latin America as a set of feudal societies in a more or less prebourgeois stage of develop-ment has fallen before the critiques of Frank and many others as well as before the political reality symbolized by the Cuban revolution and all its many consequences. Recent analysis in Latin America has centered instead around the concept of 'dependence'.[11]

8. Philip Abrams concludes a similar plea with this admonition: 'The academic and intellectual dissociation of history and sociology seems, then, to have had the effect of deterring both disciplines from attending seriously to the most important issues involved in the understanding of social transition'. 'The Sense of the Past and the Origins of Sociology', *Past and Present*, 55 (May 1972), 32.
9. Frank, 'The Myth of Feudalism', p. 3.
10. Frank's critique, now classic, of these theories is entitled 'Sociology of Development and Underdevelopment of Sociology' and is reprinted in *Latin America: Underdevelop-ment or Revolution* (New York: Monthly Review Press, 1969), pp. 21–94.
11. See Theotonio Dos Santos, *La Nueva Dependencia* (Buenos Aires: s/ediciones, 1968).

However, recently, Ernesto Laclau has made an attack on Frank which, while accepting the critique of dualist doctrines, refuses to accept the categorization of Latin American states as capitalist. Instead Laclau asserts that 'the world capitalist system. . .includes, *at the level of its definition,* various modes of production'. He accuses Frank of confusing the two concepts of the 'capitalist mode of production' and 'participation in a world capitalist economic system'.[12]

Of course, if it's a matter of definition, then there can be no argument. But then the polemic is scarcely useful since it is reduced to a question of semantics. Furthermore, Laclau insists that the definition is not his but that of Marx, which is more debatable. Rosa Luxemburg put her finger on a key element in Marx's ambiguity or inconsistency in this particular debate, the ambiguity which enables both Frank and Laclau to trace their thoughts to Marx:

Admittedly, Marx dealt in detail with the process of appropriating non-capitalist means of production [NB, Luxemburg is referring to primary products produced in peripheral areas under conditions of coerced labor] as well as with the transformation of the peasants into a capitalist proletariat. Chapter XXIV of *Capital,* Vol. 1, is devoted to describing the origin of the English proletariat, of the capitalistic agricultural tenant class and of industrial capital, with particular emphasis on the looting of colonial countries by European capital. Yet we must bear in mind that all this is treated solely with a view to so-called primitive accumulation. For Marx, these processes are incidental, illustrating merely the genesis of capital, its first appearance in the world; they are, as it were, travails by which the capitalist mode of production emerges from a feudal society. As soon as he comes to analyze the capitalist process of production and circulation, he reaffirms the universal and exclusive domination of capitalist production [NB, that is, production based on wage labor].[13]

There is, after all, a substantive issue in this debate. It is in fact the same substantive issue that underlay the debate between

12. Ernesto Laclau (*h*), 'Feudalism and Capitalism in Latin America', *New Left Review*, 67 (May–June 1971), 37–8.
13. *The Accumulation of Capital* (New York: Monthly Review Press, 1968), pp. 364–5. Luxemburg however, as is evident, lends herself further to the confusion by using the terminology of 'capitalistic' and 'non-capitalistic' modes of production. Leaving these terms aside, her vision is impeccable: 'From the aspect both of realising the surplus value and of producing the material elements of constant capital, international trade is a prime necessity for the historical existence of capitalism – an international trade which under actual conditions is essentially an exchange between capitalistic and non-capitalistic modes of production'. *Ibid.*, p. 359. She shows similar insight into the need of recruiting labor for core areas from the periphery, what she calls 'the increase in the variable capital'. See *ibid.*, p. 361.

Maurice Dobb and Paul Sweezy in the early 1950s about the 'transition from feudalism to capitalism' that occurred in early modern Europe.[14] The substantive issue, in my view, concerns the appropriate unit of analysis for the purpose of comparison. Basically, although neither Sweezy nor Frank is quite explicit on this point, and though Dobb and Laclau can both point to texts of Marx that seem clearly to indicate that they more faithfully follow Marx's argument, I believe both Sweezy and Frank better follow the spirit of Marx if not his letter[15] and that, leaving Marx quite out of the picture, they bring us nearer to an understanding of what actually happened and is happening than do their opponents.

What is the picture, both analytical and historical, that Laclau constructs? The heart of the problem revolves around the existence of free labor as the defining characteristic of a capitalist mode of production:

The fundamental economic relationship of capitalism is constituted by the *free* [italics mine] labourer's sale of his labour-power, whose necessary precondition is the loss by the direct producer of ownership of the means of production...

If we now confront Frank's affirmation that the socio-economic complexes of Latin America has been capitalist since the Conquest Period... with the currently available empirical evidence, we must conclude that the 'capitalist' thesis is indefensible. In regions with dense indigenous populations – Mexico, Peru, Bolivia, or Guatemala – the direct producers were not despoiled of their ownership of the means of production, while extra-economic coercion to maximize various systems of labour service... was progressively intensified. In the plantations of the West Indies, the economy was based on a mode of production constituted by slave labour, while in the mining areas there developed disguised forms of slavery and other types of forced labour which bore not the slightest resemblance to the formation of a capitalist proletariat.[16]

14. The debate begins with Maurice Dobb, *Studies in the Development of Capitalism* (London: Routledge and Kegan Paul, 1946). Paul Sweezy criticized Dobb in 'The Transition from Feudalism to Capitalism', *Science and Society*, 14: 2 (Spring 1950), 134–57, with a 'Reply' by Dobb in the same issue. From that point on many others got into the debate in various parts of the world. I have reviewed and discussed this debate *in extenso* in ch. 1 of *The Modern World-System*.
15. It would take us into a long discursus to defend the proposition that, like all great thinkers, there was the Marx who was the prisoner of his social location and the Marx, the genius, who could on occasion see from a wider vantage point. The former Marx generalized from British history. The latter Marx is the one who has inspired a critical conceptual framework of social reality. W. W. Rostow incidentally seeks to refute the former Marx by offering an alternative generalization from British history. He ignores the latter and more significant Marx. See *The Stages of Economic Growth: A Non-Communist Manifesto* (Cambridge: University Press, 1960).
16. Laclau, 'Feudalism and Capitalism', pp. 25, 30.

There in a nutshell it is. Western Europe, at least England from the late seventeenth century on, had primarily landless, wage-earning laborers. In Latin America, then and to some extent still now, laborers were not proletarians, but slaves or 'serfs'. If proletariat, then capitalism. Of course. To be sure. But is England, or Mexico, or the West Indies a unit of analysis? Does each have a separate 'mode of production'? Or is the unit (for the sixteenth–eighteenth centuries) the European world-economy, including England *and* Mexico, in which case what was the 'mode of production' of this world-economy?

Before we argue our response to this question, let us turn to quite another debate, one between Mao Tse-Tung and Liu Shao-Chi in the 1960s concerning whether or not the Chinese People's Republic was a 'socialist state'. This is a debate that has a long background in the evolving thought of Marxist parties.

Marx, as has been often noted, said virtually nothing about the post-revolutionary political process. Engels spoke quite late in his writings of the 'dictatorship of the proletariat'. It was left to Lenin to elaborate a theory about such a 'dictatorship', in his pamphlet *State and Revolution*, published in the last stages before the Bolshevik takeover of Russia, that is, in August 1917. The coming to power of the Bolsheviks led to a considerable debate as to the nature of the regime that had been established. Eventually a theoretical distinction emerged in Soviet thought between 'socialism' and 'communism' as two stages in historical development, one realizable in the present and one only in the future. In 1936 Stalin proclaimed that the USSR had become a socialist (but not yet a communist) state. Thus we now had firmly established *three* stages after bourgeois rule: a post-revolutionary government, a socialist state, and eventually communism. When, after the Second World War, various regimes dominates by the Communist Party were established in various east European states, these regimes were proclaimed to be 'peoples' democracies', a new name then given to the post-revolutionary stage one. At later points, some of these countries, for example Czechoslovakia, asserted they had passed into stage two, that of becoming a socialist republic.

In 1961, the 22nd Congress of the CPSU invented a fourth stage, in between the former second and third stages: that of a socialist state which had become a 'state of the whole people', a stage it was contended the USSR had at that point reached. The Programme of the Congress asserted that 'the state as an organization of the entire people will survive until the complete victory of communism'.[17] One of its commentators defines the 'intrinsic substance (and) chief distinctive feature' of this stage: 'The state of the whole people is the first state in the world with no class struggle to contend with and, hence, with no class domination and no suppression.'[18]

One of the earliest signs of a major disagreement in the 1950s between the Communist Party of the Soviet Union and the Chinese Communist Party was a theoretical debate that revolved around the question of the 'gradual transition to Communism'. Basically, the CPSU argued that different socialist states would proceed separately in effectuating such a transition whereas the CCP argued that all socialist states would proceed simultaneously.

As we can see, this last form of the debate about 'stages' implicitly raised the issue of the unit of analysis, for in effect the CCP was arguing that 'communism' was a characteristic not of nation-states but of the world-economy as a whole. This debate was transposed onto the internal Chinese scene by the ideological debate, now known to have deep and long-standing roots, that gave rise eventually to the Cultural Revolution.

One of the corollaries of these debates about 'stages' was whether or not the class struggle continued in post-revolutionary states prior to the achievement of communism. The 22nd Congress of the CPSU in 1961 had argued that the USSR had become a state without an internal class struggle, there were no longer existing antagonistic classes within it. Without speaking of the USSR, Mao Tse-Tung in 1957 had asserted in China:

The class struggle is by no means over... It will continue to be long and tortuous, and at times will even become very acute... Marxists are still a minority among the entire population as well as among the intellectuals. Therefore, Marxism must still develop through struggle... Such struggles will never end. This is the law of development of truth and, naturally, of Marxism as well.[19]

17. Cited in F. Burlatsky, *The State and Communism* (Moscow: Progress Publishers, n.d. [1961]), p. 95.
18. *Ibid.*, p. 97.
19. Mao Tse-Tung, *On The Correct Handling of Contradictions Among The People*, 7th edn, revised translation (Peking: Foreign Languages Press, 1966), pp. 37–8.

If such struggles *never* end, then many of the facile generalizations about 'stages' which 'socialist' states are presumed to go through are thrown into question.

During the Cultural Revolution, it was asserted that Mao's report *On the Correct Handling of Contradiction Among the People* cited above, as well as one other, 'entirely repudiated the "theory of the dying out of the class struggle" advocated by Liu Shao-Chi. . .'[20] Specifically, Mao argued that 'the elimination of the system of ownership by the exploiting classes through socialist transformation is not equal to the disappearance of struggle in the political and ideological spheres'.[21]

Indeed, this is the logic of a *cultural* revolution. Mao is asserting that even if there is the achievement of *political* power (dictatorship of the proletariat) and *economic* transformation (abolition of private ownership of the means of production), the revolution is still far from complete. Revolution is not an event but a process. This process Mao calls 'socialist society' – in my view a somewhat confusing choice of words, but no matter – and 'socialist society covers a fairly long historical period'.[22] Furthermore, 'there are classes and class struggle throughout the period of socialist society'.[23] The Tenth Plenum of the 8th Central Committee of the CCP, meeting from 24 to 27 September 1962, in endorsing Mao's views, omitted the phrase 'socialist society' and talked instead of 'the historical period of proletarian revolution and proletarian dictatorship, . . . the historical period of transition from capitalism to communism', which it said 'will last scores of years or even longer' and during which 'there is a class struggle between the proletariat and the bourgeosie and struggle between the socialist road and the capitalist road'.[24]

20. *Long Live The Invincible Thought of Mao Tse-Tung!*, undated pamphlet, issued between 1967 and 1969, translated in *Current Background*, 884 (18 July 1969), 14.
21. This is the position taken by Mao Tse-Tung in his speech to the Work Conference of the Central Committee at Peitaiho in August 1962, as reported in the pamphlet, *Long Live...*, p. 20. Mao's position was subsequently endorsed at the 10th Plenum of the 8th CCP Central Committee in September 1962, a session this same pamphlet describes as 'a great turning point in the violent struggle between the proletarian headquarters and the bourgeois headquarters in China'. *Ibid.*, p. 21.
22. Remarks made by Mao at 10th Plenum, cited in *ibid.*, p. 20.
23. Mao Tse-Tung, 'Talk on the Question of Democratic Centralism', 30 January 1962, in *Current Background*, 891 (8 October 1969), 39.
24. 'Communiqué of the 10th Plenary Session of the 8th Central Committee of the Chinese Communist Party', *Current Background*, 691 (5 October 1962), 3.

We do not have directly Liu's counter arguments. We might however take as an expression of the alternative position a recent analysis published in the USSR on the relationship of the socialist system and world development. There it is asserted that at some unspecified point after the Second World War, 'socialism outgrew the bounds of one country and became a world system...'[25] It is further argued that: 'Capitalism, emerging in the 16th century, became a world economic system only in the 19th century. It took the bourgeois revolutions 300 years to put an end to the power of the feudal elite. It took socialism 30 or 40 years to generate the forces for a new world system.'[26] Finally, this book speaks of 'capitalism's international division of labor'[27] and 'international socialist cooperation of labor'[28] as two separate phenomena, drawing from this counterposition the policy conclusion: 'Socialist unity has suffered a serious setback from the divisive course being pursued by the incumbent leadership of the Chinese People's Republic', and attributes this to 'the great-power chauvinism of Mao Tse-Tung and his group'.[29]

Note well the contrast between these two positions. Mao Tse-Tung is arguing for viewing 'socialist society' as process rather than structure. Like Frank and Sweezy, and once again implicitly rather than explicitly, he is taking the world-system rather than the nation-state as the unit of analysis. The analysis by USSR scholars by contrast specifically argues the existence of *two* world-systems with two divisions of labor existing side by side, although the socialist system is acknowledged to be 'divided'. If divided politically, is it united economically? Hardly, one would think; in which case what is the substructural base to argue the existence of the system? Is it merely a moral imperative? And are then the Soviet scholars defending their concepts on the basis of Kantian metaphysics?

Let us see now if we can reinterpret the issues developed in these two debates within the framework of a general set of concepts that could be used to analyze the functioning of world-

25. Yuri Sdobnikov (ed.), *Socialism and Capitalism: Score and Prospects* (Moscow: Progress Publications, 1971), p. 20. The book was compiled by staff members of the Institute of World Economy and International Relations, and the senior contributor was Professor V. Aboltin.
26. *Ibid.*, p. 21.   27. *Ibid.*, p. 26.
28. *Ibid.*, p. 24.   29. *Ibid.*, p. 25.

systems, and particularly of the historically specific capitalist world-economy that has existed for about four or five centuries now.

We must start with how one demonstrates the existence of a single division of labor. We can regard a division of labor as a grid which is substantially interdependent. Economic actors operate on some assumption (obviously seldom clear to any individual actor) that the totality of their essential needs – of sustenance, protection, and pleasure – will be met over a reasonable time span by a combination of their own productive activities and exchange in some form. The smallest grid that would substantially meet the expectations of the overwhelming majority of actors within those boundaries constitutes a single division of labor.

The reason why a small farming community whose only significant link to outsiders is the payment of annual tribute does not constitute such a single division of labor is that the assumptions of persons living in it concerning the provision of protection involve an 'exchange' with other parts of the world-empire.

This concept of a grid of exchange relationships assumes, however, a distinction between *essential* exchanges and what might be called 'luxury' exchanges. This is to be sure a distinction rooted in the social perceptions of the actors and hence in both their social organization and their culture. These perceptions can change. But this distinction is crucial if we are not to fall into the trap of identifying *every* exchange activity as evidence of the existence of a system. Members of a system (a minisystem or a world-system) can be linked in limited exchanges with elements located outside the system, in the 'external arena' of the system.

The form of such an exchange is very limited. Elements of the two systems can engage in an exchange of preciosities. That is, each can export to the other what is in *its* system socially defined as worth little in return for the import of what in its system is defined as worth much. This is not a mere pedantic definitional exercise, as the exchange of preciosities *between* world-systems can be extremely important in the historical evolution of a given world-system. The reason why this is so important is that in an exchange of preciosities, the importer is 'reaping a windfall' and not obtaining a profit. Both exchange partners can reap windfalls simultaneously but only one can obtain maximum profit, since the exchange of surplus value within a system is a zero-sum game.

We are, as you see, coming to the essential feature of a capitalist world-economy, which is production for sale in a market in which the object is to realize the maximum profit. In such a system production is constantly expanded as long as further production is profitable, and men constantly innovate new ways of producing things that will expand the profit margin. The classical economists tried to argue that such production for the market was somehow the 'natural' state of man. But the combined writings of the anthropologists and the Marxists left few in doubt that such a mode of production (these days called 'capitalism') was only one of several possible modes.

Since, however, the intellectual debate between the liberals and the Marxists took place in the era of the industrial revolution, there has tended to be a *de facto* confusion between industrialism and capitalism. This left the liberals after 1945 in the dilemma of explaining how a presumably non-capitalist society, the USSR, had industrialized. The most sophisicated response has been to conceive of 'liberal capitalism' and 'socialism' as two variants of an 'industrial society', two variants destined to 'converge'. This argument has been trenchantly expounded by Raymond Aron.[30] But the same confusion left the Marxists, including Marx, with the problem of explaining what was the mode of production that predominated in Europe from the sixteenth to the eighteenth centuries, that is before the industrial revolution. Essentially, most Marxists have talked of a 'transitional' stage, which is in fact a blurry non-concept with no operational indicators. This dilemma is heightened if the unit of analysis used is the state, in which case one has to explain why the transition has occurred at different rates and times in different countries.[31]

Marx himself handled this by drawing a distinction between 'merchant capitalism' and 'industrial capitalism'. This I believe is unfortunate teminology, since it leads to such conclusions as that of Maurice Dobb who says of this 'transitional' period:

30. Say Raymond Aron, *Dix-huit leçons de la société industrielle* (Paris: Ed. Gallimard, 1962).
31. This is the dilemma, I feel, of E. J. Hobsbawm in explaining his so-called 'crisis of the seventeenth century'. See his *Past and Present* article reprinted (with various critiques) in Trevor Aston (ed.), *The Crisis of the Seventeenth Century* (London: Routledge and Kegan Paul, 1965).

But why speak of this as a stage of capitalism at all? The workers were generally not proletarianized: that is, they were not separated from the instruments of production, nor even in many cases from occupation of a plot of land. Production was scattered and decentralized and not concentrated. *The capitalist was still predominantly a merchant* [italics mine] who did not control production directly and did not impose his own discipline upon the work of artisan-craftsmen, who both laboured as individual (or family) units and retained a considerable measure of independence (if a dwindling one).[32]

One might well say: why indeed? Especially if one remembers how much emphasis Dobb places a few pages earlier on capitalism as a mode of *production* – how then can the capitalist be primarily a merchant? – on the concentration of such ownership in the hands of a few, and on the fact that capitalism is not synonymous with private ownership, capitalism being different from a system in which the owners are 'small peasant producers or artisan-producers'. Dobb argues that a defining feature of private ownership under capitalism is that some are 'obliged to [work for those that own] since [they own] nothing and [have] no access to means of production [and hence] have no other means of livelihood'.[33] Given this contradiction, the answer Dobb gives to his own question is in my view very weak: 'While it is true that at this date the situation was transitional, and capital-to-wage-labour relations were still immaturely developed, the latter were already beginning to assume their characteristic features'.[34]

If capitalism is a mode of production, production for profit in a market, then we ought, I should have thought, to look to whether or not such production was or was not occurring. It turns out in fact that it was, and in a very substantial form. Most of this production, however, was not industrial production. What was happening in Europe from the sixteenth to the eighteenth centuries is that over a large geographical area going from Poland in the northeast westwards and southwards throughout Europe and including large parts of the Western Hemisphere as well, there grew up a world-economy with a single division of labor within which there was a world market, for which men produced largely agricultural products for sale and profit. I would think the simplest thing to do would be to call this agricultural capitalism. This then resolves the problems incurred by using the per-

32. Maurice Dobb, *Capitalism Yesterday and Today* (London: Lawrence and Wishart, 1958), p. 21.

33. *Ibid.*, pp. 6–7.   34. *Ibid.*, p. 21.

vasiveness of *wage* labor as a defining characteristic of capitalism. An individual is no less a capitalist exploiting labor because the state assists him to pay his laborers low wages (including wages in kind) and denies these laborers the right to change employment. Slavery and so-called 'second serfdom' are not to be regarded as anomalies in a capitalist system. Rather the so-called serf in Poland or the Indian on a Spanish *encomienda* in New Spain in this sixteenth-century world-economy were working for landlords who 'paid' them (however euphemistic this term) for cash crop production. This is a relationship in which labor power is a commodity (how could it ever be more so than under slavery?), quite different from the relationship of a feudal serf to his lord in eleventh-century Burgundy, where the economy was not oriented to a world market, and where labor power was (therefore?) in no sense bought or sold.

Capitalism thus means labor as a commodity to be sure. But in the era of agricultural capitalism, wage labor is only one of the modes in which labor is recruited and recompensed in the labor market. Slavery, coerced cash-crop production (my name for the so-called 'second feudalism'), sharecropping, and tenancy are all alternative modes. It would be too long to develop here the conditions under which differing regions of the world-economy tend to specialize in different agricultural products. I have done this elsewhere.[35]

What we must notice now is that this specialization occurs in specific and differing geographic regions of the world-economy. This regional specialization comes about by the attempts of actors in the market to avoid the normal operation of the market whenever it does not maximize their profit. The attempts of these actors to use non-market devices to ensure short-run profits makes them turn to the political entities which have in fact power to affect the market – the nation-states. (Again, why at this stage they could not have turned to city-states would take us into a long discursus, but it has to do with the state of military and shipping technology, the need of the European landmass to expand overseas in the fifteenth century if it was to maintain the level of income of the various aristocracies, combined with the state of political disintegration to which Europe had fallen in the Middle Ages.)

35. See my *The Modern World-System*, ch. 2.

In any case, the local capitalist classes – cash-crop landowners (often, even usually, nobility) and merchants – turned to the state, not only to liberate them from non-market constraints (as traditionally emphasized by liberal historiography) but to create new constraints on the new market, the market of the European world-economy.

By a series of accidents – historical, ecological, geographic – northwest Europe was better situated in the sixteenth century to diversify its agricultural specialization and add to it certain industries (such as textiles, shipbuilding, and metal wares) than were other parts of Europe. Northwest Europe emerged as the core area of this world-economy, specializing in agricultural production of higher skill levels, which favored (again for reasons too complex to develop) tenancy and wage labor as the modes of labor control. Eastern Europe and the Western Hemisphere became peripheral areas specializing in export of grains, bullion, wood, cotton, sugar – all of which favored the use of slavery and coerced cash-crop labor as the modes of labor control. Mediterranean Europe emerged as the semiperipheral area of this world-economy specializing in high-cost industrial products (for example, silks) and credit and specie transactions, which had as a consequence in the agricultural arena sharecropping as the mode of labor control and little export to other areas.

The three structural positions in a world-economy – core, periphery, and semiperiphery – had become stabilized by about 1640. How certain areas became one and not the other is a long story.[36] The key fact is that given slightly different starting points, the interests of various local groups converged in northwest Europe, leading to the development of strong state mechanisms, and diverged sharply in the peripheral areas, leading to very weak ones. Once we get a difference in the strength of the state machineries, we get the operation of 'unequal exchange'[37] which is enforced by strong states on weak ones, by core states on peripheral areas. Thus capitalism involves not only appropriation of the surplus value by an owner from a laborer, but an appro-

---

36. I give a brief account of this in 'Three Paths of National Development in the Sixteenth Century', *Studies in Comparative International Development*, 7: 2 (Summer 1972) 95–101, and below, ch. 2.

37. See Arghiri Emmanuel, *Unequal Exchange* (New York: Monthly Review Press, 1972).

priation of surplus of the whole world-economy by core areas. And this was as true in the stage of agricultural capitalism as it is in the stage of industrial capitalism.

In the early Middle Ages, there was to be sure trade. But it was largely either 'local', in a region that we might call the 'extended' manor, or 'long-distance', primarily of luxury goods. There was no exchange of 'bulk' goods, of 'staples' across intermediate-size areas, and hence no production for such markets. Later on in the Middle Ages, world-economies may be said to have come into existence, one centering on Venice, a second on the cities of Flanders and the Hanse. For various reasons, these structures were hurt by the retractions (economic, demographic, and ecological) of the period 1300–1450. It is only with the creating of a *European* division of labor after 1450 that capitalism found firm roots.

Capitalism was from the beginning an affair of the world-economy and not of nation-states. It is a misreading of the situation to claim that it is only in the twentieth century that capitalism has become 'world-wide', although this claim is frequently made in various writings, particularly by Marxists. Typical of this line of argument is Charles Bettelheim's response to Arghiri Emmanuel's discussion of unequal exchange:

The tendency of the capitalist mode of production to become worldwide is manifested not only through the constitution of a group of national economies forming a complex and hierarchical structure, including an imperialist pole and a dominated one, and not only through the antagonistic relations that develop between the different 'national economies' and the different states, but also through the constant 'transcending' of 'national limits' by big capital (the formation of 'international big capital', 'world firms', etc....).[38]

The whole tone of these remarks ignores the fact that capital has never allowed its aspirations to be determined by national boundaries in a capitalist world-economy, and that the creation of 'national' barriers – generically, mercantilism – has historically been a defensive mechanism of capitalists located in states which are one level below the high point of strength in the system. Such was the case of England *vis-à-vis* the Netherlands in 1660–1715, France *vis-à-vis* England in 1715–1815, Germany *vis-à-vis* Britain in the nineteenth century, the Soviet Union *vis-à-vis* the US in the

38. Charles Bettelheim, 'Theoretical Comments', in Emmanual, *Unequal Exchange*, p. 295.

twentieth. In the process a large number of countries create national economic barriers whose consequences often last beyond their initial objectives. At this later point in the process the very same capitalists who pressed their national governments to impose the restrictions now find these restrictions constraining. This is not an 'internationalization' of 'national' capital. This is simply a new political demand by certain sectors of the capitalist classes who have at all points in time sought to maximize their profits within the real economic market, that of the world-economy.

If this is so, then what meaning does it have to talk of structural positions within this economy and identify states as being in one of these positions? And why talk of three positions, inserting that of 'semiperiphery' in between the widely used concepts of core and periphery? The state machineries of the core states were strengthened to meet the needs of capitalist landowners and their merchant allies. But that does not mean that these state machineries were manipulable puppets. Obviously any organization, once created, has a certain autonomy from those who pressed it into existence for two reasons. It creates a stratum of officials whose own careers and interests are furthered by the continued strengthening of the organization itself, however the interests of its capitalist backers may vary. Kings and bureaucrats wanted to stay in power and increase their personal gain constantly. Secondly, in the process of creating the strong state in the first place, certain 'constitutional' compromises had to be made with other forces within the state boundaries and these institutionalized compromises limit, as they are designed to do, the freedom of maneuver of the managers of the state machinery. The formula of the state as 'executive committee of the ruling class' is only valid, therefore, if one bears in mind that executive committees are never mere reflections of the wills of their constituents, as anyone who has ever participated in any organization knows well.

The strengthening of the state machineries in core areas has as its direct counterpart the decline of the state machineries in peripheral areas. The decline of the Polish monarchy in the sixteenth and seventeenth centuries is a striking example of this phenomenon.[39] There are two reasons for this. In peripheral

39. See J. Siemenski, 'Constitutional Conditions in the Fifteenth and Sixteenth Centuries', in *Cambridge History of Poland*, vol. 1, W. F. Reddaway *et al.* (eds.), *From the Origins*

countries, the interests of the capitalist landowners lie in an opposite direction from those of the local commercial bourgeoisie. Their interests lie in maintaining an open economy to maximize their profit from world-market trade (no restrictions in exports and access to lower-cost industrial products from core countries) and in elimination of the commercial bourgeoisie in favor of outside merchants (who pose no local political threat). Thus, in terms of the state, the coalition which strengthened it in core countries was precisely absent.

The second reason, which has become ever more operative over the history of the modern world-system, is that the strength of the state machinery in core states is a function of the weakness of other state machineries. Hence intervention of outsiders via war, subversion, and diplomacy is the lot of peripheral states.

All this seems very obvious. I repeat it only in order to make clear two points. One cannot reasonably explain the strength of various state machineries at specific moments of the history of the modern world-system primarily in terms of a genetic–cultural line of argumentation, but rather in terms of the structural role a country plays in the world-economy at that moment in time. To be sure, the initial eligibility for a particular role is often decided by an accidental edge a particular country has, and the 'accident' of which one is talking is no doubt located in part in past history, in part in current geography. But once this relatively minor accident is given, it is the operations of the world-market forces which accentuate the differences, institutionalize them, and make them impossible to surmount over the short run.

The second point we wish to make about the structural differences of core and periphery is that they are not comprehensible unless we realize that there is a third structural position: that of the semiperiphery. This is not the result merely of establishing arbitrary cutting-points on a continuum of characteristics. Our logic is not merely inductive, sensing the presence of a third category from a comparison of indicator curves. It is also deductive. The semiperiphery is needed to make a capitalist world-economy run smoothly. Both kinds of world-system, the

to Sobieski (to 1696) (Cambridge: University Press, 1950), pp. 416–40; Janusz Tazbir, 'The Commonwealth of the Gentry', in Aleksander Gieysztor *et al., History of Poland* (Warszawa: PWN – Polish Scientific Publications, 1968), pp. 169–271.

world-empire with a redistributive economy and the world-economy with a capitalist market economy, involve markedly unequal distribution of rewards. Thus, logically, there is immediately posed the question of how it is possible politically for such a system to persist. Why do not the majority who are exploited simply overwhelm the minority who draw disproportionate benefits? The most rapid glance at the historic record shows that these world-systems have been faced rather rarely by fundamental system-wide insurrection. While internal discontent has been eternal, it has usually taken quite long before the accumulation of the erosion of power has led to the decline of a world-system, and as often as not, an external force has been a major factor in this decline.

There have been three major mechanisms that have enabled world-systems to retain relative political stability (not in terms of the particular groups who will play the leading roles in the system, but in terms of systemic survival itself). One obviously is the concentration of military strength in the hands of the dominant forces. The modalities of this obviously vary with the technology, and there are to be sure political prerequisites for such a concentration, but nonetheless sheer force is no doubt a central consideration.

A second mechanism is the pervasiveness of an ideological commitment to the system as a whole. I do not mean what has often been termed the 'legitimation' of a system, because that term has been used to imply that the lower strata of a system feel some affinity with or loyalty towards the rulers, and I doubt that this has ever been a signifcant factor in the survival of world-systems. I mean rather the degree to which the staff or cadres of the system (and I leave this term deliberately vague) feel that their own well-being is wrapped up in the survival of the system as such and the competence of its leaders. It is this staff which not only propagates the myths; it is they who believe them.

But neither force nor the ideological commitment of the staff would suffice were it not for the division of the majority into a larger lower stratum and a smaller middle stratum. Both the revolutionary call for polarization as a strategy of change and the liberal encomium to consensus as the basis of the liberal polity reflect this proposition. The import is far wider than its use in the analysis of contemporary political problems suggests. It is the normal condition of either kind of world-system to have a three-layered structure. When and if this ceases to be the case, the world-system disintegrates.

In a world-empire, the middle stratum is in fact accorded the role of maintaining the marginally desirable long-distance luxury trade, while the upper stratum concentrates its resources on controlling the military machinery which can collect the tribute, the crucial mode of redistributing surplus. By providing, however, for an access to a limited portion of the surplus to urbanized elements who alone, in premodern societies, could contribute political cohesiveness to isolated clusters of primary producers, the upper stratum effectively buys off the potential leadership of coordinated revolt. And by denying access to political rights for this commercial-urban middle stratum, it makes them constantly vulnerable to confiscatory measures whenever their economic profits become sufficiently swollen so that they might begin to create for themselves military strength.

In a world-economy, such 'cultural' stratification is not so simple, because the absence of a single political system means the concentration of economic roles vertically rather than horizontally throughout the system. The solution then is to have three *kinds* of states, with pressures for cultural homogenization within each of them – thus, besides the upper stratum of core states and the lower stratum of peripheral states, there is a middle stratum of semiperipheral ones.

This semiperiphery is then assigned as it were a specific economic role, but the reason is less economic than political. That is to say, one might make a good case that the world-economy as an economy would function every bit as well without a semiperiphery. But it would be far less *politically* stable, for it would mean a polarized world-system. The existence of the third category means precisely that the upper stratum is not faced with the *unified* opposition of all the others because the *middle* stratum is both exploited and exploiter. It follows that the specific economic role is not all that important, and has thus changed through the various historical stages of the modern world-system. We shall discuss these changes shortly.

Where then does class analysis fit in all of this? And what in such a formulation are nations, nationalities, peoples, ethnic groups? First of all, without arguing the point now,[40] I would contend that all these latter terms denote variants of a single phenomenon which I will term 'ethno-nations'.

Both classes and ethnic groups, or status groups, or ethno-nations are phenomena of world-economies and much of the enormous confusion that has surrounded the concrete analysis of their functioning can be attributed quite simply to the fact that they have been analyzed as though they existed within the nation-states of this world-economy, instead of within the world-economy as a whole. This has been a Procrustean bed indeed.

The range of economic activities being far wider in the core than in the periphery, the range of syndical interest groups is far wider there.[41] Thus, it has been widely observed that there does not exist in many parts of the world today a proletariat of the kind which exists in, say, Europe or North America. But this is a confusing way to state the observation. Industrial activity being disproportionately concentrated in certain parts of the world-economy, industrial wage workers are to be found principally in certain geographic regions. Their interests as a syndical group are determined by their collective relationship to the world-economy. Their ability to influence the political functioning of this world-economy is shaped by the fact that they command larger percentages of the population in one sovereign entity than another. The form their organizations take have, in large part, been governed too by these political boundaries. The same might be said about industrial capitalists. Class analysis is perfectly capable of accounting for the political position of, let us say, French skilled workers if we look at their structural position and interests in the world-economy. Similarly with ethno-nations. The meaning

40. See my fuller analysis in 'Social Conflict in Post-Independence Black Africa: The Concepts of Race and Status-Group Reconsidered' in Ernest Q. Campbell (ed.), *Racial Tensions and National Identity* (Nashville: Vanderbilt University Press, 1972), pp. 207–26, and below, ch. 10.
41. 'Range' in this sentence means the number of different occupations in which a significant proportion of the population is engaged. Thus peripheral society typically is overwhelmingly agricultural. A core society typically has its occupations well-distributed over all of Colin Clark's three sectors. If one shifted the connotation of range to talk of style of life, consumption patterns, even income distribution quite possibly one might reverse the correlation. In a typical peripheral society, the differences between a subsistence farmer and an urban professional are probably far greater than those which could be found in a typical core state.

of ethnic consciousness in a core area is considerably different from that of ethnic consciousness in a peripheral area precisely because of the different class position such ethnic groups have in the world-economy.[42]

Political struggles of ethno-nations or segments of classes within national boundaries of course are the daily bread and butter of local politics. But their significance or consequences can only be fruitfully analyzed if one spells out the implications of their organizational activity or political demands for the functioning of the world-economy. This also incidentally makes possible more rational assessments of these politics in terms of some set of evaluative criteria such as 'left' and 'right'.

The functioning then of a capitalist world-economy requires that groups pursue their economic interests within a single world market while seeking to distort this maket for their benefit by organizing to exert influence on states, some of which are far more powerful than others but none of which controls the world market in its entirety. Of course, we shall find on closer inspection that there are periods where one state is relatively quite powerful and other periods where power is more diffuse and contested, permitting weaker states broader ranges of action. We can talk then of the relative tightness or looseness of the world-system as an important variable and seek to analyze why this dimension tends to be cyclical in nature, as it seems to have been for several hundred years.

We are now in a position to look at the historical evolution of this capitalist world-economy itself and analyze the degree to which it is fruitful to talk of distinct stages in its evolution as a system. The emergence of the European world-economy in the 'long' sixteenth century (1450–1640) was made possible by an historical conjuncture: on those long-term trends which were the culmination of what has been sometimes described as the 'crisis of feudalism' was superimposed a more immediate cyclical crisis plus climatic changes, all of which created a dilemma that could only be resolved by a geographic expansion of the division of labor. Furthermore, the balance of intersystem forces was such as to make

42. See my 'The Two Modes of Ethnic Consciousness: Soviet Central Asia in Transition?' in Edward Allworth (ed.), *The Nationality Question in Soviet Central Asia* (New York: Praeger, 1973), pp. 168–75, and below, ch. 11.

this realizable. Thus a geographic expansion did take place in conjunction with a demographic expansion and an upward price rise.

The remarkable thing was not that a European world-economy was thereby created, but that it survived the Hapsburg attempt to transform it into a world-empire, an attempt seriously pursued by Charles V. The Spanish attempt to absorb the whole failed because the rapid economic–demographic–technological burst forward of the preceding century made the whole enterprise too expensive for the imperial base to sustain, especially given many structural insufficiencies in Castilian economic development. Spain could afford neither the bureaucracy nor the army that was necessary to the enterprise, and in the event went bakrupt, as did the French monarchs making a similar albeit even less plausible attempt.

Once the Hapsburg dream of world-empire was over – and in 1557 it was over forever – the capitalist world-economy was an established system that became almost impossible to unbalance. It quickly reached an equilibrium point in its relations with other world-systems: the Ottoman and Russian world-empires, the Indian Ocean proto-world-economy. Each of the states or potential states within the European world-economy was quickly in the race to bureaucratize, to raise a standing army, to homogenize its culture, to diversify its economic activities. By 1640, those in north-west Europe had succeeded in establishing themselves as the core states; Spain and the northern Italian city-states declined into being semi-peripheral; northeastern Europe and Iberian America had become the periphery. At this point, those in semiperipheral status had reached it by virtue of decline from a former more pre-eminent status.

It was the system-wide recession of 1650–1730 that consolidated the European world-economy and opened stage two of the modern world-economy. For the recession forced retrenchment, and the decline in relative surplus allowed room for only one core state to survive. The mode of struggle was mercantilism, which was a device of partial insulation and withdrawal from the world market of *large* areas themselves hierarchically constructed – that is, empires within the world-economy (which is quite different from world-empires). In this struggle England first ousted the Netherlands from its commercial primacy and then resisted successfully

France's attempt to catch up. As England began to speed up the process of industrialization after 1760, there was one last attempt of those capitalist forces located in France to break the imminent British hegemony. This attempt was expressed first in the French Revolution's replacement of the cadres of the regime and then in Napoleon's continental blockade. But it failed.

Stage three of the capitalist world-economy begins then, a stage of industrial rather than of agricultural capitalism. Henceforth, industrial production is no longer a minor aspect of the world market but comprises an ever larger percentage of world gross production – and even more important, of world gross surplus. This involves a whole series of consequences for the world-system.

First of all, it led to the further geographic expansion of the European world-economy to include now the whole of the globe. This was in part the result of its technological feasibility both in terms of improved military firepower and improved shipping facilities which made regular trade sufficiently inexpensive to be viable. But, in addition, industrial production *required* access to raw materials of a nature and in a quantity such that the needs could not be supplied within the former boundaries. At first, however, the search for new markets was not a primary consideration in the geographic expansion since the new markets were more readily available within the old boundaries, as we shall see.

The geographic expansion of the European world-economy meant the elimination of other world-systems as well as the absorption of the remaining minisystems. The most important world-system up to then outside of the European world-economy, Russia, entered in semiperipheral status, the consequence of the strength of its state machinery (including its army) and the degree of industrialization already achieved in the eighteenth century. The independences in the Latin American countries did nothing to change their peripheral status. They merely eliminated the last vestiges of Spain's semiperipheral role and ended pockets of noninvolvement in the world-economy in the interior of Latin America. Asia and Africa were absorbed into the periphery in the nineteenth century, although Japan, because of the combination of the strength of its state machinery, the poverty of its resource base (which led to a certain disinterest on the part of world capitalist forces), and its geographic remoteness from the core areas, was able quickly to graduate into semipheripheral status.

The absorption of Africa as part of the periphery meant the end of slavery world-wide for two reasons. First of all, the manpower that was used as slaves was now needed for cash-crop production in Africa itself, whereas in the eighteenth century Europeans had sought to *discourage* just such cash-crop production.[43] In the second place, once Africa was part of the periphery and not the external arena, slavery was no longer economic. To understand this, we must appreciate the economics of slavery. Slaves receiving the lowest conceivable reward for their labor are the least productive form of labor and have the shortest life span, both because of undernourishment and maltreatment and because of lowered psychic resistance to death. Furthermore, if recruited from areas surrounding their workplace the escape rate is too high. Hence, there must be a high transport cost for a product of low productivity. This makes economic sense only if the purchase price is virtually nil. In capitalist market trade, purchase always has a real cost. It is only in long-distance trade, the exchange of preciosities, that the purchase price can be in the social system of the purchaser virtually nil. Such was the slave trade. Slaves were bought at low immediate cost (the production cost of the items actually exchanged) and none of the usual invisible costs. That is to say, the fact that removing a man from West Africa lowered the productive potential of the region was of *zero* cost to the European world-economy since these areas were not part of the division of labor. Of course, had the slave trade totally denuded Africa of all possibilities of furnishing further slaves, then a real cost to Europe would have commenced. But that point was never historically reached. Once, however, Africa

43. A. Adu Boahen cites the instructions of the British Board of Trade in 1751 to the Governor of Cape Castle (a small British fort and trading settlement in what is now Ghana) to seek to stop the local people, the Fante, from cultivating cotton. The reason given was the following: 'The introduction of culture and industry among the Negroes is contrary to the known established policy of this country, there is no saying where this might stop, and that it might extend to tobacco, sugar and every other commodity which we now take from our colonies; and thereby the Africans, who now support themselves by wars, would become planters and their slaves be employed in the culture of these articles in Africa, which they are employed in in America'. Cited in A. Adu Boahen, *Topics in West Africa History* (London: Longmans, Green and Co., 1966), p. 113.

was part of the periphery, then the real cost of a slave in terms of the production of surplus in the world-economy went up to such a point that it became far more economical to use wage labor, even on sugar or cotton plantations, which is precisely what transpired in the nineteenth-century Caribbean and other slave labor regions.

The creation of vast new areas as the periphery of the expanded world-economy made possible a shift in the role of some other areas. Specifically, both the United States and Germany (as it came into being) combined formerly peripheral and semiperipheral regions. The manufacturing sector in each was able to gain political ascendancy, as the peripheral subregions became less economically crucial to the world-economy. Mercantilism now became the major tool of semiperipheral countries seeking to become core countries, thus still performing a function analogous to that of the mercantilist drives of the late seventeeth and eighteenth centuries in England and France. To be sure, the struggle of semiperipheral countries to 'industrialize' varied in the degree to which it succeeded in the period before the First World War: all the way in the United States, only partially in Germany, not at all in Russia.

The internal structure of core states also changed fundamentally under industrial capitalism. For a core area, industrialism involved divesting itself of substantially all agricultural activities (except that in the twentieth century further mechanization was to create a new form of working the land that was so highly mechanized as to warrant the appellation industrial). Thus whereas, in the period 1700–40, England not only was Europe's leading industrial exporter but was also Europe's leading agricultural exporter – this was at a high point in the economy-wide recession – by 1900, less than 10 percent of England's population were engaged in agricultural pursuits.

At first under industrial capitalism, the core exchanged manufactured products against the periphery's agricultural products – hence, Britain from 1815 to 1873 as the 'workshop of the world'. Even to those semiperipheral countries that had some manufacture (France, Germany, Belgium, the us), Britain in this period supplied about half their needs in manufactured goods. As, however, the mercantilist practices of this latter group both

cut Britain off from outlets and even created competition for
Britain in sales to peripheral areas, a competition which led to
the late nineteenth-century 'scramble for Africa', the world
division of labor was reallocated to ensure a new special role for
the core: less the provision of the manufactures, more the
provision of the machines to make the manufactures as well as the
provision of infrastructure (especially, in this period, railroads).

The rise of manufacturing created for the first time under
capitalism a large-scale urban proletariat. And in consequence for
the first time there arose what Michels has called the 'anti-capitalist
mass spirit',[44] which was translated into concrete organizational
forms (trade unions, socialist parties). This development intruded
a new factor as threatening to the stability of the states and of
the capitalist forces now so securely in control of them as the
earlier centrifugal thrusts of regional anti-capitalist landed elements had been in the seventeenth century.

At the same time that the bourgeoisies of the core countries
were faced by this threat to the internal stability of their state
structures, they were simultaneously faced with the economic crisis
of the latter third of the nineteenth century resulting from the
more rapid increase of agricultural production (and indeed of light
manufactures) than the expansion of a potential market for these
goods. Some of the surplus would have to be redistributed to
someone to allow these goods to be bought and the economic
machinery to return to smooth operation. By expanding the
purchasing power of the industrial proletariat of the core countries, the world-economy was unburdened simultaneously of two
problems: the bottleneck of demand, and the unsettling 'class
conflict' of the core states – hence, the social liberalism or welfare-
state ideology that arose just at that point in time.

The First World War was, as men of the time observed, the
end of an era; and the Russian Revolution of October 1917 the
beginning of a new one – our stage four. This stage was to be
sure a stage of revolutionary turmoil but it also was, in a seeming
paradox, the stage of the *consolidation* of the industrial capitalist
world-economy. The Russian Revolution was essentially that of
a semiperipheral country whose internal balance of forces had

44. Rober Michels, 'The Origins of the Anti-Capitalist Mass Spirit', in *Man in Contemporary
    Society* (New York: Columbia University Press, 1955), vol. 1, pp. 740–65.

been such that as of the late nineteenth century it began on a decline towards a peripheral status. This was the result of the marked penetration of foreign capital into the industrial sector which was on its way to eliminating all indigenous capitalist forces, the resistance to the mechanization of the agricultural sector, the decline of relative military power (as evidenced by the defeat by the Japanese in 1905). The Revolution brought to power a group of state managers who reversed each one of these trends by using the classic technique of mercantilist semiwithdrawal from the world-economy. In the process of doing this, the now USSR mobilized considerable popular support, especially in the urban sector. At the end of the Second World War, Russia was reinstated as a very strong member of the semiperiphery and could begin to seek full core status.

Meanwhile, the decline of Britain which dates from 1873 was confirmed and its hegemonic role was assumed by the United States. While the US thus rose, Germany fell further behind as a result of its military defeat. Various German attempts in the 1920s to find new industrial outlets in the Middle East and South America were unsuccessful in the face of the US thrust combined with Britain's continuing relative strength. Germany's thrust of desperation to recoup lost ground took the noxious and unsuc-cessful form of Nazism.

It was the Second World War that enabled the United States for a brief period (1945–65) to attain the same level of primacy as Britain had in the first part of the nineteenth century. United States growth in this period was spectacular and created a great need for expanded market outlets. The Cold War closure denied not only the USSR but eastern Europe to US exports. And the Chinese Revolution meant that this region, which had been destined for much exploitative activity, was also cut off. Three alternative areas were available and each was pursued with assiduity. First, western Europe had to be rapidly 'reconstructed', and it was the Marshall Plan which thus allowed this area to play a primary role in the expansion of world productivity. Secondly, Latin America became the reserve of US investment from which now Britain and Germany were completely cut off. Thirdly, southern Asia, the Middle East and Africa had to be decolonized. On the one hand, this was necessary in order to reduce the share of the surplus taken by the western European intermediaries, as Canning covertly supported the Latin American revolutionaries against Spain in the 1820s.[45] But also, these countries had to be decolonized in order to mobilize productive potential in a way that had never been achieved in the colonial era. Colonial rule after all had been an *inferior* mode of relationship of core and periphery, one occasioned by the strenuous late-nineteenth-century conflict among industrial states but one no longer desirable from the point of view of the new hegemonic power.[46]

But a world capitalist economy does not permit true imperium. Charles V could not succeed in his dream of world-empire. The Pax Britannica stimulated its own demise. So too did the Pax Americana. In each case, the cost of *political* imperium was too high economically, and in a capitalist system, over the middle run when profits decline, new *political* formulae are sought. In this case the costs mounted along several fronts. The efforts of the USSR to further its own industrialization, protect a privileged market area (eastern Europe), and force entry into other market areas led to an immense spiralling of military expenditure, which on the Soviet side promised long-run returns whereas for the US it was merely a question of running very fast to stand still. The economic resurgence of western Europe, made necessary both to provide markets for US sales and investments and to counter the USSR military thrust, meant over time that the west European state structures collectively became as strong as that of the US, which led in the late 1960s to the 'dollar and gold crisis' and the retreat of Nixon from the free-trade stance which is the definitive mark of the self-confident leader in a capitalist market system. When the cumulated Third World pressures, most notably Vietnam, were added on, a restructuring of the world division of labor was inevitable, involving probably in the 1970s a quadripartite division of the larger part of the world surplus by the US, the European Common Market, Japan, and the USSR.

Such a decline in US state hegemony has actually *increased* the freedom of action of capitalist enterprises, the larger of which

45. See William W. Kaufman, *British Policy and the Independence of Latin America, 1804–28* (New Haven: Yale University Press, 1951).
46. Cf. Catherine Coquery-Vidrovitch, 'De l'impérialisme britannique à l'impérialisme contemporaine – l'avatar colonial', *L'Homme et la société*, 18 (October–December 1970), 61–90.

have now taken the form of multinational corporations which are able to maneuver against state bureaucracies whenever the national politicians become too responsive to internal worker pressures. Whether some effective links can be established between multinational corporations, presently limited to operating in certain areas, and the USSR remains to be seen, but it is by no means impossible.

This brings us back to one of the questions with which we opened this paper, the seemingly esoteric debate between Liu Shao-Chi and Mao Tse-Tung as to whether China was, as Liu argued, a socialist state, or whether, as Mao argued, socialism was a *process* involving continued and continual class struggle. No doubt to those to whom the terminology is foreign the discussion seems abstrusely theological. The issue, however, as we said, is real. If the Russian Revolution emerged as a reaction to the threatened further decline of Russia's structural position in the world-economy, and if fifty years later one can talk of the USSR as entering the status of a core power in a *capitalist* world-economy, what then is the meaning of the various so-called socialist revolutions that have occurred on a third of the world's surface? First let us notice that it has been neither Thailand nor Liberia nor Paraguay that has had a 'socialist revolution' but Russia, China and Cuba. That is to say, these revolutions have occurred in countries that, in terms of their internal economic structures in the pre-revolutionary period, had a certain minimum strength in terms of skilled personnel, some manufacturing, and other factors which made it plausible that, within the framework of a capitalist world-economy, such a country could alter its role in the world division of labor within a reasonable period (say 30–50 years) by the use of the technique of mercantilist semi-withdrawal. (This may not be all that plausible for Cuba, but we shall see.) Of course, other countries in the geographic regions and military orbit of these revolutionary forces had changes of regime without in any way having these characteristics (for example, Mongolia or Albania). It is also to be noted that many of the countries where similar forces are strong or where considerable counterforce is required to keep them from emerging also share this status of minimum strength. I think of Chile or Brazil or Egypt – or indeed Italy.

Are we not seeing the emergence of a political structure for *semiperipheral* nations adapted to stage four of the capitalist world-system? The fact that all enterprises are nationalized in these countries does not make the participation of these enterprises in the world-economy one that does not conform to the mode of operation of a capitalist market system: seeking increased efficiency of production in order to realize a maximum price on sales, thus achieving a more favorable allocation of the surplus of the world-economy. If tomorrow U.S. Steel became a worker's collective in which all employees without exception received an identical share of the profits and all stockholders are expropriated without compensation, would U.S. Steel thereby cease to be a capitalist enterprise operating in a capitalist world-economy?

What then have been the consequences for the world-system of the emergence of many states in which there is no private ownership of the basic means of production? To some extent, this has meant an internal reallocation of consumption. It has certainly undermined the ideological justification in world capitalism, both by showing the political vulnerability of capitalist entrepreneurs and by demonstrating that private ownership is irrelevant to the rapid expansion of industrial productivity. But to the extent that it has raised the ability of the new semiperipheral areas to enjoy a larger share of the world surplus, it has once again depolarized the world, recreating the triad of strata that has been a fundamental element in the survival of the world-system.

Finally, in the peripheral areas of the world-economy, both the continued economic expansion of the core (even though the core is seeing some reallocation of surplus internal to it) and the new strength of the semiperiphery has led to a further weakening of the political and hence economic position of the peripheral areas. The pundits note that 'the gap is getting wider', but thus far no one has succeeded in doing much about it, and it is not clear that there are very many in whose interests it would be to do so. Far from a strengthening of state authority, in many parts of the world we are witnessing the same kind of deterioration Poland knew in the sixteenth century, a deterioration of which the frequency of military coups is only one of many signposts. And all of this leads us to conclude that stage four has been the stage of the *consolidation* of the capitalist world-economy.

Consolidation, however, does not mean the absence of contradictions and does not mean the likelihood of long-term survival. We thus come to projections about the future, which has always been man's great game, his true *hybris*, the most convincing argument for the dogma of original sin. Having read Dante, I will therefore be brief.

There are two fundamental contradictions, it seems to me, involved in the workings of the capitalist world-system. In the first place, there is the contradiction to which the nineteenth-century Marxian corpus pointed, which I would phrase as follows: whereas in the short run the maximization of profit requires maximizing the withdrawal of surplus from immediate consumption of the majority, in the long run the continued production of surplus requires a mass demand which can only be created by redistributing the surplus withdrawn. Since these two considerations move in opposite directions (a 'contradiction'), the system has constant crises which in the long run both weaken it and make the game for those with privilege less worth playing.

The second fundamental contradiction, to which Mao's concept of socialism as process points, is the following: whenever the tenants of privilege seek to coopt an oppositional movement by including them in a minor share of the privilege, they may no doubt eliminate opponents in the short run; but they also up the ante for the next oppositional movement created in the next crisis of the world-economy. Thus the cost of 'cooption' rises ever higher and the advantages of cooption seem ever less worthwhile.

There are today no socialist systems in the world-economy any more than there are feudal systems because there is only *one* world-system. It is a world-economy and it is by definition capitalist in form. Socialism involves the creation of a new kind of *world*-system, neither a redistributive world-empire nor a capitalist world-economy but a socialist world-government. I don't see this projection as being in the least utopian but I also don't feel its institution is imminent. It will be the outcome of a long struggle in forms that may be familiar and perhaps in very few forms, that will take place in *all* the areas of the world-economy (Mao's continual 'class struggle'). Governments may be in the hands of persons, groups or movements sympathetic to this transformation but *states* as such are neither progressive nor reactionary. It is movements and forces that deserve such evaluative judgments.

Having gone as far as I care to in projecting the future, let me return to the present and to the scholarly enterprise which is never neutral but does have its own logic and to some extent its own priorities. We have adumbrated as our basic unit of observation a concept of world-systems that have structural parts and evolving stages. It is within such a framework, I am arguing, that we can fruitfully make comparative analyses – of the wholes and of parts of the whole. Conceptions precede and govern measurements. I am all for minute and sophisticated quantitative indicators. I am all for minute and diligent archival work that will trace a concrete historical series of events in terms of all its immediate complexities. But the point of either is to enable us to see better what has happened and what is happening. For that we need glasses with which to discern the dimensions of difference, we need models with which to weigh significance, we need summarizing concepts with which to create the knowledge which we then seek to communicate to each other. And all this because we are men with hybris and original sin and therefore seek the good, the true, and the beautiful.

2 ✦ Three paths of national development in sixteenth-century Europe

In the search to comprehend the world-system of our day, few have turned towards analysis of the political economy of sixteenth-century Europe. Yet such an analysis is extremely relevant, not only because the modern world-system was created there then, but because most of the processes that explain the workings of this system are to be found there in their pristine form, and hence can be examined with greater clarity.

The modern world-system originated in the sixteenth century, the 'long' sixteenth century as Fernand Braudel has called it, that is, from 1450 to 1640. This was the period in which was created a European world-economy whose structure was unlike any that the world had known before. The singular feature of this world-economy was the discontinuity between economic and political institutions. This discontinuity made possible and was made possible by the creation of capitalist forms of production, not only in commerce and industry, but most important of all, in agriculture.

World-economies had existed before in history – that is, vast arenas within which a sophisicated division of labor existed based on a network of trade, both long-distance and local. But wherever such a world-economy had evolved previously, sooner or later an imperium expanded to fill the geographical space of this economy, a single political structure – such as Rome, Byzantium, China. The imperial framework established political constraints which prevented the effective growth of capitalism, set limits on economic growth and sowed the seeds of stagnation and/or disintegration.

By a series of historical accidents too complex to develop here, the nascent European world-economy of the sixteenth century knew no such imperium. The only serious attempt to create one

– that of Charles V and the Hapsburgs – was a failure. The failure of Charles V was the success of Europe.

The way the European world-economy operated in bare outline was simple enough. The geographical limits of this world-economy, determined largely by the state of technology at the time, included northwest Europe, which became the core of the system during this period, eastern Europe (but not Russia) which, along with Spanish America, became its periphery, and the Christian Mediterranean area which, having been at the outset an advanced core area, became transformed in the course of the sixteenth century into a semiperiphery.

Core, semiperiphery and periphery all refer to positions in the economic system. The core areas were the location of a complex variety of economic activities – mass-market industries such as there were (mainly textiles and shipbuilding), international and local commerce in the hands of an *indigenous* bourgeoisie, relatively advanced and complex forms of agriculture (both pastoralism and high-productivity forms of tillage with a high component of medium-sized, yeoman-owned land). The peripheral areas, by contrast, were monocultural, with the cash crops being produced on large estates by coerced labor. The semiperipheral areas were in the process of deindustrializing. The form of agricultural labor control they used was intermediate between the freedom of the lease system and the coercion of slavery and serfdom. It was for the most part sharecropping (*métayage, mezzadria*). The semiperiphery, in transition, still retained for the time being some share in international banking and high-cost, quality industrial production.

All this added up to a world-economy in the sense that the various areas came to be dependent upon each other for their specialized roles. The profitability of specific economic activities became a function of the proper functioning of the system as a whole: profitability was generally served by increasing the overall productivity of the system.

Groups seeking to protect their economic interests in the political arena found that while the economy spread over a vast world, this world was made up of a multitude of political entities of varying forms. In the core states there evolved relatively strong state systems, with an absolute monarch and a patrimonial state bureaucracy working primarily for this monarch. The venality of office and the development of standing armies based on mercenaries were the critical elements in the establishment of such a bureaucracy.

By contrast, the critical feature of the periphery was the *absence* of the strong state. In eastern Europe the kings gradually lost all effective power to the 'kinglets' – the aristocrats turned capitalist farmers – the Junkers with their *Gutswirtschaft* in east Elbia, the nobles with their private armies and strong *Sejm* (parliament) in Poland, etc. In Spanish America, there was no indigenous state authority at all, the relatively weak bureaucracy operating in the interests of Castile (or Portugal in the case of Brazil), and the local *encomenderos* and *donatários* playing the role of east European aristocratic capitalist farmers.

The semiperiphery once again was in between. By the end of the long sixteenth century, the decline of state authority was clear in Spain and in the large city-states of northern Italy (where the power of foreign monarchs and local estate-owners grew). Southern France (Languedoc), which was economically parallel, was an area of strong and multifarious resistance to the expansion of French central authority, one of the key loci of political uprising.

The operation of this system will be made clearer if we look successively at three particular areas, each representative of one role in the world-system: Poland in the periphery, Venice in the semiperiphery, and England in the core.

In the fourteenth and fifteenth centuries the social structure of Poland was not markedly different from that of France or England. The state was somewhat less strong because of the impact of the era of invasions just previously, but not markedly so. The demographic contraction of Europe, to increased rights of the tiller of the soil *vis-à-vis* the landowner (the decline of feudalism). Polish merchants flourished and Polish towns were growing, at least to the same extent again as in the west. And indeed the signs of religious resistance to the dominion of the Mediterranean lands were as visible there as in Germany or England. Indeed, when the Reformation began, it would spread to Poland too, and at first would show the same vigor there – amongst the same groups – as in western Europe.

In the fourteenth and fifteenth centuries Poland had begun to expand her export of wheat and wood via the Baltic to the Low Countries and from there to England and northern France. When the population of Europe began rapidly to expand in the fifteenth and sixteenth centuries, there came to be an even larger market for Poland's products. There was great financial return available to Polish landowners able to increase production to meet the increased demand.

Polish nobles began to use various devices at their disposal to expand their demesne, that is, land whose productive activity they directly managed. This was not too difficult. The problem was less to acquire land than to acquire an adequate supply of farm labor. The rate of exploitation was increasing, given the lure of profit. Peasants had however a recourse. There were vast un-occupied lands in parts of Poland, especially in areas of western Ukraine, then a part of Poland. Peasants simply ran away – either to colonize new lands or to the towns. In order to prevent this, Polish nobles secured legislation tying the peasants to the land – the so-called second feudalism. This was less a case of reciprocal rights and duties than of simple coercion of low-cost estate labor.

What happened to the increased production for the market? It was shipped, much of it via the Vistula, to Gdánsk (Danzig), then by ship to the Low Countries, especially Amsterdam. In the beginning the Polish nobles on their estates sold their goods to Polish merchants who took them to Gdánsk. But since the nobles had ancient exemptions from taxation which the merchants did not enjoy, it soon became obvious that it was more profitable for the polish arostocrats to organize their own transport to Gdánsk. This began the decline of the Polish bourgeoisie, which had the additional advantage for the nobility of eliminating a rival element on the local *political* scene. Although the tax exemption was only supposed to apply to products grown on noble land, soon the nobles bought the products of independent peasants and mixed them with their own produce, thus further economically under-cutting the Polish bourgeoisie.

But Polish aristocrats did not wish literally to transport these goods. They needed technical personnel. For this role, they employed non-Poles – Jews, Germans, Armenians. (It is striking that at the very moment that Jews were being expelled from the states of western Europe they were being welcomed into the peripheral areas of eastern Europe.) Obviously a non-Polish bourgeoisie offered no *political* threat to the Polish aristocracy.

In Gdánsk the produce was sold largely to German merchants and placed on ships, increasingly on Dutch ships, for transshipment. As the long sixteenth century went on, this channel of trade became increasingly secured by a system which can only be called international debt peonage.

The Polish aristocracy was faced with a chronic shortage of funds – the same as the nobilities of western Europe at this time. The era of economic expansion was one of expanded investment and, even more importantly, of expanded luxury consumption. To keep up, aristocrats had to borrow. The German merchants of Gdánsk lent them money against the following year's produce. This led to liquidity problems for the German merchants who, in turn, borrowed money from Dutch international merchant-bankers against the following year's shipments. As with all such cycles of debt, it was hard to extricate oneself. This meant that the creditor assured himself not only of a good price for his purchases but also of the exclusion of rival purchasers.

Meanwhile, in Poland, as the nobility increasingly transformed itself into capitalist farmers exploiting low-cost labor, and the indigenous bourgeoisie declined (which meant also the relative decline of the towns), the kind found both his tax base and his possibilities of political maneuver constrained. Over time, the effects cumulated, as the throne lost power to the parliament, and the central parliament lost it to local ones. (Incidentally, also, as part of this picture, the Counter-Reformation triumphed totally.)

Without a strong state and a strong indigenous bourgeoisie, there was no effective pressure to establish productive devices for local handicrafts. As the efficiency of western European products grew, they undersold Polish products, and a once significant local handicraft industry all but disappeared.

By the end of the sixteenth century, Poland epitomized what we would call, in twentieth-century parlance, a neocolonial state. It was a producer of primary cash crops which it exchanged internationally for the manufactured goods of other countries. The local landowning classes were linked economically to the heartlands of international capitalism, governing enclaves which were part of a world economy, but the combination of which could in no sense be said to make up a national economy.

Poland was an open economy and most of its surplus was drained abroad. Forces that might sustain local nationalism were in acute decline and the partition of Poland in the eighteenth century was simply the logical culmination of a long process of gestation. Poland became, in the course of the sixteenth century, an underdeveloped country in the European world-economy.

Venice at first sight seems to present an entirely different picture. In the High Middle Ages, Venice had been the core state of a smaller Mediterranean regional economy, a prefiguration of the European world-economy. Not only was it a center of trade, of finance and of textile production, but it had an imperium stretching down the Adriatic (Dalmatia) to the Aegean. Crete and Cyprus played the same role *vis-à-vis* Venice that the West Indies would later play *vis-à-vis* first Spain, then England. They were centers of sugar estates farmed by slaves, as well as slave marts for the surrounding region. The slaves were primarily Slavs and Tartars from the Balkans and the Black Sea, not black Africans, but the social system was the same.

Venice was linked to another center of regional economy, Bruges in Flanders, by an overland trade route via the Rhine and the Alps. Venice's merchant fleet serviced Mediterranean transport as the Dutch fleet would in the later sixteenth century come to service European sea transport. And her navy protected her position against rivals.

Venice was a thriving metropolis where the wealthier merchant classes controlled the state and the intermediate skilled workers were effectively 'unionized' via the guild system. The underclasses were of non-Venetian origin.

When the Portuguese went around the Cape of Good Hope in 1497, they came momentarily to monopolize the pepper and space trade from the Orient that had been one of the pillars of the Venetian economy. But this was only a temporary setback for Venice. For by the 1530s, and in collaboration with Arab merchants in the Indian Ocean and the Ottoman Turks who by now controlled not only Syria but Egypt, the Mediterranean spice trade revived and continued to expand. Neither the fall of

Constantinople nor Portuguese explorations therefore had much to do with Venetian decline.

For Venice did decline. It declined as a center of trade because, with the creation of a European world-economy, whose great waterways in the sixteenth century were the Baltic Sea and the Atlantic Ocean, Venice was no longer geographically central. Furthermore sugar production on Mediterranean islands had gradually exhausted the land and the manpower by the mid fifteenth century. New lands and peoples had to be exploited – first the Atlantic islands (Madeira, Canary Islands, Azores, São Tomé and Príncipe), then the West Indies and Brazil.

With an expanding population but with increased numbers of bad harvests and consequent epidemics (due to slightly changed climatic conditions in the sixteenth century), Venice began to have problems of food supply. This was aggravated by recurrent quarrels with the Turks which, irregularly but often, cut them off from Syrian and Egyptian breadbaskets. East European grain serviced first northwest Europe and then Iberia. There was little left over to reach the Italian city-states by the long sea voyage past Gibraltar.

One solution was to begin to turn some capital into the exploitation of Venice's immediate countryside, the Terraferma. But the money expended there then could not be spent on renewing Venetian industry.

Venice had been a center both of shipbuilding and of textiles. In the case of shipbuilding, Venice was facing a wood shortage similar to its grain shortage, while Amsterdam was cornering the major expanding source of wood supply at this time, the countries of the Baltic Sea. Furthermore, Amsterdam's technological advances, particularly the invention of the light and swift *fluyt*, further out-dated Venetian ships.

As for Venetian textiles, they were of high quality but very dear. No doubt this was splendid for the Renaissance nobility of the Italian city-states which indulged in the luxuries for which we remember them (not only fine clothing and furnishings, but art and architecture). But Venice was not geared to the new mass markets that were emerging in the sixteenth century – the middle farmers of northern Europe, the artisans, the lesser bureaucrats – all of whom had some money because of economic expansion and the general inflation, and who wished to purchase inexpensive and stylish (albeit less durable) cloths. England was to acquire much of this market at this time with the development of the 'new draperies' – light, colorful, and much less costly.

One of the factors which made it possible for England to develop a new textile technology, whereas Venice did not, was that England was not burdened by Venice's yoke of a large fixed capital investment and a relatively rigid wage structure.

In England, when manufacturers found wage levels too high, they transferred their enterprises to the countryside where they found cheap water power and, even more important, underemployed farm labor willing and legally free to engage in part-time industrial labor. In Venice the guilds were strong enough to prevent such runaway 'factories'. In England, the guilds protested too, but less effectively, because they were less entrenched.

Venice seemed to shine very brightly as late as the first decades of the seventeenth century. But it was glitter and façade by then. Its trading role had been undermined, its industrial base outmoded and undercut. It took only the combined tragedies of a series of epidemics and the Thirty Years War (which cut them off from their remaining important textile outlet, Germany) for it all to collapse.

Meanwhile, 'wise money' had gone into the agricultural enterprises of the countryside. This was particularly true of church money. The decline of Venice also meant a decline of the Renaissance humanism its ruling classes had supported. Venice joined the rest of northern Italy in being deindustrialized and agrarianized. This process did not result in the total elimination of industry and banking. Northern Italy was not Poland. It did not become the periphery of the European world economy, only the semiperiphery. The cause of Poland's 'underdevelopment' had been her slight backwardness at the beginning of the long sixteenth century. True, the backwardness had only been slight. But the very process of development of capitalism within a European world-economy transformed the slight gap into a very large one. The refeudalization of Poland was an essential element in the industrial and commercial advance of the core states.

Venice had the disadvantage of being too advanced, and rigidly so. She could not adapt to the demands of an expanding world economy, and geography, once in her favor, was now against her. So from being ahead of northwest Europe, she fell far behind. It would not be until the late nineteenth century that northern Italy would once again begin to industrialize (but Poland would not do so until the mid twentieth century).

How then did England do it? England, in the late Middle Ages, was a colony of Europe, an exporter of raw materials (wool) for continental manufactures. Her trade was heavily in the hands of Italian and Hanseatic merchants.

In the fifteenth century, England undertook, with partial success, the indigenization of her commercial network. The Italians and Hanseates were circumscribed, if not yet entirely eliminated (note, however, that England was moving in the opposite direction from Poland in this regard). One of the reasons England could do this was outside assistance. English import–export merchants, organized in the Merchant Adventurers' Company, established themselves in symbiotic relationship with the most powerful commercial network of the early sixteenth century, the merchants of Antwerp. The rise of Antwerp contributed to the strengthening of the indigenous English bourgeoisie.

In England, as elsewhere in Europe, the demographic decline of the fourteenth and early fifteenth centuries had led to a loosening of feudal bonds because of the increased bargaining position of the peasant. One consequence in England had been the pastoralization of much land. Sheep-raising required less manpower per acre than food products and offered at the time comparatively greater profits. Where land was not converted to pastoral use, large estates tended to be broken up and smaller units, managed by small and medium-sized producers (owners or tenants), began to be the pattern.

England's response to the economic expansion of the sixteenth century was to greatly acentuate these trends. This was the era of the first enclosures. But we must be careful here. For there were two kinds of enclosures – those made by the large landlord to expand pastoral acreage, and those made by the small landowner (the yeoman) to increase productivity on the tilled land.

In both these processes, the need of the landowner was not more manpower as in Poland but less. Men were forced off the land rather than forced to stay on it. Some went to the cities, as they were to go in the later enclosures of the eighteenth century, to become proletarians. But many more went in the sixteenth century to newly colonized forest areas where they became the unemployed and underemployed available for the new rural industries, the wage laborers of an increasingly commercial agriculture, and the vagabonds and brigands of which Elizabethan literature is so full.

It was in order to contain the social menace of this expulsion from the land that the forerunner of today's social welfare legislation, the Elizabethan Poor Laws, were invented (similar legislation was being enacted in other parts of northwest Europe at this time). This legislation was designed to head off urban rebellions by keeping the poor both from starving and from residing in the cities. It succeeded in its objective.

There was another solution for surplus population that was beginning to be used – emigration, first of all to Ireland, and then in the seventeenth century to the Americas. The incorporation of the Celtic fringe into England's national economy first starts seriously at this time. Wales was legally integrated with England and began to specialize as a cattle area with largely English landlords. The overflow of Welshmen pushed off the land went to England as subproletarians and filled the ranks of England's army as mercenaries.

A key factor in England's ability to cope with the new world economy was the relatively strong Tudor state, beginning with the so-called Henrician administrative revolution of the 1530s. The roots of England's state machinery are in part to be found in the legal homogeneity deriving from the Norman conquest and the relative isolation of an insular state. But neither factor was probably as important as the weakening of the nobility in the great internecine wars of the late Middle Ages (the Hundred Years War, the Wars of the Roses) combined with the emergence of other social groups amongst whom the monarchy could find allies, albeit temporary ones.

The absolute monarchy was of course not absolute, either in theory or in fact. It represented rather the first weak effort to establish state supremacy against local lords and outside powers – very strong by comparison with the situation in peripheral areas of the European world economy, but incredibly weak by comparison with twentieth-century governments.

The absolute monarchs were the focal point of the two great conflicting forces of the core states of the nascent capitalist world-economy: those new productive forces which were making it possible for England (and France) to develop economically and for the monarch to assert himself internally; and those hierarchies derived from earlier times of which the monarch was the pinnacle and the exemplar and which were the other pillar of the monarch's strength. The famous gentry were among the first category. Gentry is a term that has caused much confusion because it indicates in this context less a legal category deriving from medieval law than an emerging social class of capitalist farmers whose social origins ran the gamut from the peerage to gentlemen esquires to the yeomanry.

Finally, the secret of England in this period was that she was able to strengthen her industrial base, not only *vis-à-vis* the periphery of the European world economy, but even *vis-à-vis* her chief rival-to-be, France. Indeed, John Nef argues that the period 1540–1640 in England can be called the first industrial revolution. One of the elements that contributed to this was the enormous growth of London and the relatively small size of England, the combination of which meant a very large internal market for a not too large producing area.

The Tudor monarchs juggled well and stayed on top of a tumultuous situation, giving the English economy enough time to make the transition from colony to core state. While Poland became a monoculture and northern Italy was deindustrialized, England was developing a complex structure of multiple economic activities. England turned inwards just sufficiently to minimize the negative effects of outside forces that could have limited these developments, while gearing her economic activities for the capitalist world-economy of which she was now becoming a core state.

The story of the long sixteenth century is far more elaborate than we have indicated here. We have made no mention of the role of the Western Hemisphere – its slaves, its serfs, its bullion. Nor have we spoken of the price of inflation, so central a feature of the economic expansion of the time. We have only touched upon the process of class formation within the world-economy and its constituent states. The role of religious turmoil has been scarcely alluded to. We have furthermore omitted the whole story of the Hapsburg Empire that failed and of the decline of Spain, or the story of France which was torn between imperial and national aspirations, or of Amsterdam which was to provide the vital fluid of the later sixteenth century, or of the international banking networks. No mention has been made of the areas that were external to the European world-economy of the time but in trade relation with it – Russia, the Indian Ocean, east Asia – and the ways in which the political developments of an external area were crucially different from that of a peripheral area (Russia versus Poland, Malaysia or India versus Brazil or New Spain).

We have sought merely to illustrate briefly how the economic development of particular states in modern times is and has been a function of their role in a world-economy, and how the political developments within such states have reflected the pressures that derive from the consequences for various groups of the condition of this world-economy at a given time.

3 ❧ The present state of the debate on world inequality

It has never been a secret from anyone that some have more than others. And in the modern world at least, it is no secret that some countries have more than other countries. In short, world inequality is a phenomenon about which most men and most groups are quite conscious.

I do not believe that there has ever been a time when these inequalities were unquestioned. That is to say, people or groups who have more have always felt the need to justify this fact, if for no other reason than to try to convince those who have less that they should accept this fact with relative docility. These ideologies of the advantaged have had varying degrees of success over time. The history of the world is one of a constant series of revolts against inequality – whether that of one people or nation *vis-à-vis* another or of one class within a geographical area against another.

This statement is probably true of all of recorded history, indeed of all historical events, at least since the Neolithic Revolution. What has changed with ther advent of the modern world in the sixteenth century is neither the existence of inequalities nor of the felt need to justify them by means of ideological constructs. What has changed is that even those who defend the 'inevitability' of inequalities in the present feel the need to argue that eventually, over time, these inequalities will disappear, or at the very least diminish considerably in scope. Another way of saying this is that of the three dominant ideological currents of the modern world – conservatism, liberalism, and Marxism – two at least (liberalism and Marxism) are committed in theory and the abstract to egalitarianism as a principle. The third, conservatism, is not, but conservatism is an ideology that has been very much on the defensive ever since the French Revolution. The proof of this is that most conservatives decline to fly the banner openly but hide their conservative ideas under the mantle of liberalism or occasionally even Marxism.

Surely it is true that in the universities of the world in the twentieth century, and in other expressions of intellectuals, the contending ideologies have been one variant or another of liberalism and Marxism. (Remember at this point we are talking of ideologies and not of political movements. Both 'Liberal' parties and Social-Democratic parties in the twentieth century have drawn on liberal ideologies.)

One of the most powerful thrusts of the eighteenth-century Enlightenment, picked up by most nineteenth and twentieth century thought systems, was the assumption of progress, reformulated later as evolution. In the context of the question of equality, evolution was interpreted as the process of moving from an imperfect, unequal allocation of privileges and resources to some version of equality. There was considerable argument about how to define equality. (Reflect on the different meanings of 'equality of opportunity' and 'to each according to his needs'. There was considerable disagreement about who or what were the obstacles to this desired state of equality. And there was fundamental discord about how to transform the world from its present imperfection to the desired future, primarily between the advocates of gradualism based on education to advocates of revolution based on the use at some point in time of violence.

I review this well-known history of modern ideas simply to underline where I think our current debates are simply the latest variant of now classic debates and where I think some new issues have been raised which make these older formulations outdated.

If one takes the period 1945–60, both politically and intellectually, we have in many ways the apogee of the liberal–Marxist debate. The world was politically polarized in the so-called Cold War. There were two camps. One called itself the 'free world' and argued that it and it alone upheld the first part of the French Revolution's trilogy, that of 'liberty'. It argued that its economic system offered the hope over time of approximating 'equality' through a path which it came to call 'economic development' or sometimes just 'development'. It argued too that it was gradually achieving 'fraternity' by means of education and political reform (such as the 1954 Supreme Court decision in the United States, ending the legality of segregation).

The other camp called itself the 'socialist world' and argued that it and it alone represented the three objectives of the French Revolution and hence the interests of the people of the world. It argued that when movements inspired by these ideas would come to power in all non 'socialist' countries (and however they came to power), each would enact legislation along the same lines and by this process the whole world would become 'socialist' and the objective would be achieved.

These somewhat simplistic ideological statements were of course developed in much more elaborate form by the intellectuals. It has become almost traditional (but I think nonetheless just) to cite W. W. Rostow's *The Stages of Economic Growth* as a succinct, sophisticated, and relatively pure expression of the dominant liberal ideology which informed the thinking of the political leadership of the United States and its western allies. Rostow showed no modesty in his subtitle: which was 'a non-Communist Manifesto'.

His basic thesis is no doubt familiar to most persons interested in these problems. Rostow saw the process of change as a series of stages through which each national unit had to go. They were the stages through which Rostow felt Great Britain had gone, and Great Britain was the crucial example since it was defined as being the first state to embark on the evolutionary path of the modern industrial world. The inference, quite overtly drawn, was that this path was a model, to be copied by other states. One could then analyze what it took to move from one stage to another, why some nations took longer than others, and could prescribe (like a physician) what a nation must do to hurry along its process of 'growth'. I will not review what ideological function such a formulation served. This has been done repeatedly and well. Nonetheless, this viewpoint, somewhat retouched, still informs the developmentalist ideas of the major western governments as well as that of international agencies. I consider Lester Pearson's 'Partners in Progress' report in the direct line of this analytic framework.

In the socialist world in this period there was no book quite the match of Rostow's. What there was instead was an encrusted version of evolutionary Marxism which also saw rigid stages through which every state or geographical entity had to go. The differences were that the stages covered longer historical time and the model country was the USSR. These are the stages known as slavery–feudalism–capitalism–socialism. The absurdities of the rigid formulation which dates from the 1930s and the inappropriateness of applying this on a *national* level have been well argued recently by an Indian Marxist intellectual, Irfan Habib, who argues not only the meaningfulness of the concept of the 'Asiatic mode of production' but also the illogic of insisting that the various historical modes of extracting a surplus must each, necessarily, occur in all countries and follow in a specific order. Habib argues:

The materialist conception of history need not necessarily prescribe a set universal periodisation, since what it essentially does is to formulate an analytic method for the development of class societies, and any periodisation, theoretically, serves as no more than the illustration of the application of such a method...The crucial thing is the definition of principal contradiction (i.e., class-contradictions) in a society, the marking out of factors responsible for intensifying them, and the delineation of the shaping of the social order, when a particular contradiction is resolved. It is possible that release from the set P–S–F–C-pattern [primitive communism–slavery–feudalism–capitalism] may lead Marxists to apply themselves better to this task, since they would no longer be obliged to look for the same 'fundamental laws of the epoch' (a favourite Soviet term), or 'prime mover', as premised for the supposedly corresponding European epoch.[1]

I give this excerpt from Habib because I very much agree with his fundamental point that this version of Marxist thought, so prevalent between 1945 and 1965, is a sort of 'mechanical copying' of liberal views. Basically, the analysis is the same as that represented by Rostow except that the names of the stages are changed and the model country has shifted from Great Britain to the USSR. I will call this approach the developmentalist perspective, as espoused either by liberals or Marxists.

There is another perspective that has slowly pushed its way into public view during the 1960s. It has no commonly accepted name, in part because the early formulations of this point of view have

1. Irfan Habib, 'Problems of Marxist Historical Analysis in India', *Enquiry* (Monsoon, 1969). Reprinted in S. A. Shah (ed.), *Towards National Liberation: Essays on the Political Economy of India* (Montreal: n.p., 1973), pp. 8–9.

often been confused, partial, or unclear. It was first widely noticed in the thinking of the Latin American structuralists (such as Prebisch and Furtado) and those allied to them elsewhere (such as Dudley Seers). It later took the form of arguments such as the 'development of underdevelopment' (A. G. Frank, in the heritage of Baran's *The Political Economy of Growth*), the 'structure of dependence' (Theontonio Dos Santos), 'unequal exchange' (Arghiri Emmanuel), 'accumulation of world capital' (Samir Amin), 'subimperialism' (Ruy Mauro Marini). It also surfaced in the Chinese Cultural Revolution as Mao's concept of the continuity of the class struggle under socialist regimes in single countries.[2]

What all these concepts have in common is a critique of the developmentalist perspective. Usually they make it from a Marxist tradition but it should be noted that some of the critics, such as Furtado, come from a liberal heritage. It is no accident that this point of view has been expressed largely by persons from Asia, Africa and Latin America or by those others particularly interested in these regions (such as Umberto Melotti of *Terzo Mondo*).[3]

I would like to designate this point of view the 'world-system perspective'. I mean by that term that it is based on the assumption, explicitly or implicitly, that the modern world comprises a single capitalist world-economy, which has emerged historically since the sixteenth century and which still exists today. It follows from such a premise that national states are *not* societies that have separate, parallel histories, but parts of a whole reflecting that whole. To the extent that stages exist, they exist for the system as a whole. To be sure, since different parts of the world play and have played differing roles in the capitalist world-economy, they have dramatically different internal socio-economic profiles and hence distinctive politics. But to understand the internal class contradictions and political struggles of a particular state, we must first situate it in the world-economy. We can then understand the ways in which various political and cultural thrusts may be efforts to alter or preserve a position within this world-economy which is

2. See my 'Class Struggle in China?' *Monthly Review*, 25: 4 (September 1973), 55–8.
3. See U. Melotti, 'Marx e il Terzo Mondo', *Terzo Mondo*, 13–14 (September–December 1971). Melitto subtitles the work: 'Towards a Multilinear Schema of the Marxist Conception of Historical Development'.

to the advantage or disadvantage of particular groups located within a particular state.[4]

What thus distinguishes the developmentalist and the world system perspective is not liberalism versus Marxism nor evolutionism versus something else (since both are essentially evolutionary). Rather I would locate the distinction in two places. One is in mode of thought. To put it in Hegelian terms, the developmentalist perspective is mechanical, whereas the world-system perspective is dialectical. I mean by the latter term that at every point in the analysis, one asks not what is the formal structure but what is the consequence for both the whole and the parts of maintaining or changing a certain structure at that particular point in time, given the totality of particular positions of that moment in time. Intelligent analysis demands knowledge of the complex texture of social reality (historical concreteness) within a long-range perspective that observes trends and forces of the world-system, which can explain what underlies and informs the diverse historically concrete phenomena. If synchronic comparisons and abstracted generalizations are utilized, it is only as heuristic devices in search of a truth that is ever contemporary and hence ever changing.

This distinction of scientific methodology is matched by a distinction of praxis, of the politics of the real world. For what comes through as the second great difference between the two perspectives (the developmentalist and the world-system) is the prognosis for action. This is the reason why the latter perspective has emerged primarily from the intellectuals of the Third World. The developmentalist perspective not only insists that the model is to be found in the old developed countries (whether Great Britain – USA or USSR) but also that the fundamental international political issues revolve around the relations among the hegemonic powers of the world. From a world-system perspective, there are no 'models' (a mechanical notion) and the relations of the hegemonic powers are only one of many issues that confront the world-system.

4. I have developed this argument at length elsewhere. See *The Modern World-System: Capitalist Agriculture and the Origins of the European World-Economy* (New York and London: Academic Press, 1974) and 'The Rise and Future Demise of the World Capitalist System: Concepts for Comparative Analysis', *Comparative Studies in Society and History* 16: 4 (October 1974), 387–415, and above, ch. 1.

The emergence of the world-system perspective is a consequence of the dramatic challenge to European political domination
of the world which has called into question all Europo-centric
constructions of social reality. But intellectual evolution itself is
seldom dramatic. The restructuring of the allocation of power in
the world has made itself felt in the realm of ideas, particularly
in the hegemonic areas of the world, via a growing malaise that
intellectuals in Europe (including of course North America) have
increasingly felt about the validity of their answers to a series of
'smaller' questions – smaller, that is, than the nature of the
world-system as such.

Let us review successively six knotty questions to which answers
from a developmentalist perspective have increasingly seemed
inadequate.

Why have certain world-historical events of the last two centuries
taken place where and when they have? The most striking
'surprise', at the moment it occurred and ever since, is the
Russian Revolution. As we all know, neither Marx nor Lenin nor
anyone else thought that a 'socialist revolution' would occur in
Russia earlier than anywhere else. Marx had more or less predicted
Great Britain as the likely candidate, and after Marx's death, the
consensus of expectation in the international socialist movement
was that it would occur in Germany. We know that even after
1917 almost all the leading figures of the CPSU expected that the
'revolution' would have to occur quickly in Germany if the Soviet
regime was to survive. There was however no socialist revolution
in Germany and nonetheless the Soviet regime did survive.

We do not want for explanations of this phenomenon, but we
do lack convincing answers. Of course, there exists an explanation
that turns Marx on his head and argues that socialist revolutions
occur not in the so-called 'advanced capitalist' countries but
precisely in 'backward' countries. But this is in such blatant
contradiction with other parts of the developmentalist perspective
that its proponents are seldom willing to state it baldly, even less
defend it openly.

Nor is the Russian Revolution the only anomaly. There is a
long-standing debate about the 'exceptionalism' of the United
States. How can we explain that the USA replaced Great Britain
as the hegemonic industrial power of the world, and in the

process managed to avoid giving birth to a serious internal socialist movement? And if the USA could avoid socialism, why could not Brazil or Russia or Canada? Seen from the perspective of 1800, it would have been a bold social scientist who would have predicted the particular success of the USA.

Again there have been many explanations. There is the 'frontier' theory. There is the theory that underlines the absence of a previously entrenched 'feudal' class. There is the theory of the US as Britain's 'junior partner' who overtook the senior. But all of these theories are precisely 'exceptionalist' theories, contradicting the developmentalist paradigm. And furthermore, some of these variables apply to other countries where they did not seem to have the same consequences.

We could go on. I will mention two more briefly. For a long time, Great Britain's primacy (the 'first' industrial power) has been unquestioned. But was Britain the 'first' and if so why was she? This is a question that only recently has been seriously adumbrated. In April 1974 at another international colloquium held here in Montreal on the theme of 'Failed Transitions to Industrialism: The Case of 17th Century Netherlands and Renaissance Italy', one view put forward quite strongly was that neither Italy nor the Netherlands was the locus of the Industrial Revolution precisely because they were too far *advanced* economically. What a striking blow to a developmentalist paradigm.

And lastly one should mention the anomaly of Canada: a country which economically falls into a category below that of the world's leading industrial producers in structural terms, yet nonetheless is near the very top of the list in per capita income. This cannot be plausibly explained from a developmentalist perspective.

If the world has been 'developing' or 'progressing' over the past few centuries, how do we explain the fact that in many areas things seem to have gotten worse, not better? Worse in many ways, ranging from standard of living, to the physical environment, to the quality of life. And more to the point, worse in some places but better in others. I refer not merely to such contemporary phenomena as the so-called 'growing gap' between the industrialized countries and the Third World, but also to such earlier phenomena as the deindustrialization of many areas of the world (starting with the widely known example of the Indian textile industry in the late eighteenth and early nineteenth century).

You may say that this contradicts the liberal version of the developmentalist perspective but not its Marxist version, since 'polarization' was seen as part of the process of change. True enough, except that 'polarization' was presumably within countries and not between them. Furthermore, it is not clear that it is 'polarization' that has occurred. While the rich have gotten richer and the poor have gotten poorer, there is surely a fairly large group of countries now somewhere in between on many economic criteria, to cite such politically diverse examples as Mexico, Italy, Czechoslovakia, Itan, and South Africa.

Furthermore, we witness in the 1970s a dramatic shift in the distribution of the profit and the international terms of trade of oil (and possibly other raw materials). You may say it is because of the increased political sophistication and strength of the Arab world. No doubt this has occurred, but is this an explanation? I remind this group that the last moment of time in which there was a dramatic amelioration of world terms of trade of primary products was in the period 1897–1913, a moment which represented in political terms the apogee of European colonial control of the world.

Once again it is not that there are not a large number of explanations for the rise in oil prices. It is rather that I find these explanations, for what they're worth, in contradiction with a developmentalist perspective.

Why are there 'regressions'? In 1964, S. N. Eisenstadt published an article entitled 'Breakdowns of Modernization', in which he discussed the fact that there seemed to be cases of 'reversal' of regimes to 'a lower, less flexible level of political and social differentiation...'[5]

In seeking to explain the origins of such 'reversals', Eisenstadt restricted himself to hesitant hypotheses:

The problem of why in Turkey, Japan, Mexico, and Russia there emerge in the initial stages of modernization elites with orientations to change and ability to implement relatively effective policies, while they did not develop in these initial phases in Indonesia, Pakistan, or Burma, or why elites with similar differences tended to develop also in later stages of modernization, is an

5. S. N. Eisenstadt, 'Breakdowns of Modernization', *Economic Development and Cultural Change* 12: 4 (July 1964), 367.

extremely difficult one and constitutes one of the most baffling problems in comparative sociological analysis. There are but four available indications to deal with this problem. Very tentatively, it may perhaps be suggested that to some extent it has to do with the placement of these elites in the preceding social structure, with the extent of their internal cohesiveness, and of the internal transformation of their own value orientation.[6]

As is clear, Eisenstadt's tentative explanation is to be found in anterior factors operating internally in the state. This calls into question the concept of stages through which all not only must pass but all *can* pass, but it leaves intact the state framework as the focus of analysis and explanation. This of course leads us logically to ask how these anterior factors developed. Are they pure historical accident?

Similarly after the political rebellion of Tito's Yugoslavia against the USSR, the latter began to accuse Yugoslavia of 'revisionism' and of returning to capitalism. Later, China took up the same theme against the USSR.

But how can we explain how this happens? There are really two varieties of explanation from a developmentalist perspective. One is to say that 'regression' seems to have occurred, but that in fact 'progress' had never taken place. The leaders of a movement, whether a nationalist movement or a socialist movement, only pretended to favor change. In fact they were really always 'neocolonialist' stooges or 'revisionists' at heart. Such an explanation has partial truth, but it seems to me to place too much on 'false consciousness' and to fail to analyze movements in their immediate and continuing historical contexts.

The second explanation of 'regression' is a change of heart – 'betrayal'. Yes, but once again, how come sometimes, but not always? Are we to explain large-scale social phenomena on the basis of the accident of the biographic histories of the particular leaders involved? I cannot accept this, for leaders remain leaders in the long run only if their personal choices reflect wider social pressures.

If the fundamental paradigm of modern history is a series of parallel national processes, how do we explain the persistence of nationalism, indeed quite often its primacy, as a political force in the modern world? Developmentalists who are liberals deplore nationalism or explain it away as a transitional 'integrating'

6. *Ibid.*, pp. 365–6.

phenomenon. Marxists who are developmentalists are even more embarrassed. If the class struggle is primary – that is, implicitly the intranational class struggle – how do we explain the fact that the slogan of the Cuban revolution is 'Patria o muerte – venceremos?' And how could we explain this even more astonishing quotation from Kim Il Sung, the leader of the Democratic People's Republic of Korea:

> The homeland is a veritable mother for everyone. We cannot live nor be happy outside of our homeland. Only the flourishing and prosperity of our homeland will permit us to go down the path to happiness. The best sons and daughters of our people, all without exception, were first of all ardent patriots. It was to recover their homeland that Korean Communists struggled, before the Liberation, against Japanese imperialism despite every difficulty and obstacle.[7]

And if internal processes are so fundamental, why has not the reality of international workers' solidarity been greater? Remember the First World War.

As before, there are many explanations for the persistence of nationalism. I merely observe that all these explanations have to *explain away* the primacy of internal national processes. Or to put it another way, for developmentalists nationalism is sometimes good, sometimes bad. But when it is the one or the other, it is ultimately explained by developmentalists in an ad hoc manner, adverting to its meaning for the world-system.

An even more difficult problem for the developmentalists has been the recrudescence of nationalist movements in areas smaller than that of existing states. And it is not Biafra or Bangladesh that is an intellectual problem, because the usual manner of accounting for secessionist movements in Third World countries has been the failure to attain the stage of 'national integration'.

No, the surprise has been in the industrialized world: Blacks in the USA, Québec in Canada, Occitania in France, the Celts in Great Britain, and lurking in the background the nationalities question in the USSR. It is not that any of these 'nationalisms' is new. They are all long-standing themes of political and cultural conflict in all these countries. The surprise has been that, as of say 1945 or even 1960, most persons in these countries, using a developmentalist paradigm, regarded these movements or claims

---

7. *Activité Révolutionnaire du Camarade Kim Il Sung* (Pyongyang: Editions en langues étrangères, 1970). Livre illustré, 52nd page (edition unpaginated). Translation mine.

as remnants of a dying past, destined to diminish still further in vitality. And lo, a phoenix reborn.

The explanations are there. Some cry, anachronism – but if so, then the question remains, how come such a flourishing anachronism? Some say, loud shouting but little substance, a last bubble of national integration. Perhaps, but the intellectual and organizational development of these ethno-national movements seem to have moved rapidly and ever more firmly in a direction quite opposite to national integration. In any case, what in the developmentalist paradigm explains this phenomenon?

One last question, which is perhaps only a reformulation of the previous five. How is it that the 'ideal types' of the different versions of the developmentalist perspective all seem so far from empirical reality? Who has not had the experience of not being quite certain which party represents the 'industrial proletariat' or the 'modernizing elite' in Nigeria, or in France of the Second Empire for that matter? Let us be honest. Each of us, to the extent that he has ever used a developmentalist paradigm, has stretched empirical reality to a very Procrustean bed indeed.

Can the world-system perspective answer these questions better? We cannot yet be sure. This point of view has not been fully thought through. But let me indicate some possible lines of argument.

If the world-system is the focus of analysis, and if in particular we are talking of the capitalist world-economy, then divergent historical patterns are precisely to be expected. They are not an anomaly but the essence of the system. If the world-economy is the basic economic entity comprising a single division of labor, then it is natural that different areas perform different economic tasks. Anyway it is natural under capitalism, and we may talk of the core, the periphery and the semiperiphery of the world-economy. Since however political boundaries (states) are smaller than the economic whole, they will each reflect different groupings of economic tasks and strengths in the world market. Over time, some of these differences may be accentuated rather than diminished – the basic inequalities which are our theme of discussion.

It is also clear that over time the loci of economic activities keep changing. This is due to many factors – ecological exhaustion, the impact of new technology, climate changes, and the socioeconomic consequences of these 'natural' phenomena. Hence some areas 'progress' and others 'regress'. But the fact that particular states change their position in the world-economy, from semiperiphery to core say, or vice versa, does not in itself change the nature of the system. These shifts will be registered for individual states as 'development' or 'regression'. The key factor to note is that within a capitalist world-economy, all states cannot 'develop' simultaneously *by definition*, since the system functions by virtue of having unequal core and peripheral regions.[8]

Within a world-economy, the state structures function as ways for particular groups to affect and distort the functioning of the market. The stronger the state machinery, the more its ability to distort the world market in favor of the interests it represents. Core states have stronger state machineries than peripheral states.

This role of the state machineries in a capitalist world-economy explains the persistence of nationalism, since the primary social conflicts are quite often between groups located in different states rather than between groups located within the same state boundaries. Furthermore, this explains the ambiguity of class as a concept, since class refers to the economy which is worldwide, but class consciousness is a political, hence primarily national, phenomenon. Within this context, one can see the recrudescence of ethno-nationalisms in industrialized states as an expression of class consciousness of lower caste-class groups in societies where the class terminology has been preempted by nation-wide middle strata organized around the dominant ethnic group.

If then the world-system is the focus of analysis rather than the individual states, it is the natural history of this system at which we must look. Like all systems, the capitalist world-economy has both cyclical and secular trends, and it is important to distinguish them.

On the one hand, the capitalist world-economy seems to go through long cycles of 'expansion' and 'contraction'. I cannot at this point go into the long discussion this would require. I will limit myself to the very brief suggestion that 'expansion' occurs

8. As to how particular states can change their position, I have tried to furnish an explanation in 'Dependence in an Interdependent World: The Limited Possibilities of Transformation within the Capitalist World-Economy', *African Studies Review* 17: 1 (April 1974), 1–26, and below, ch. 4.

when the totality of world production is less than world effective demand, as permitted by the existing social distribution of world purchasing power, and that 'contraction' occurs when total world production exceeds world effective demand. These are cycles of 75–100 years in length in my view and the downward cycle is only resolved by a political reallocation of world income that effectively expands world demand. I believe we have just ended an expansionary cycle and we are in the beginning of a contractual one.

These cycles occur within a secular trend that has involved the physical expansion and politico-structural consolidation of the capitalist world-economy as such, but has also given birth to forces and movements which are eating away at these same structural supports of the existing world-system. In particular, these forces which we call revolutionary forces are calling into question the phenomenon of inequality so intrinsic to the existing world-system.

The trend towards structural consolidation of the system over the past four centuries has included three basic developments.

The first has been the capitalization of world agriculture, meaning the ever more efficient use of the world's land and sea resources in large productive units with larger and larger components of fixed capital. Over time, this has encompassed more and more of the earth's surface, and at the present we are probably about to witness the last major physical expansion, the elimination of all remaining plots restricted to small-scale, so-called 'subsistence' production. The counterpart of this process has been the steady concentration of the world's population as salaried workers in small, dense pockets – that is, proletarianization and urbanization. The initial impact of this entire process has been to render large populations more exploitable and controllable.

The second major structural change has been the development of technology that maximizes the ability to transform the resources of the earth into useable commodities at 'reasonable' cost levels. This is what we call industrialization, and the story is far from over. The next century should see the spread of industrial activity from the temperate core areas in which it has hitherto been largely concentrated to the tropical and semitropical peripheral areas. Industrialization too has hitherto tended to consolidate the system in providing a large part of the profit that makes the system worth the while of those who are on top of it, with a large enough surplus to sustain and appease the world's middle strata. Mere extension of industrial activity will not change a peripheral area into a core area, for the core areas will concentrate on ever newer, specialized activities.

The third major development, at once technological and social, has been the strengthening of all organizational structures – the states', the economic corporate structures, and even the cultural institutions – *vis-à-vis* both individuals and groups. This is the process of bureaucratization, and while it has been uneven (the core states are still stronger than the peripheral states, for example), all structures are stronger today than previously. Prime ministers of contemporary states have the power today that Louis XIV sought in vain to achieve. This too has been stabilizing because the ability of these bureaucracies physically to repress opposition is far greater than in the past.

But there is the other side of each of these coins. The displacement of the world's population into urban areas has made it easier ultimately to organize forces against the power structures. This is all the more so since the ever-expanding, market-dependent, propertyless groups are simultaneously more educated, more in communication with each other, and hence *potentially* more politically conscious.

The steady industrialization of the world has eaten away at the political and hence economic justifications for differentials in rewards. The technological advances, while still unevenly distributed, have created a new military equality of destructive potential. It is true that one nation may have a thousand times the fire power of another, but if the weaker one has sufficient to incur grievous damage, of how much good is it for the stronger to have a thousand times as much strength? Consider not merely the power of a weaker state with a few nuclear rockets but the military power of urban guerillas. It is the kind of problem Louis XIV precisely did *not* need to worry about.

Finally, the growth of bureaucracies in the long run has created the weakness of topheaviness. The ability of the presumed decision makers to control not the populace but the bureaucracies has effectively diminished, which again creates a weakness in the ability to enforce politico-economic will.

Where then in this picture do the forces of change, the

movements of liberation, come in? They come in precisely as not totally coherent pressures of groups which arise out of the structural contradictions of the capitalist world-economy. These groups seem to take organizational form as movements, as parties, and sometimes as regimes. But when the movements become regimes, they are caught in the dilemma of becoming part of the machinery of the capitalist world-economy they are presuming to change. Hence the so-called 'betrayals'. It is important neither to adulate blindly these regimes, for inevitably they 'betray' in part their stated goals, nor to be cynical and despairing, for the movements which give birth to such regimes represent real forces, and the creation of such regimes is part of a long-run process of social transformation.

What we need to put in the forefront of our consciousness is that both the party of order and the party of movement are currently strong. We have not yet reached the peak of the political consolidation of the capitalist world-economy. We are already in the phase of its political decline. If your outlook is developmentalist and mechanical, this pair of statements is an absurdity. From a world-system perspective, and using a dialectical mode of analysis, it is quite precise and intelligible.

This struggle takes place on all fronts – political, economic, and cultural – and in all arenas of the world, in the core states, in the periphery (largely in the Third World), and in the semiperiphery (many but not all of which states have collective ownership of basic property and are hence often called 'socialist' states).

Take a struggle like that of Vietnam, of Algeria, or Angola. They were wars of national liberation. They united peoples in these areas. Ultimately, the forces of national liberation won or are winning political change. How may we evaluate its effect? On the one hand, these colonial wars fundamentally weakened the internal supports of the regimes of the USA, France and Portugal. They sapped the dominant forces of world capitalism. These wars made many changes possible in the countries of struggle, the metropolises, and in third countries. And yet, and yet – one can ask if the net result has not been in part further to intregrate these countries, even their regimes, into the capitalist world-economy. It did both of course. We gain nothing by hiding this from ourselves. On the other hand, we gain nothing by showing olympian neutrality in the form of equal disdain for unequal combatants.

The process of analysis and the process of social transformation are not separate. They are obverse sides of one coin. Our praxis informs, indeed makes possible, our analytic frameworks. But the work of analysis is itself a central part of the praxis of change. The perspectives for the future of inequality in the world-system are fairly clear in the long run. In the long run the inequalities will disappear as the result of a fundamental transformation of the world-system. But we all live in the short run, not in the long run. And in the short run, within the constraints of our respective social locations and our social heritages, we labor in the vineyards as we wish, towards what ends we choose. We are here today because we want to be. We will make of this colloquium what we want to make of it, and we will draw whatever political conclusions we wish to draw.

4 ❧ Dependence in an interdependent world: the limited possibilities of transformation within the capitalist world-economy

'Dependence' has become the latest euphemism in a long list of such terms. No doubt its original intent was critical. The term itself emerged out of the 'structuralist' theories of Latin American scholars and was meant as a rebuttal to 'developmentalist' or 'modernization' theories and 'monetarist' policy views.[1] André Gunder Frank has traced its intellectual origins and its limitations in a recent combative paper entitled 'Dependence is dead; long live dependence and the class struggle'.[2]

We live in a capitalist world-economy, one that took definitive shape as a European world-economy in the sixteenth century (see Wallerstein 1974a) and came to include the whole world geographically in the nineteenth century. Capitalism as a system of production for sale in a market for profit and appropriation of this profit on the basis of individual or collective ownership has only existed in, and can be said to require, a world-system in which the political units are not coextensive with the boundaries of the market economy. This has permitted sellers to profit from strengths in the market whenever they exist but enabled them simultaneously to seek, whenever needed, the instrusion of political entities to distort the market in their favor. Far from being a system of free competition of all sellers, it is a system in which competition becomes relatively free only when the economic advantage of upper strata is so clear-cut that the unconstrained operation of the market serves effectively to reinforce the existing system of stratification.

---

1. See, as a mere beginning, Bodenheimer 1971, Caputo and Pizarro 1970, Cardoso 1971, Cockcroft et al. 1972, Bulletin of the Institute of Development Studies 1971.
2. See Frank 1972a; see also for a similar point of view Frères du Monde 1971.

This is not to say that there are no changes in position. Quite the contrary. There is constant and patterned movement between groups of economic actors as to who shall occupy various positions in the hierarchy of production, profit, and consumption. And there are secular developments in the structure of the capitalist world-system such that we can envisage that its internal contradictions as a system will bring it to an end in the twenty-first or twenty-second century.

The important thing for living men, and for scholars and scientists as their collective intellectual expression, is to situate the options available in the contemporary situation in terms of the patterns we can discern in the historical past. In this task, conceptual clarification is the most constant need, and as life goes on and new experiences occur, we learn, if we are wise, to reject and reformulate the partial truths of our predecessors, and to unmask the ideological obscurantism of the self-interested upholders of encrusted privilege.

The years 1945–70 were a period of exceptional obscurantism in all fields of study, and African studies has been in this sense typical. Liberal ideology prevailed in the world of social science reflecting the easy and unquestioned economic hegemony of the United States. But liberalism has come onto hard days – not least of all in the analysis of 'development'. If the decline of Cold War polarization in the 1960s effectively reduced the political bargaining power of African states, the beginning of a worldwide economic contraction of effective demand of the 1970s is likely to sweep African aspirations aside as those who are on top of the world heap struggle with each other to remain there. In the 1960s, African scholars began to worry about 'growth without development'. In the 1970s and 1980s, there is the clear possibility of neither growth nor development.

To understand the issues, we must successively treat the structure of the world-economy, its cyclical patterns including the present conjuncture, and the ways in which the position of particular states may change within this structure. This will, I believe, explain 'the limited possibilities of transformation within the capitalist world-economy'.

The structure of the world-economy as a single system has come increasingly in recent years to be analyzed in terms of a core–

periphery image, an image which has been linked with the discussion of 'dependence'. And thus it has been argued, for example, that Third World countries are not 'underdeveloped' nations but 'peripheral capitalist' nations.[3] This is far clearer terminology, but it leads unfortunately to further confusion if the unicity of the world-system is not borne clearly in mind. Ikonicoff argues, for example, that peripheral capitalist economies 'operate by economic laws and growth factors [that] are clearly different from those of the economies one might call the model of classic capitalism' (1972, p. 692). This is only so because our model of 'classic capitalism' is wrong, since both in the sixteenth century and today the core and the periphery of the world-economy were not two separate 'economies' with two separate 'laws' but one capitalist economic system with different *sectors* performing different functions.

Once one recognizes the unicity of the system, one is led to ask if the conception of a bi-modal system is adequate. Clearly, it leaves much unexplained, and thus we have seen the emergence of such terms as 'subimperial' states (see Marini 1969) or 'go-between nations' (see Galtung 1972, pp. 128–9). Both of these terms seem to me unwise as they emphasize only one aspect of their role, each an important one, but not in my opinion the key one. I prefer to call them semiperipheral countries to underline the ways they are at a disadvantage in the existing world-system. More important, however, is the need to explicate the *complexity* of the role which semiperipheral states play within the system as well as the fact that the system could not function without being *tri*-modal.

Before this explication, it is necessary to spell out one more fact. The capitalist system is composed of owners who sell for profit. The fact that an owner is a group of individuals rather than a single person makes no essential difference. This has long been recognized for joint-stock companies. It must now also be recognized for sovereign states. A state which collectively owns all the means of production is merely a collective capitalist firm as long as it remains – as all such states are, in fact, presently compelled to remain – a participant in the market of the capitalist world-

3. See, for example, the whole special issue of *Revue Tiers-Monde* 1972, especially the introduction by Ikonicoff.

economy. No doubt such a 'firm' *may* have different modalities of internal division of profit, but this does not change its essential economic role *vis-à-vis* others operating in the world market.[4] It, of course, remains to discuss in which sector of the world-system the 'socialist' states are located.

The capitalist world-system needs a semiperipheral sector for two reasons: one primarily political and one politico-economic. The political reason is very straightforward and rather elementary. A system based on unequal reward must constantly worry about political rebellion of oppressed elements. A polarized system with a small distinct high-status and high-income sector facing a relatively homogeneous low-status and low-income sector including the overwhelming majority of individuals in the system leads quite rapidly to the formation of classes *für sich* and acute, disintegrating struggle. The major political means by which such crises are averted is the creation of 'middle' sectors, which tend to think of themselves primarily as better off than the lower sector rather than as worse off than the upper sector. This obvious mechanism, operative in all kinds of social structures, serves the same function in world-systems.

But there is another reason that derives from the particular needs of this kind of social structure, a capitalist world-system. The multiplicity of states within the single economy has two advantages for sellers seeking profit. First, the absence of a single political authority makes it impossible for anyone to legislate the general will of the world-system and hence to curtail the capitalist mode of production. Second, the existence of state machineries makes it possible for the capitalist sellers to organize

4. I have argued this at length in my paper, 'The Rise and Future Demise of the World Capitalist System: Concepts for Comparative Analysis' (1974b, and above, ch. 1). Samir Amin makes just about the same point:

> The predominance of the capitalist mode of production expresses itself also on another level, that of the *world-system* which constitutes a characteristic of contemporary reality. At this level, the formations (central and peripheral) are organized in a single hierarchical system. The disintegration of this system – with the founding of socialist states, true or self-styled – does not change anything in this hypothesis...Socialism cannot be in fact the juxtaposition of national socialisms, regressive with respect to integrated (but not egalitarian) world character of capitalism. Nor can it be a *socialist system* separate from the world-system. It is precisely for this reason that there are not two world markets: the capitalist market and the socialist market; but only *one* – the former – in which eastern Europe participates, albeit marginally.
>
> (1972b, p. 13)

the frequently necessary artificial restraints on the operation of the market.

But this system has one disadvantage for the sellers. The state machineries can reflect other pressures than of those who sell products on the market, for example, of those who sell labor. What regularly happens in core countries is the operation of a guild principle which, in fact, raises wage levels. It is this to which Arghiri Emmanuel refers when he says: 'The value of labor power is, so far as its determination is concerned, a magnitude that is, in the immediate sense, *ethical*: it is *economic* only in an indirect way, through the mediation of its moral and historical element, which is itself determined, in the last analysis, by economic causes' (1972, p. 120).

The rising wages of the workers in the core countries, combined with the increasing *economic* disadvantage of the leading economic producers, given constant technological progress, and heaviest investment in rapidly outdated fixed capital by precisely the leading producers, leads to an inevitable decline in comparative costs of production. For individual capitalists, the ability to shift capital, from a declining leading sector to a rising sector, is the only way to survive the effects of cyclical shifts in the loci of the leading sectors. For this there must be sectors able to profit from the wage-productivity squeeze of the leading sector. Such sectors are what we are calling semiperipheral countries. If they weren't there, the capitalist system would as rapidly face an *economic* crisis as it would a *political* crisis. (How, incidentally, this shift of capital investment would operate in a world capitalist system composed of only state-owned enterprises is an interesting question, but not one for the moment we are called upon to analyze.)

How then can we tell a semiperipheral country when we see one? Even if we admit a tri-modal system, it would be an oversimplification not to bear in the front of our mind that each structural sector contains states of varying degrees of political and economic strength. Furthermore, each sector contains some states that are seeking to move (or *not* to move) from one structural position to another (and for whom such a move is plausible) and other states that for the moment are mired in the location where they find themselves.

Nonetheless, it is important to spell out some defining characteristics of a semiperipheral state, as opposed to a core or a peripheral state. If we think of the exchange between the core and the periphery of a capitalist system being that between high-wage products and low-wage products, there then results an 'unequal exchange' in Emmanuel's conception, in which a peripheral worker needs to work many hours, at a given level of productivity, to obtain a product produced by a worker in a core country in one hour. And vice versa. Such a system is *necessary* for the expansion of a world market if the primary consideration is *profit*. Without *unequal* exchange, it would not be *profitable* to expand the size of the division of labor.[5] And without such expansion, it would not be profitable to maintain a capitalist world-economy, which would then either disintegrate or revert to the form of a redistributive world-empire.[6]

What products are exchanged in this 'unequal exchange' are a function of world technology. If in the sixteenth century, peripheral Poland traded its wheat for core Holland's textiles, in the mid-twentieth-century world, peripheral countries are often textile producers whereas core countries export wheat as well as electronic equipment. The point is that we should not identify any particular product with a structural sector of the world-economy but rather observe the wage patterns and margins of profit of particular products at particular moments of time to understand who does what in the system.

In a system of unequal exchange, the semiperipheral country stands in between in terms of the kinds of products it exports and in terms of the wage levels and profit margins it knows. Furthermore, it trades or seeks to trade in both directions, in one mode with the periphery and in the opposite with the core. And

5. See Samir Amin: 'Central capital is not at all constrained to emigrate because of a lack of possible [investment] outlets in the center; but it will emigrate to the periphery if it can get a higher remuneration there...It is thus here that we insert the *necessary* theory of *unequal exchange*. The products exported by the periphery are interesting to the degree that – other things being equal annd here this expressions means *of equal productivity* – the remuneration for labor is less than it is in the center. And this is possible to the degree that society is forced by various means – economic and extra-economic – to play this new role: furnish cheap manpower to the export sector' (1972a, pp. 707–8).

6. It would take us far astray to develop this here. What I mean by 'redistributive world-empire' is defined in my 'The Rise and Future Demise...'. It would be interesting to see if it were not such processes as these which account for the stifling of nascent capitalist elements in such ancient systems as the Roman Empire.

herein lies the singularity of the semiperiphery as opposed to both the periphery and the core. Whereas, at any given moment, the more of *balanced* trade a core country or a peripheral country can engage in, the better off it is in absolute terms, it is often in the interest of a semiperipheral country to *reduce* external trade, even if balanced, since one of the major ways in which the aggregate profit margin can be increased is to capture an increasingly large percentage of its *home* market for its *home* products.

This, then, leads to a second clear and distinctive feature of a semiperipheral state. The direct and immediate interest of the state as a political machinery in the control of the market (internal and international) is greater than in either the core of the peripheral states, since the semiperipheral states can *never* depend on the market to maximize, *in the short run*, their profit margins.

The 'politicization' of economic decisions can be seen to be most operative for semiperipheral states at moments of active change of status, which are two: (1) the actual breakthrough from peripheral to semiperipheral status and (2) strengthening of an already semiperipheral state to the point that it can lay claim to membership in the core.

The political economies of the various sectors of the world-economy show distinct differences in patterns at various moments of the long-run cycles of the world-economy. It was rather convincingly established by the price historians who began writing in the late 1920s that for a very long period the European world-economy (and, at least since the nineteenth century, the whole world) has gone through a series of systemic expansions and contractions (see a summary and synthesis of this literature in Braudel and Spooner, pp. 378–486). It should be obvious that when the system as a whole is in economic crisis, some parts of it may have to pay a price in relative position as a result of the conflict engendered by the enforced redistribution that follows on economic contraction. But what does that mean for the nations of the periphery and the semiperiphery? Is world economic crisis their bane or their salvation? As one might guess, the answer is not easy.

Clearly, as a general rule, there is more pressure for reallocation of roles and rewards in all systems at moments of contraction than at moments of expansion, since in moments of expansion even groups that are less rewarded may obtain an *absolute* expansion in reward, whereas in moments of contraction even those who are most highly rewarded are threatened with *absolute* decline, in which case one way to maintain an evenness in absolute reward is to seek an increase in *relative* reward. This general proposition applies to world-systems as well.

A pressure to reallocate roles and rewards can have two different outlets: one is circulation of the groups who play different roles, and hence what is increase for one is decrease for another. A second is the redistribution of rewards among different roles in a more egalitarian direction. Within the modern world-system, much historical change has been justified in the name of the latter objective, but the reality thus far of most such change has been the former. One fundamental explanation is that the framework of the capitalist world-system limits critically the possibilities of transformation of the reward system within it, since disparity of reward is the fundamental motivating force of the operation of the system as it is constructed.

To be very concrete, it is not possible theoretically for all states to 'develop' simultaneously. The so-called 'widening gap' is not an anomaly but a continuing basic mechanism of the operation of the world-economy. Of course, *some* countries can 'develop'. But the some that rise are at the expense of others that decline. Indeed, the rest of this paper will be devoted to indicating some of the mechanisms used by the minority that at given moments rise (or fall) in status within the world-economy.

There is an alternative system that can be constructed, that of a socialist world government in which the principles governing the economy would not be the market but rather the optimum utilization and distribution of resources in the light of a collectively arrived at notion of substantive rationality. I say this not in order to develop further how such a prospective system would operate, were it in existence, but rather to emphasize that the nationalization or socialization of all productive enterprises within the bounds of a nation-state is not and theoretically cannot be a sufficient defining condition of a socialist system, even if the whole nation thinks of socialism as its objective. As long as these nations remain part of a capitalist world-economy, they continue to produce for this world market on the basis of the same principles as any other producer. Even if *every* nation in the world were to permit only state ownership of the means of production, the world-system would still be a capitalist system, although doubtless the political parameters would be very different from what they presently are.

Let me be very clear. I am not suggesting that it does not matter if a country adopts collective ownership as a political requirement of production. The moves in this direction are the result of a series of progressive historical developments of the capitalist world-economy and represent themselves a major motive force for further change. Nor am I in any way suggesting the immutability of the capitalist system. I am merely suggesting that ideological intent is not synonymous with structural change, that the only *system* in the modern world that can be said to have a mode of production is the *world*-system, and that this system currently (but not eternally) is capitalist in mode.

It is important to cut through the ideological veneer if we are to notice the differences among those countries in the periphery seeking to become semiperipheral in role, those countries in the semiperiphery seeking to join the core, and those countries in the core fighting against a declining economic position.

The shift to which most attention has been paid in recent years is the shift from being peripheral to being semiperipheral, although it is usually discussed abstractly as though it were a question of shifting from periphery to core.[7] But this is not the shift that is, in fact, made. Countries have not moved, nor are any now moving, from being primarily exporters of low-wage products to being substantial exporters of high-wage products as well as being their own major customer for these high-wage products. Rather, some move from the former pattern to that of

7. For example, Samir Amin's discussion (1972a) argues that there are two models of capital accumulation, each a 'system', one peripheral and one self-centered ('*auto-centré*'). But when he cites a case that uses what he argues is the correct strategy of 'self reliance', Vietnam, he talks of Vietnam having reached 'an effective first stage of the transition' (p. 717). But what is the structural composition of this 'first stage' in terms of the world-economy which Amin agrees is single? This is not spelled out. But it is I should think very important to spell out. Amin is in favor of 'self reliance' but not of 'autarchy', for example. In practice, Amin distinguishes not only between most peripheral countries and Vietnam, but also between two stages of 'peripheral domination', which leads to his calling Brazil a 'very advanced underdeveloped nation' (pp. 720–1).

having a higher-wage sector which produces *part* of what is consumed on the internal market but is still in a dependent relationship for the other part of national consumption. The essential difference between the semiperipheral country that is Brazil or South Africa today and the semiperipheral country that is North Korea or Czechoslovakia is probably less in the economic role each plays in the world-economy than in the political role each plays in conflicts among core countries and the direction of their exported surplus value.

We must start with the clear realization that not all peripheral countries at any given time are in an equal position to lay claim to a shift in status. As Reginald Green somewhat depressingly puts it: 'The attainment of a dynamic toward national control over and development of the economy must start from the existing structural and institutional position, both territorial and international' (1970, p. 277). We know, by looking backward in history, that among peripheral countries some have changed status and others have not. The Santiago meeting of UNCTAD in 1972 underlined among other things the differing *interests* of different Third World countries in various proposals. The United Nations has developed a list of 'hard core' poor nations, of which sixteen are in Africa (about half of all African states), eight in Asia and Oceania, and only one (Haiti) in Latin America. It is not clear that politico-economic decisions on the reallocation of world resources, such as those that have been favored by the Group of 77, would in fact do very much to alter the relative status of these 'hard core' countries (see Colson 1972, especially pp. 826–30).

The fact that some make it and some don't is a continuing source of puzzlement for many writers. For example, Cardoso and Faletto, in their discussion of populism in Latin American countries as a mode of profiting from world economic crises, note that these movements have been more successful in some than others. Whereas in some they simply led to an 'intensified oligarchic control of agricultural-exporting groups, usually taking authoritarian-military forms', in others they have led to 'more open polyclass' rule and consequently more industrialization. They explain differing results as the result of different schemes of domination that managed to prevail in each country (Cardoso and

Faletto 1969, p. 80). This seems less an explanation than a restatement of the phenomenon.

Similarly, Green notes the limitations of the 'staple thesis', suggesting it is unable to account for why the 'dynamic external trade sector' with 'spill-over demand' worked in Canada and Scandinavia but elsewhere led to 'fossilization' (1970, p. 280). He suggests that the key issue is how countries 'mobilise and harness the potential resource flows from these enclaves to the creation of national educational, institutional, and productive capacity to create a dynamic for development broader than the original export units' (p. 293). No doubt, but once again this implies some missing element in the equation and assumes all countries can make it.

Is it not rather the case that only a minority of peripheral countries can fit into an expanding world market or conquer part of a contracting one at any given time? And that those who do, of course, manifest their 'success' by this missing 'extra ingredient'. It would seem to be more fruitful to look at the possible alternative strategies in the light of the fact that only a minority can 'make it' within the framework of the world-system as it is than to search for the universal recipe. We may of course, be dismayed by the ethics of such a choice – I am myself[8] – but that would only lead us to ask about the possibilities of some more radical systemic transformation, not to look for a reformist panacea.

Basically there are three strategies: the strategy of seizing the chance, the strategy of promotion by invitation, and the strategy of self-reliance. They are different, to be sure, but perhaps (unfortunately) less different than their protagonists proclaim.

By seizing the chance, we mean simply the fact that at moments of world-market contraction, where typically the price level of primary exports from peripheral countries goes down more rapidly than the price level of technologically advanced industrial exports from core countries, the governments of peripheral states

8. R. H. Tawney calls the approach to self-improvement in a capitalist world by individual achievement via the use of talent the Tadpole Philosophy, 'since the consolation which it offers for social evils consists in the statement that exceptional individuals can succeed in evading them'. And he concludes: 'As though the noblest use of exceptional powers were to scramble to shore, undeterred by the thought of drowning companions!' (1952, p. 109). Developmental ideology is merely the global version of this Tadpole Philosophy.

are faced with balance-of-payments problems, a rise in unemployment, and a reduction of state income. One solution is 'import substitution', which tends to palliate these difficulties. It is a matter of 'seizing the chance' because it involves aggressive state action that takes advantage of the weakened political position of core countries and the weakened economic position of domestic opponents of such policies. It is a classic solution and accounts, for example, for the expansion of industrial activity in Russia and Italy in the late nineteenth century (see, for example, Von Laue 1963) or of Brazil and Mexico (see Furtado 1970, especially pp. 85–9) – or South Africa (see Horowitz 1967, chapter 15) – in the wake or the Great Depression of 1929. A war situation, providing destruction is somewhat limited, and 'reconstruction', aggressively pursued, may provide the same 'chance'. Was this not the case for North Korea in the 1950s? (See Kuark 1963.)

In each of these cases, we are dealing with relatively strong peripheral countries, countries that had some small industrial base already and were able to expand this base at a favorable moment. As Theontonio Dos Santos puts it:

The capacity to react in the face of these [economic] crises depends in large part on the internal composition of the dependent countries. If they possess a very important complementary industrial sector, the latter can profit from the crisis in the following manner: In the course of the crisis, the export sector is weakened, imports diminish and their cost tends to rise because of the financial crisis which devalues national currencies... The consequence is thus an encouragement of national industry which has a relatively important market, a high sales price, and weak international competition; if this sector has some unused capacity, it can utilize it immediately, and with a favorable state policy, it can use the small existing foreign exchange to import cheaply machines, for the surplus production in dominant countries causes their prices to go down relatively. (1971, p. 737)

'Seizing the chance' as a strategy has certain built-in problems, for industrial development leads these prospective semiperipheral countries to import both machines and manufactured primary materials from the core countries, essentially substituting new dependence for the old, from which 'no dependent country has yet succeeded in liberating itself' (Dos Santos 1971, p. 745). This problem is far more serious today than in the 1930s, and *a fortiori* than in earlier centuries because of the world level of technology. Merhav has argued that what he calls 'technological dependence' inevitably leads, on the one hand, to the emergence of a monopolistic structure because the scales of output that must be adopted to introduce modern methods are large relative to the extent of the initial market; and on the other hand, these markets will be only practically expanded through income generated by investment, since a large proportion of the capital goods must be imported. In addition, the monopolistic structure itself will restrict the volume of investment...So that the two effects reinforce each other...[9]

Furthermore, such (national) monopolies are created 'even in industries which in the advanced countries are more nearly competitive in structure...' (Merhav 1969, p. 65). Thus, despite the industrialization 'investment is less than what it could be with the existing resources'.[10]

The national political alliance of 'development populism' furthermore is subject to internal contradictions in countries based on private enterprise since it involves a temporary coming together of the industrial bourgeoisie and the urban workers to favor certain kinds of state action, but once these actions are engaged in, the two groups have opposite interests in terms of wage scales. Thus, Marini suggests that holding such a 'developmentalist alliance' together depends on

the possibility of maintaining a tariff policy and a monetary policy that allows, at the expense of the agricultural sector and of the traditional sectors, intertwining at one and the same time the rhythm of industrial inversion and, if not a significant rise in real wages, at least an increase in absolute terms of the number of individuals from the popular sectors who are progressively incorporated into the industrial system.   (1969, p. 107)

Marini indicates the great political difficulties for Latin America in keeping up such a policy for long periods of time. But hasn't this been equally true for Eastern European countries in the last twenty years, where all enterprises have been state-run? Was not the crisis that brought Gierek to power in Poland the result of the breakdown of the 'developmentalist alliance' that Gomulka originally symbolized? Had not Gomulka's backtrackings led to severe worker unrest, as concessions to the agricultural sector were being paid for by urban workers in terms of real wages?

9. Merhav 1969, pp. 59–60. The ways in which technological dependence is both economically irrational and self-perpetuating in the capitalist world economy is explained with great clarity by Urs Müller-Plantenburg (1971). However, it is not at all clear from his analysis why the forces he adumbrates (see the summary on p. 77) which force a private entrepreneur in a peripheral country into an irrational technology should not operate equally for a state-run enterprise.
10. Merhav 1969, p. 60. 'What it could be' reminds one of Paul Baran's concept of 'potential economic surplus' (see Baran 1967, ch. 2).

Technological dependence plus internal political pressures from the agricultural sector have a possible solution, as Marini points out. Speaking of the policies of the Brazilian military that came to power after 1964, he says:

Thus, both by their policies of reinforcing their alliance with the large landowners (*el latifundio*) and by their policy of integration to imperialism, the Brazilian bourgeoisie cannot count on a growth of the internal market sufficient to absorb the growing production that results from technological modernization. There remains no alternative but to try to expand outward, and thus they turn necessarily to obtaining a guaranteed external market for their production. The low cost of production which the present wage policy and industrial modernization tend to create points in the same direction: export of manufactured products.

(1969, pp. 85–6)

This same analysis, virtually unchanged, could be used to explain the 'outward policy' of the present South African government and their attempts to achieve a common market in southern Africa.[11] At a smaller scale, is this not what has been involved in the abortive attempts of President Mobutu of Zaïre to build new structures of economic cooperation in Equatorial Africa?

The image thus far projected is of an attempt by an indigenous 'developmentalist' sector in a peripheral country to 'seize its chance' and strengthen its 'industrial sector', thus becoming a 'semiperipheral' country. Then, we have suggested, over time the combination of internal pressure (the 'agricultural sector') and external *force majeure* ('technological dependence') leads to the recuperation of the rebel and the stabilization of the new economic structures such that the development of an 'internal market' originally projected is abandoned[12] and an 'external market' is substituted, but one in which the semiperipheral country largely serves as a purveyor of products it is no longer worth the while of the core country to manufacture.

But have we not got beyond the 'recuperated rebel' scenario?

11: This has been the clear hope of the South African leadership. See Lombard *et al.* 1968.
12. See André Gunder Frank: 'But this import *substitute* development *did not* create its own market, or at least its own internal market. This development if anything created a post-war internal market for externally-produced and imported producer goods, and foreign investment...rather than raising internal wages...Instead, to pay for the imports of producers goods required to sustain industrial production, as well as to sustain the latter's profitability, this dependent capitalism again resorted – perforce – to the increasing super-exploitation of labor, both in the export and the domestic sectors, as in Brazil and Mexico (and India?)' (1972b, p. 41).

We may have, as the increasingly sophisticated techniques of the burgeoning multinational corporations seem to enable the world-system to arrive at the same result by means of what I am calling 'semiperipheral development by invitation'.

The whole system of direct investment across frontiers grew up in part because of the flowering of infant industry protectionism and in part because of some political limitations to growth of enterprises in core countries (such as anti-trust legislation). The multinational corporations quickly realized that operating in collaboration with state bureaucracies posed no real problems. For these national governments are for the most part weak both in terms of what they have to offer and in their ability to affect the overall financial position of the outside investor. As Hymer points out, governments of underdeveloped nations are roughly in the relationship to a multinational corporation that a state or municipal government in the United States stands to a national corporation. While the government of the metropolis can, by taxation, 'capture some of the surplus generated by the multinational corporation', the competition among peripheral countries 'to attract corporate investment eats up their surplus' (Hymer 1972, p. 128).

Why then do the underdeveloped countries compete for this investment? Because, as the examples of the Ivory Coast and Kenya demonstrate, there are distinct advantages in winning this competition even at the disadvantageous terms such aided development is offered. For example, Samir Amin who has been one of the most vocal critics of the Ivory Coast path of development points out:

Up to now [1971] every one has gotten something out of the Ivory Coast's prosperity via foreign capitalist enterprise: in the countryside, the traditional chiefs, transformed into planters, have become richer, as have the immigrant workers from [Upper Volta] who come out of a traditional, stagnant, very poor milieu; in the town, unemployment remains limited in comparison with what it is already in the large urban centres of older African countries.

(1971b, p. 92)

No doubt, as Amin says, the Ivory Coast has gone from being 'the primitive country that it was in 1950' to being a 'veritable under developed country, well integrated, as its elder sister, Senegal, into the world capitalist system' (1971b, p. 93). No doubt, too, as Amin suggests, only Nkrumah's pan-African proposals 'would have made it possible to begin to resolve the true problem of development' (p. 280). But Nkrumah did not survive, as we know. The effective choice of the Ivory Coast bourgeoisie may not, therefore, have been between the Ivory Coast path and that recommended by Nkrumah and Amin, but between the Ivory Coast path and that of Dahomey. Given such a choice, there seems little need to explain further why they chose as they did (see my discussion in Wallerstein 1971, pp. 19–33).

The path of promotion by invitation seems to have two differences with the path of 'seizing the chance'. Done in more intimate collaboration (economic and political) with external capitalists, it is more a phenomenon of moments of expansion than of moments of contraction. Indeed, such collaborative 'development' is readily sacrificed by core countries when they experience any economic difficulties themselves. Second, it is available to countries with less prior industrial development than the first path but then it peaks at a far lower level of import-substitution light industries rather than the intermediate level of heavier industries known in Brazil or South Africa.

One might make the same analysis for Kenya, except that the neighbor of Kenya is Tanzania, and thus for Tanzania the path of *ujamaa* has survived and is indeed the prime example of the third road of development for a peripheral country, that of 'self-reliance'. Tanzania has been determined *not* to be a 'complicit victim', in Sfia's trenchant phase (see Sfia 1971, p. 580).

A sympathetic analysis of Taanzania's attempts by Green (1970) starts with the assumption that 'in Africa the closed-national strategy of structural change for development will be even harder to implement than in Latin America' and that 'economic decolonization and development will be agonizingly slow even with efficient policy formulation and execution and the best likely external economic developments' (pp. 284–5). Green terminates with the cautious conclusion that: 'The Tanzania experience to date [1969] is that even in the short term a clearly enunciated and carefully pursued strategy of development including economic independence as a goal can be consistent with an accelerating rate of economic as well as social and political development' (p. 324). Let us accept that Tanzania has done modestly well. We may applaud, but may we generalize the advice? One thing to consider is whether Tanzania's path has not been possible for the same reason as Kenya's and the Ivory Coast's, that it is a path being pursued not by all peripheral countries, but by very few. In this case, both Tanzania's poverty and her rarity among Africa's regimes stand her in good stead of thus far minimizing the external pressure brought to bear against her economic policies. Core capitalist countries calculate risks for Tanzania as well as Kenya. Tanzania's model of self-reliance would seem more convincing if Zambia were successfully to adopt it.

It is from eastern Europe that we get, interestingly enough, a caution to small countries on the limits of the path of self-reliance. The Hungarian economist, Béla Kádár, sums up his prudence thus:

The necessity to comply increasingly with world economy as well as the development of international cooperation implies further restrictions in decisions on nationalization. It is an apparent contradiction, and yet in order to ensure national development sacrifices will have to be made by submitting to a greater degree of dependence. This is the price of profits and it is not at all certain that it is bought too costly. Many examples could be quoted showing that excessive striving after autarchy and extreme protectionism lead to increased external economic dependence and to the curtailment of sovereignty.

(1972, p. 21)

One of the most pessimistic elements in the analysis of the difficulties of peripheral countries to transform their states is to be found in Quijano's hypothesis of the 'marginalization' of the masses. It has become a commonplace of the literature on peripheral countries that, since the Second World War at least, there has been a steady influx into the towns, in part the result of growing population density in 'rural areas without corresponding growing need for manpower, in part the secondary effect of the spread of education and facility of movement which makes such moves seem attractive. It is further commonly agreed that this urban influx is too large to be absorbed in the wage employment and is thus 'unemployed'.

Quijano argues that this process is not reversible within the system because this growing urban manpower,

with respect to the employment needs of the hegemonic sectors [of the peripheral economic structures] that are monopolistically organized, is *surplus*; and with respect to intermediate sectors organized in a competitive mode and consequently characterized by the permanent instability of these very fragile enterprises with very peripheral occupations, this manpower is *floating*, for it must be intermittently employed, unemployed or underemployed depending on the contingencies that affect the economic sector. (1971, p. 335)

Quijano is pointing essentially to the same phenomenon of which Marx spoke when he referred to 'pauperization'. Marx was historically wrong about western Europe but that was in large part because he underestimated the politico-economic consequences of the unicity of the world-economy.

The point of marginalization as Amin notes is that in peripheral countries wages are not 'both cost and revenue that creates demand...but on the contrary only cost, demand being found elsewhere: externally or in the revenue of the privileged social sectors' (1972a, p. 711). The conclusion we can draw from such a hypothesis is that at the national peripheral level the problem is relatively insoluble. At best, marginalization can be minimized (as in the Ivory Coast, at the expense of Upper Volta, among others). But it also points to one of the long-run contradictions of the system as it presently exists: for one day, the 'demand' of these marginalized workers will in fact be needed to maintain the profit rates. And when that comes, we will be faced, in a way that we are not now, with the question of the transition to socialism.[13]

Let us look, far more briefly, because less relevant to Africa, to the mode by which semiperipheral countries have historically made it into the core. Which are such countries? England rose from the semiperipheral status it still had at the beginning of Elizabeth's reign to membership in the core by the time of the seventeenth-century recession. The United States and Germany followed a similar path in the nineteenth century. The USSR is on the same path today. But many other lesser countries have worked their way forward, if to less spectacular heights: Belgium, Sweden,

13. Perhaps to keep his spirits up, Samir Amin seems to suggest in his postface to *L'Accumulation à l'échelle mondiale* (1971a) that we are in the transition now. Yes, to be sure, if we use the word loosely. But no, if it implies in any sense a short run. In any case, he is absolutely right when he says: 'For if there is a problem, it is a problem of *transition* and not of perspective' (p. 597). But then he goes on: 'The essential point is never to lose from view the necessity of reinforcing the socialist cohesion of the whole of the nation.' I fear, as he does at other points, the easy slide of such a concept into ideological justification of a stratum in power. I would say the essential problem is never to lose from view the necessity of reinforcing the cohesion, such as it is, of socialist political forces throughout the world-economy.

and much more doubtfully in terms of the economic structure, Canada. If I add Canada, it becomes clear that fairly 'developed' countries may to some extent still be subordinate to other countries in the hierarchy of the world-economy. Still it would be hard to convince anyone in either Canada or, say, Sierra Leone that there were not many significant differences in the way each relates to the world-economy, the consequent social and political structure within each country, and the perspectives of the immediate future.

To gauge the degree to which semiperipheral countries are able today to utilize the classic mechanisms of advancement in the world economy, we should review both how this classic mechanism worked and the role that wage differentials have played in the structuring of the world-economy. What in a national society determines the general wage level that so manifestly varies from country to country, and in particular seems always to be relatively high in core countries and relatively low in peripheral countries? Obviously, a given employer wishes to pay the least he can for the services he purchases, given the labor market, and the employee wishes to get as high a wage as he can. From the viewpoint of larger social forces, however, as mediated through the state, wage levels affect both sale of products externally (a motive pressing for lower wages) and sale of products internally (a motive pressing for higher wages). Furthermore, the collective organization of workers leads both to legislation and convention assuring at given times given minima, with the expectations socialized into the psyches of the members of the society. Thus, as Arghiri Emmanuel argues, 'Regardless of market conditions, there are wage levels that are impossible, because unthinkable, in a particular country, at a particular period, for a particular racial or ethnic group of wage earners' (1972, p. 119).

Emmanuel argues the case that it is precisely the relative rigidity of national wage levels combined with the tendency to equivalence in international profit margins that accounts for unequal exchange within the world-economy. Nonetheless, it is precisely this same rigidity which has made possible historically the shift of semiperipheral countries, which, in fact, have *medium* wage levels, to the status of core countries.

The problem of breakthrough for a semiperipheral country is

that it must have a market available large enough to justify an advanced technology, for which it must produce at a lower cost than existing producers. Obviously, there are a number of elements involved in this which are interrelated in a complex way.

One way to enlarge a market for national products is to control access of other producers to the one market a given state politically controls, its own: hence, prohibitions, quotas, tariffs. A second is to expand the political boundaries thus affected via unification with neighbors or conquest. Or, conversely, instead of increasing the costs of imported goods, a state seeks to lower the costs of production, thus affecting simultaneously the home market and external markets. Subsidies for production in whatever form are a mode of reallocation of national costs, such that the effective price of other goods is raised relative to the item subsidized. Reducing costs of production by reducing wage levels is a two-edged sword since it increases external sales at the risk of lowering internal sales, and only makes sense if the balance is positive. A fourth way to increase the market is to increase the internal level of purchasing power which, combined with the natural competitive advantages of low or zero transportation costs, should result in increased internal sales. If this is done by raising wage levels, this is the converse two-edged sword of the previous one, increasing internal sales at the risk of lowering external sales. Finally, the state or other social forces can affect the 'tastes', primarily of internal consumers, by ideology or propaganda, and thus expand the market for its products.

Obviously, in addition, it is critical not merely to have optimal cost levels, but to have a certain *absolute* size of the market. Furthermore, the steady advance of technology involving machinery with larger and larger components of fixed capital constantly raises the threshold. Thus, the possibility of a state passing from semiperipheral to core status has always been a matter of juggling elements that move in varied directions to achieve a nearly perfect mix.

For example, the mix that England achieved in the 'long' sixteenth century involved a combination of a *rural* textile industry (thus free from the high guild-protection wage costs of traditional centres of textile production such as Flanders, southern Germany, and northern Italy), with a process of agricultural improvement of arable land in medium-sized units (thus simultaneously providing a yeoman class of purchasers with an evicted class of vagrants and migrants who provided much of the labor for the textile industry), plus a deliberate decision to push for the new market of *low*-cost textiles (the 'new draperies') to be sold to the new middle stratum of artisans, less wealthy burghers, and richer peasants who had flourished in the expanding cycle of the European world-economy (see Wallerstein 1974a for this argument in detail). Germany, too, in the nineteenth century operated on the advantages of a medium wage level, based on the historic legacy of a declining artisan class to create a sufficiently large internal market, yet with a cost of production sufficient to compete with Britain especially in areas to the east and south, where it had transportation advantages. This is not, however, the only mix that can work. There is the 'white settler' phenomenon where high wage levels *precede* industrialization and distance from world centers of production (providing the natural protection of high transportation costs for imports). Once again, Emmanuel pushes the point to clarify what is happening. He reminds us that of Britain's five colonies of settlement – the United States, Canada, Australia, New Zealand, and the Cape – the first four have today the highest per capita incomes in the world whereas South Africa is at the level of Greece or Argentina. Yet it had the same colonists, the same links to Britain.

One factor alone was different, namely, what happened to the indigenous population. Whereas in the other four colonies the total extermination of the natives was undertaken, in South Africa the colonists confined themselves to relegating them to the ghettos of apartheid. The result is that in the first four countries wages have reached very high levels, while in South Africa, despite the selective wages enjoyed by the white workers, the average wage level has remained relatively very low, hardly any higher than that in the underdeveloped countries, and below that of the Balkans, Portugal, and Spain.

(Emmanuel 1972, p. 125)

The high-wage route (that is, high in relation to the wages in the leading industrial countries of the world) is not likely to be easily repeated. First, it requires special political conditions (a settler population attracted in the first place by the immediately or potentially *high* standard of living) plus the technological level of a past era, where world distances mattered more and technological dependence (as discussed above) mattered less.

The model of the twentieth century has been the USSR. But what exactly is this model? First of all, let us not forget that the Soviet Union built its structure on a semiperipheral country to be sure – Russia – but one that was nonetheless the fifth industrial producer in the world (in absolute terms) in 1913. It was not a state in which the process of marginalization had gone very far at all.[14] The state entered into the picture to keep industrial wage levels at a medium level[15] and rural wage levels such that there was an extensive urban labor reserve.[16] Last but not least, the USSR was a very large country, which made possible the relatively long period of autarchy which it practiced. And even so, its long stunting of the internal market because of wage levels has forced into the Krushchev–Brezhnev revision of this policy as part of the preparation for future competition in the world market as an exporter of manufactured products. If the USSR with its relatively strong pre-revolutionary industrial base, its firm political control over external trade and internal wages, and its enormous size has, nonetheless, if you will, barely made it into the core of the world-economy, what hope is there for semi-industrialized countries, true semiperipheral ones – as the Brazil, the Chile, or the South Africa of today, to take three politically different examples – to expand their market, and primarily their internal market, sufficiently to transform their role in the world-economy?[17] All that one has said of the economic processes that are worsening the ability of peripheral countries to maneuver in the world-economy point to pessimism here, too, except one consideration which we have not yet discussed: the impact of world contraction on this picture.

14. Amin says it was 'unknown', but I suspect that this is an exaggeration. See Amin 1972a, p. 714.
15. Emmanuel suggests that this is a distinction between a competitive economy and a planned one, although sixteenth-century England and nineteenth-century Germany belie this explanation. In any case, he is right in his concrete description of what happened in the USSR: 'The state being the dictator of specializations of prices, there is no need for high wages to appropriate an increased share of the world economic product. On the contrary, since the share is given by the real potential of production, the state is all the better able to increase accumulation if wages, and consumption generally, are kept down at very low levels' (1972, p. 130).
16. As Amin says, 'the *kolkhoz* and administrative oppression fulfilled [the] function [of forcing the masses to be a passive reserve of manpower] that, in the English model, was performed by the enclosure acts and the poor laws' (1972a, p. 715).
17. To *s'autocentrer*, to use Amin's awkward-to-translate word. See the discussion in Amin 1971a, pp. 610ff.

If high wages are so advantageous in terms of unequal exchange, why doesn't everyone raise their wage levels, or at least every state? Obviously, because the advantage is a function also of low absolute competition (quite apart from price level). To be sure, capital will always flow to high profit areas, but it 'flows'. There is always a lag. The way it works, in fact, is that whenever some producer is undercut in the cost of production, there will be a tendency over time to uncover a new specialization requiring a momentarily rare skill, which 'in the international division of labor at that moment, is free from competition on the part of the low-wage countries' (Emmanuel 1972, p. 145). And this is possible because we socially legitimate the variety of products which are technologically feasible.

This process, however, can most easily operate in moments of economic expansion, when it is easier to create new markets for new products than to fight over old ones. But in moments of contraction, the calculus changes. As has become clear once again in the 1970s, core countries are quite willing to expend considerable energy fighting over old ones.[18]

What is the impact of such a fight on the possibilities of semiperipheral countries moving towards core status and peripheral ones moving towards semiperipheral status? I believe that the 'slippage' of core countries offers, still today, opportunities for the semiperiphery but makes the outlook even more bleak for the periphery.

At moments of world-economic downturns, the weakest segment of the world-economy in terms of bargaining power tends to be squeezed first. The relative decline in world output reduces the market for the exports of the peripheral countries, and faster than it does the prices of their imports. Peripheral countries may even discover new protectionist barriers against their exports as other countries seek to 'take back' areas of production once thought to be of such low profitability as to be worthy only of peripheral countries. To be sure, a few peripheral countries who

18. Actually, the in-fighting began earlier. 'When the U.S. balance of payments was strong, its reserves apparently unlimited, and its dollar untouched by any hint of possible devaluation, the government could face the massive outflow of capital by U.S. companies with equanimity. In today's conditions, this is no longer possible. Under President Johnson, the government was forced to introduce a number of measures to stem the tide of U.S. investment overseas' (Tugendhat 1971, p. 43).

have the relatively strongest technological base may use the impetus of the crisis to push forward with import substitution. But the bulk of the periphery simply 'stagnates'.

What happens in the semiperiphery is rather different. In an expanding world-economy, semiperipheral countries are beggars, seeking the 'aid' of core countries to obtain a part of the world market against *other semiperipheral* countries. Thus, becoming the agent of a core country, the subimperial role, is if not a necessary condition of further economic gain at least the facile road to it. It is no accident, thus, that ideologically semiperipheral countries are often the loudest exponents of particular *weltanschauungen* and the strongest denouncers of evil practices – of other semiperipheral countries.

As long, therefore, as expansion continues, the mode of economic prosperity for producing groups in semiperipheral areas is via the reinforcement of dependency patterns *vis-à-vis* core countries. However, when world contraction comes, the squeeze is felt by core countries who proceed to fight each other, each fearing 'slippage'. Now the semiperipheral countries may be courted, as the outlets for core products become relatively rarer. The bargaining relationship of a core and semiperipheral country changes in exactly the way the bargaining relationship between seignior and serf changed in moments of economic contraction in the Middle Ages, in favor of the lower stratum, enabling the latter to get some structural and even institutional changes as part of the new exchange.

There is much talk of the new multipolar world of the 1970s. Let us take one such analysis and see its implications for our problem. Anouar Abdel-Malek predicts a period of tripolar peaceful coexistence, in which there will be an attempt to maintain equilibrium between three sectors: Europe, around the USSR; Asia, around China; America, around the USA, the latter spreading out in triangular form to include Oceania and sub-Saharan Africa. Without debating whether this particular geography is accurate, it is difficult to disagree with Abdel-Malek's conclusion:

The world enters at an accelerated pace into an *era of great mobility* where, paradoxically, the growth of the power potential held by the principal states will permit a dialectic of neutralization-improvement of position (*valorization*) far more subtle than at present, wherein careful intelligence on the part of national and revolutionary movements in the dependent sector of the world will enable them to take advantage of, in the sense of bringing into being, optimal international alliances, those most likely to bear the enormous autochtonous effort of liberation and of revolution.   (1971, pp. 63–4)

But will not the economic difficulties lead to increased strife among the core countries? Curiously, as we so clearly see, it does not. It leads them to limit their strife in order to face, each in its turn, the harder bargaining it must do with its dependent semiperipheral clients. Conversely, we may see new movements towards alliances between semiperipheral countries, which will take the political form of changes in regimes to place themselves in a position to make such alliances. Can not the Allende regime in Chile be seen as one such effort? And can not the deteriorating relationship of the USSR with the 'revolutionary forces', particularly in semiperipheral regimes, be seen as the simple consequence of the promotion of the USSR from semiperiphery to core and hence a change in its interests within the framework of a capitalist world-economy?

Who in Africa could at the present time take advantage of such a thrust forward by semiperipheral countries? Not many. South Africa, were the rest of Africa ready to serve as its market. But a segregated South Africa will find political resistance where a Black South Africa would not. And so the African continent may well have to sit this cycle out in terms of the advantages outlined above for semiperipheral countries.

But if over the next twenty years, a number of semiperipheral states, using the mechanism of state ownership (wholly or in large part) combined with a transnational, ideologically justified alliance, do in fact manage to make some clear gains, how will that change the world-economy? These gains may well be at the expense of some core countries, but also at the expense of peripheral ones. Is this more than a circulation of power?

No, if we look at the national and world economics of it. But yes, if we look at its political implications. Establishing a system of state ownership within a capitalist world-economy does not mean establishing a socialist economy. It may not mean improving the economic well-being of the majority of the population. It is merely a variant of classic mercantilism. But it does change the world political scene because it clarifies the role of monopolistic limitation via the state in the unequal exchange of world capitalism, and thereby in the long run affects the political mobilization of those forces who are discontented with the 'limited possibilities of transformation' within the present system.

If one justifies political changes not because there are clear economic benefits to the world-economy as a whole but because they unveil more clearly the contradictions of the present system, the impossibility of maximizing rationally the social good within it, then we must be sure that we do not, by the process of justifying the present changes, in fact create new ideological screens.

But we have been creating these ideological screens for fifty years. By identifying state ownership with socialism, we have contributed to a massive confusion that has had nefarious political consequences. State-ownership countries have, in fact, lower standards of living than those countries that have predominantly private enterprises; and, in addition, social inequality in these so-called socialist countries is still manifestly enormous. This is not because they have state-owned enterprises but because they have been up to now largely semiperipheral countries in a capitalist world economy.

For twenty-five years liberal reformists have advocated international aid as a major means of overcoming the economic dilemmas of underdeveloped nations. We have seen how little it has helped. Are we not in danger of falling into the same trap if, using new terms, we create an analogous left-wing myth that self-reliance will overcome, in any immediate sense, the dependence of peripheral countries?

State ownership is not socialism. Self-reliance is not socialism. These policies may represent intelligent political decisions for governments to take. They may be decisions that socialist movements should endorse. But a socialist government when it comes will not look anything like the USSR, or China, or Chile, or Tanzania of today. Production for use and not for profit, and rational decision on the cost benefits (in the widest sense of the term) of alternative uses is a different mode of production, one that can only be established within the single division of labor that is the world-economy and one that will require a single government.

In the meantime, to return to Africa, what sensible men can do is to use the subtleties of careful intelligence, as Abdel-Malek suggests, to push those changes that are immediately beneficial and to coordinate with others elsewhere the long-run strategies that will permit more fundamental transformation. One step towards more careful intelligence is to call a spade a spade, mercantilism mercantilism, and state-owned capitalist enterprise state-owned capitalist enterprise.

Addendum

I now believe that the formulations in this essay are incomplete and can lead to some confusion. In particular, I do not clarify the distinctions between semiperipheral states that have socialist governments and those that do not. In a subsequent essay (ch. 5 below), I do discuss this question quite specifically.

References

Abdel-Malek, A. (ed.). 1971. *Sociologie de l'impérialisme*. Paris: Anthropos

Amin, Samir. 1971a. *L'accumulation à l'échelle mondiale*. Paris: Anthropos
    1971b. *L'Afrique de l'Ouest bloquée*. Paris: de Minuit
    1972a. 'le modèle théorique d'accumulation et de développement dans le monde contemporain'. *Revue Tiers-Monde*, 13: 52 (October–December)
    1972b. 'Sullo sviluppo diseguale delle formazioni sociali'. *Terzo Mondo*, 18 (December)

Baran, Paul. 1957. *The Political Economy of Growth*. New York: Monthly Review Press

Bodenheimer, Suzanne. 1971. 'Dependency and Imperialism: The Roots of Laatin American Underdevelopment'. *Politics and Society*, 1: 3 (May) 327–57

Braudel, F. P. and F. Spooner. 1967. 'Prices in Europe from 1450 to 1750'. In E. E. Rich (ed.). *The Economy of Expanding Europe in the Sixteenth and Seventeenth Centuries*. Vol. IV of *Cambridge Economic History of Europe*. Cambridge: Cambridge University Press

Bulletin of the Institute of Development Studies. 1971. 3: 4 (August). Special issue on 'Conflict and Dependence'

Caputo, Orlando and Robert Pizarro. 1970. *Imperialismo, dependencia, y relaciones internacionales*. Santiago: CESO, Universidad de Chile

Cardoso, Fernando Henrique. 1971. *Politique et développement dans les sociétés dépendantes*. Paris: Anthropos

Cardoso, Fernando Henrique and Enzo Faletto. 1969. *Dependencia y desarollo en América Latina*. Mexico: Siglo XXI

Cockcroft, James D. *et al.* (eds.). 1972. *Dependence and Underdevelopment: Latin America's Political Economy*. Garden City: Anchor Books

Colson, Jean-Philippe. 1972. 'Le groupe de 77 et le problème de l'unité des pays du tiers-monde'. *Revue Tiers-Monde,* 13: 52 (October–December)

Dos Santos, Theotonio. 1971. 'Théorie de la crise économique dans les pays sous-développés'. In A. Abdel-Malek (ed.), *Sociologie de l'impérialisme.* Paris: Anthropos

Emmanuel, Arghiri. 1972. *Unequal Exchange.* New York: Monthly Review Press

Frank, André Gunder, 1972a. 'La dépendance est morte. Vive la dépendance et la lutte de classes!' *Partisans,* 68 (November–December), 52–70.

1972b. 'That the Extent of the Internal Market Is Limited by the International Division of Labor and the Relations of Production'. Paper for IDEP–IDS–CLASCO Conference on Strategies for Economic Development: Africa Compared with Latin America, Dakar, 4–17 September. Mimeographed.

Frères du Monde. 1971. 69, 28–60. 'Une lutte historique de classes à l'échelle mondiale'.

Furtado, Celso. 1970. *Economic Development of Latin America.* New York: Cambridge University Press

Galtung, Johan. 1972. 'Structural Theory of Imperialism'. *African Review,* 1: 4 (April)

Green, Reginald Herbold. 1970. 'Political Independence and the National Economy: An Essay on the Political Economy of Decolonization'. In Christopher Allen and R. W. Johnson (eds.), *African Perspectives.* Cambridge: Cambridge University Press

Horwitz, Ralph. 1967. *The Political Economy of South Africa.* New York: Praeger

Hymer, Stephen. 1972. 'The Multinational Corporation and the Law of Uneven Development'. In Jagdish N. Bhagwati (ed.), *Economics and World Order.* New York: Macmillan

Ikonicoff, Moises. 1972. 'Sous-développement, tiers monde ou capitalisme périphérique'. *Revue Tiers-Monde,* 13: 52 (October–December)

Kádár, Bélar. 1972. 'Small Countries in World Economy'. Reprint no. 34 of Center for Afro-Asian Research of the Hungarian Academy of Sciences

Kuark, Yoon T. 1963. 'North Korea's Industrial Development During the Post-War Period.' *China Quarterly,* 14 (April–June), 51–64

Lombard, J. A. *et al.* 1968. *The Concept of Economic Co-operation in Southern Africa.* Pretoria: Bureau for Economic Policy and Analysis, Publication no. 1

Marini, Ruy Mauro. 1969. *Subdesarollo y revolución.* Mexico: Siglo XXI

Merhav, Meir. 1969. *Technological Dependence, Monopoly and Growth.* Oxford: Pergamon Press

Müller-Plantenburg, Urs. 1871. 'Technologie et dépendance'. *Critiques de l'Economie Politique,* 3 (April–June), 68–82

Quijano, Anibal. 1971. 'Pole marginal de l'économie et main-d'oeuvre marginalisée'. In A. Abdel-Malek (ed.), *Sociologie de l'imperialisme.* Paris: Anthropos

Revue Tiers-Monde. 1972. 13: 52 (October–December). Special issue on 'Le capitalisme périphérique'

Sfia, Mohamed-Salah. 1971. 'Le système mondial de l'imperialisme: d'une forme de domination à l'autre'. In A. Abdel-Malek (ed.), *Sociologie de l'imperialisme.* Paris: Anthropos

Tawney, R. H. 1952. *Equality.* 4th edn, revised. London: Allen and Unwin

Tugendhat, Christopher. 1971. *The Multinationals.* London: Eyre and Spottiswoode

Von Laue, Theodore H. 1963. *Sergei Witte and the Industrialization of Russia.* New York: Columbia University Press

Wallerstein, Immanuel. 1971. 'The Range of Choice: Constraints on the Policies of Governments of Contemporary Independent African States'. In Michael F. Lofchie (ed.), *The State of Nations.* Berkeley: University of California Press, pp. 19–33

1974a. *The Modern World-System: Capitalist Agriculture and the Origins of the European World-Economy in the Sixteenth Century.* New York and London: Academic Press

1974b. 'The Rise and Future Demise of the World Capitalist System: Concepts for Comparative Analysis'. *Comparative Studies in Society and History,* 16: 4 (September), pp. 387–415 and above, ch. 1.

5 ❧ Semiperipheral countries and the contemporary world crisis

If the philosophy of praxis affirms theoretically that every 'truth' believed to be eternal and absolute has had practical origins and has represented a 'practical' value..., it is still very difficult to make the people grasp 'practically' praxis itself, without in so doing shaking the convictions that are necessary for action...This is the reason why the proposition [in Marx] about the passage from the reign of necessity to that of freedom must be analyzed and elaborated with subtlety and delicacy.   Antonio Gramsci[1]

We find ourselves at the beginning of one of those periodic downturns, or contractions, or crises that the capitalist world-economy has known with regularity since its origins in Europe in the sixteenth century. The present moment of the history of the world-economy is marked by a number of striking phenomena:

(1) The heyday of US world hegemony is over. This means that at no level – economic production and productivity, political cohesiveness and influence, cultural self-assurance and productivity, political cohesiveness and influence, cultural self-assurance, military strength – will the US ever again match its unquestioned primacy of the period 1945–67.

However, the decline from a peak is scarcely precipitous: the US is still today the most powerful state in the world and will remain so for some time. The US still incarnates the political interests of the world's capitalist forces. Nonetheless, it is weaker than it once was and is going to become still weaker.

(2) The unity of what was a bloc of socialist nations is more or less

Prepared for a seminar on 'the Problems of the Capitalist World-Economy and its Repercussions on Developing Countries', Caracas, 1975.

1. Antonio Gramsci, 'Problems of Marxism', in Quinton Hoare and Geoffrey Nowell Smith (eds.), *Selections from the Prison Notebooks* (New York: International Publications 1971), p. 406. The proposition in Marx to which Gramsci is referring is found in the 'Introduction' to the *Critique of Hegel's Philosophy of Right*.

definitely broken, and the USSR and China are both challenging each other's socialist credentials. This obviously has an immense impact on the pattern of interstate relations. But it also marks a turning point in the history of the international workers' movement at least as important, and probably as longlasting, as the one that resulted in the definitive split of the Third from the Second International at the time of the Russian Revolution. One of the most important consequences of this present split is the destruction of the myth about the monolith of party and state in socialist countries, a myth sedulously cultivated by political forces of all hues from the 1920s to the 1960s. We are now forced to take seriously the reality of continuing internal class struggle *within* socialist countries.

(3) At the end of this present downturn (which may not come until 1990) there will probably be a new inter*state* political alignment of forces at the world level, reflecting a new phase in the economic history of the capitalist world-economy. If one limits onself to the five most significant present-day economic–military entities – the US, the European Common Market, Japan, the USSR, and China – the *least* likely regrouping is the one which prevailed during the previous era, that of the first three joined together as the 'Free World' against the latter two united as the 'Socialist Bloc'. Which if any of the other permutations will consolidate into effective working alliances is risky to predict but necessary to consider.[2]

Assuming rather than discussing these three phenomena, this paper examines the consequences of such a world-economic downturn (both in general, and this one specifically) for that group of *states* one might call *semi*peripheral, as well as the consequences for revolutionary socialist forces throughout the world. It is crucial that the argument move back and forth from the abstraction (but terribly meaningful one) of inter*state* struggles, whether political or economic, to the underlying pattern of class forces and their transnational political expressions.

Semiperipheral states play a particular role in the capitalist world-economy, based on the double antinomy of class (bourgeois–

2. I have in fact speculated on this matter cautiously in 'Old Problems and New Syntheses: The Relation of Revolutionary Ideas and Practices', Sixth Sorokin Lecture (University of Saskatchewan, 1975), and below, ch. 15.

proletarian) and function in the division of labor (core–periphery). The core–periphery distinction, widely observed in recent writings, differentiates those zones in which are concentrated high-profit, high-technology, high-wage diversified production (the core countries) from those in which are concentrated low-profit, low technology, low-wage, less diversified production (the peripheral countries). But there has always been a series of countries which fall in between in a very concrete way, and play a different role. The productive activities of these semiperipheral countries are more evenly divided. In part they act as a peripheral zone for core countries and in part they act as a core country for some peripheral areas. Both their internal politics and their social structure are distinctive, and it turns out that their ability to take advantage of the flexibilities offered by the downturns of economic activity is in general greater than that of either the core or the peripheral countries. It is in this context that we propose to look specifically at this group of countries in the present world situation.

We begin by outlining the principal market consequences of long-term economic fluctuations, the better to understand the shift in the range of political possibilities at different moments of the cycle. What in fact causes long-term cyclical shifts? The immediate answer is an acute disequilibrium in the world market between the immediate capacity for production of high-cost, high-profit economic goods and effective demand. The long-term tendency to 'over supply' is inevitable in the pattern of separate decision making processes by producers in a capitalist market. 'Over supply' leads to a shift in the terms of trade (between the core and the periphery), a shift in the loci of profitable investment world-wide and the loci of employment opportunities. This in turn affects the wage structure in those parts of the world-economy based on fully proletarianized labor, as well the degree to which workers in other areas will continue to draw part or all of their income from sources other than wage employment. When these shifts result in a strengthened world-wide effective demand, concordant expansion of the capitalist world-economy can once more take place. Subsequently the balance will shift acutely in favor of core producers; in other words, the percentage of surplus extraction that ends up in the hands of producers located in the core steadily grows. When it becomes so great as to limit marked demand, another crisis results. This at least has been the pattern up to now and, *mutatis mutandis*, this cyclical pattern persists, despite various major changes in the economic and political organization of the world-economy in the twentieth century.

One aspect of these shifts is the shift in bargaining power of various groups with each other. The central issue here is whether the producer (of the high-cost, high-profit commodity) has on his side the virtue of scarcity or the misfortune of glut *vis-à-vis* his potential customers. The first great European expansion (of land area, population, trade, and prices) took place between 1150 and 1300, under a feudal mode of production, and was followed by a corresponding contraction from 1300 to 1450. One major difference between the two periods was the relative bargaining power of lord and serf. The period of expansion was precisely a period of juridical ensconcement of feudal services, a period thus of increased exaction of surplus by the lord from his serf, exaction that took the form largely of unpaid labor (the *corvée*) on the lord's domains. When contraction occurred, this bargaining relationship altered. The 'overproduction' of agricultural products led to a contracting demand (for any given producer's goods). It also led via a series of intermediate factors (wars, famines, and epidemics) to a population decline and a labor shortage (particularly of skilled labor). Suddenly the lords were squeezed and the serfs could demand higher 'wages' (whose prerequisite was the conversion of the *corvée* to money-rent).[3] At each succeeding moment of crisis in the history of the capitalist world-economy, a similar shift of 'bargaining power' has taken place. It is taking place again today, the most spectacular example being the rise in oil prices effectuated by OPEC.

Today surplus is still being extracted, possibly even the same amount. But the *world-wide* distribution of the surplus is different. And *intermediate* elements in the surplus extraction chain gain at

3. For a more detailed analysis of the 'crisis of feudalism' in the late Middle Ages, see my *The Modern World-System: Capitalist Agriculture and the Origins of the European World-Economy in the Sixteenth Century* (New York & London: Academic Press, 1974), pp. 21–8.

the expense of those at the *core* ore the system. In present-day terms, this means among other things a shift in relative profit advantage to the *semiperipheral nations*. In moments of world economic downturn, semiperipheral countries can usually expand control of their home market at the expense of core producers, and expand their access to *neighboring* peripheral markets, again at the expense of core producers.

The reason for this is relatively straightforward. As long as the products of core producers are relatively 'scarce', they can pick and choose among semiperipheral bidders for their investment in (semi-) manufactures and for their purchase of commodities. When the core producers face a situation of 'over-supply', they begin to compete intensely with each other to maintain their share in a comparatively shrinking world market for their finished goods (especially machinery). At that time, semiperipheral countries can, up to a point, pick and choose among core producers not only in terms of the sale of their commodities (viz., OPEC oil) but also in terms both of welcoming their investment in manufactures and of purchasing their producer's goods.

These shifts in advantage are reflected in the policies of states, in the degree of their 'nationalism' and militance, and in the pattern of their international diplomatic alliances. They often result in shifts in regime where the previous regime is insufficiently flexible to respond to the changed world political situation. And of course the ability of core powers to intervene illicitly in the state affairs of each semiperipheral state decreases somewhat in moments of downturn, for precisely the reasons discussed above in terms of production and trade patterns.

But state policies are only the surface of the continual turbulence of class politics lying more or less visibly beneath. Another consequence of world-wide downturn is a shift in the location of wage employment. *Grosso modo*, unemployment tends to rise in the core, albeit unevenly. But there is probably a *de facto* compensation in an increase of real employment in the semiperiphery. Such a shift in employment patterns translates itself into real wage patterns. In the core, two things happen. The real wages of wage workers as a whole (within the bounds of any state) decrease because so many are unemployed. Insofar, however, as prices decrease those *who remain employed* may well have an *increase* in real wages. The result is a combination of a politics that reflects disillusionment with and rejection of the system by those who become unemployed (usually generating increased class consciousness), and a politics that reflects the 'clinging to a lifeboat' of those still employed (or who, being so no longer, still hope to become so once again by ousting others still employed). The latter often provide the mass base for fascist movements.

In the semiperiphery, however, the situation is different. The 'semiperiphery' includes a wide range of countries in terms of economic strength and political background. It includes the economically stronger countries of Latin America: Brazil, Mexico, Argentina, Venezuela, possibly Chile and Cuba. It includes the whole outer rim of Europe: the southern tier of Portugal, Spain, Italy and Greece; most of eastern Europe; parts of the northern tier such as Norway and Finland. It includes a series of Arab states: Algeria, Egypt, Saudi Arabia; and also Israel. It includes in Africa at least Nigeria and Zaïre, and in Asia, Turkey, Iran, India, Indonesia, China, Korea, and Vietnam. And it includes the old white Commonwealth: Canada, Australia, South Africa, possibly New Zealand. Furthermore, it is obvious that such a purely 'economic' grouping includes two very different varieties of states. There are 'socialist' states, that is, those with governments ruled by a Marxist–Leninist party, which has nationalized the basic means of production. And there are those states in which there is still the possibility of 'private' capital and therefore indigenous property-owning bourgeoisie, or the legal possibility for others to translate their income into capitalist investment. This latter set varies in terms of the degree to which the governments in power are overtly repressive of all or part of the population. The point is, there are very real differences between the manners in which socialist and non-socialist governments respond to the crisis in the world-economy, reflecting the different set of internal contradictions to which each is subject. But before examining these differences, we must pose a general problem in the strategy of change.

Within the existing framework of the capitalist world-economy, a downturn is more or less advantageous to all semiperipheral countries, but only *a few* are able to translate that advantage into a real shift in economic position (to that of a 'core power') at any given moment in history. To do this, such a semiperipheral country must garner a heavy portion of the collective advantage of the semiperiphery as a whole to itself in particular; that is, a semiperipheral country rising to core status does so, not merely at the expense of some or all core powers, but also at the expense of other semiperipheral powers. This is simply the state-level adaptation of the traditional 'dog eat dog' workings of capitalism. This is *not* 'development' but successful expropriation of world surplus.

One need not accept this path as inevitable, much less laud it as the path of virtue, and dub it 'growth, progress, and development'. What R. H. Tawney said of individuals in an unequal world is equally true of states:

It is possible that intelligent tadpoles reconcile themselves to the inconveniences of their position, by reflecting that, though most of them will live and die as tadpoles and nothing more, the more fortunate of the species will one day shed their tails, distend their mouths and stomachs, hop nimbly on to dry land, and croak addresses to their former friends on the virtues by means of which tadpoles of character and capacity can rise to be frogs. This conception of society may be described, perhaps, as the Tadpole Philosophy, since the consolation which it offers for social evils consists in the statement that exceptional individuals can succeed in evading them...And what a view of human life such an attitude implies! As though opportunities for talents to rise could be equalized in a society where the circumstances surrounding it from birth are themselves unequal! As though they could, it were natural and proper that the position of the mass of mankind should permanently be such that they can attain civilization only by escaping from it! As though the noblest use of exceptional powers were to scramble to shore, undeterred by the thought of drowning companions![4]

For those who do not wish to 'scramble to shore', the alternative is to seek to transform the system as a whole rather than profit from it. This I take to be the defining feature of a socialist movement. The touchstone of legitimacy of such a movement would be the extent to which the totality of its actions contributed, to the maximum degree possible, to the rapid transformation of the present world-system, involving the eventual replacement of the capitalist world-economy by a socialist world government. For a movement in power in a semiperipheral state, this presumably requires a strategy different from governments who seek relative advantage, that is, who attempt to 'develop'.

Let us first analyze the 'non-socialist' states, keeping in mind

4. R. H. Tawney, *Equality* (New York: Capricorn Books, 1961), pp. 108–9.

that a state's use of 'socialist' slogans is not a prime criterion in identifying its form. Many 'non-socialist' states claim to be on a socialist path – India, for example. If we take the traditional criterion of collective ownership of the means of production as a base line, we find that only a certain group of countries, those that once were grouped in a 'socialist bloc', have eliminated all or virtually all private ownership of the means of production, both internal and external. In the others, some substantial sector of production remains in the hands of private owners, although some countries have moved systematically to eliminate *external* owners and a few have moved systematically to minimize *internal* private owners. But a *combined* and *systematic* move against external *and* internal private owners is the hallmark of the 'socialist bloc'.

What are the class alignments of these 'non-socialist' states, as defined above? They obviously vary considerably among the semiperipheral states. While nearly all have an indigenous bourgeoisie, it tends to be smaller and weaker than comparable groups in core countries, and it tends to be located only in certain sectors of national economic activities. The degree to which this indigenous bourgeoisie is structurally linked to corporations located in core countries varies, but the percentage tends to be far larger than is true of the bourgeoisie within any core country; indeed, this is one of the defining structural characteristics that differentiates a contemporary core and 'non-socialist' semiperipheral country.

The working classes may be divided into three sectors: the well-paid, highly skilled 'professionals'and semiprofessionals; the less skilled but fully proletarianized workers (that is, whose real family income comes exclusively or primarily from wage employment); and the semiproletarianized sector (whose real family income comes only partially, if at all, from wage employment), including most 'migrant workers' and the bulk of the 'peasantry'. If we compare these three sectors between core and 'non-socialist' semiperipheral countries, we note a series of contrasts. The professional sector is smaller in semiperipheral countries but, in terms of real income, is frequently *better paid* than persons in equivalent positions in core countries. (Compare the real income of senior civil servants in Canada and the USA, of managerial personnel in Brazil and Germany, of university professors in Iran and France, etc.) The sector of fully proletarianized, less skilled workers is again smaller in semiperipheral than in core countries and on the whole receives *much less* real income than its counterpart in core countries. As for the sector of semiproletarianized workers, it is a myth to believe it has disappeared in core countries, but it is certainly far smaller than in semiperipheral countries, and probably receives more real income (although to my knowledge no serious statistical analyses have ever been done).

Thus the mark of a 'non-socialist' semiperipheral country in comparison to a core country is: a larger external and a weaker internal property-owning bourgeoisie; a better-paid professional sector and a more poorly paid sector of fully proletarianized workers, but a far larger (and probably worse off) sector of semiproletarianized workers. What happens to these five groups in times of world-economic downturn? And in particular, to which of these strata is it advantageous that the semiperipheral state as a *state* expand its national product, better its terms of trade, shift its economic role in the world-economy?

The external bourgeoisie, which today means largely the multinational corporation, is not necessarily hurt by semiperipheral 'development'. Since the whole point of a multinational corporation is to be able to manipulate the *locations* in which it realizes its profit, at least in bookkeeping terms, it is capable of accommodating to fluctuations in the roles particular states play in the world-economy, *provided* the state in question does not undertake any *efficacious* measures to reduce its *world-wide* profit. For example, Exxon has not thus far lost one penny as Saudi Arabia's national income has been increasing vertiginously since 1973. The Saudi Arabian state's increased share of world surplus has occurred to someone's disadvantage, but that someone is not Exxon. Thus, the key point for a multinational corporation is state policy (not polemic), and this in turn is in large part a function of the interplay of the other economic strata plus the various states as states in the *internal* politics of a given semiperipheral country, always holding constant the steadfast devotion of multinationals to their own profit levels.

The indigenous property-owning bourgeoisie, known as the 'national bourgeoisie' in much literature, has been underestimated in recent writings. In reaction to an older tradition of both liberals and Marxists to see in such a national bourgeoisie a sort of heroic figure who would one day turn on the imperialist outsiders and lead the country through its phase of nationalist bourgeois democratic development, there has been drawn a counter-picture of an inefficacious, stunted, irreducibly comprador bourgeoisie, incapable of identifying its interest with those of the nation, and having missed its historical calling. This critique is far closer to the mark than the older mythology. But its danger is that on the one hand it exaggerates its truth and on the other it misses a crucial function of the 'national bourgeoisie' in the contemporary world. It exaggerates its truth by comparing existing 'national bourgeoisies' in semiperipheral countries with idealized counterparts of yesteryear, supposedly found in an earlier epoch in England, France, Germany, and the USA. In fact the role of the national bourgeoisie in earlier historical epochs was far more complex, far more ambivalent, and far less "heroic' or nationalist than this comparison assumes.

This is not to suggest that the national bourgeoisie did not play a central role in the economic growth of western Europe. Of course it did, and the changing structure of the capitalist world-economy makes it highly improbable that any national bourgeoisie could play a comparable role in the twentieth century. For one thing, the economic and political strength of multinational corporations is far greater. But there is a second function the national bourgeoisie historically played which is still plausible today. Even if it can no longer assume a central role is fostering collective national advance ('development'), national private enterprise still can play a critical role in individual and familial social mobility. The state bureaucrat, the university graduate, the technician may still aspire via a combination of individual competence and astuteness, political influence, and corruption to translate his training into wealth as part of a 'career pattern' as he moves into his 'middle years'. But, and this is crucial, he can only do this to a significant degree if the society legitimizes large-scale property holding in the form of economic enterprises. It is this 'option' that complete public ownership of the means of production closes off. In particular, it eliminates the option of creating 'family wealth', and hence greatly reduces the ability to transmit privilege from generation to generation.

Here the analysis of the indigenous property-owning bourgeois and the skilled professional blurs together. For the latter nearly always aspires to be the former, and these aspirations are most realizable in precisely the category of country we are discussing: 'non-socialist' semiperipheral countries. These 'realistic' aspirations have a profound impact on the politics of these countries. In general, both groups – the indigenous bourgeoisie and the professional strata – look upon the state as their negotiating instrument with the rest of the capitalist world-economy. In that narrow sense, they are 'nationalist'; that is, they will always be ready to brandish the flag if they believe it has a blackmail effect, and to put the flag in cold storage for a price. No doubt, there are isolated 'idealist' individuals who act differently, but in general it is hard to persist in such 'idealism' given the social setting, except by becoming a full-time revolutionary, which of course some do.

Does world economic contraction change the politics? To be sure. It is precisely easier to gain profit for this class via economic nationalism. Therefore such 'economic nationalism' is widespread in world depressions in all those semiperipheral areas that are juridically sovereign (for example, Mexico, Brazil, Italy, South Africa in the 1930s; Canada in the 1880s, etc.). We shall see such policies utilized in the present downturn. But the *meaning* of such nationalism is not given by the form. 'Protectionist' measures can turn out to be merely obstacles whose very existence encourages the multinationals to determine new ways of hurdling them.[5] 'Import substitution' may simply involve substituting one kind of import dependence for another, thereby creating an even worse 'technological dependence'.[6] In such a case world-economic downturn merely accelerates a process that in the long run was part of the built-in program of multinational corporations.

It is worth distinguishing between the effect of world-economic downturn on the *structure* of national economic enterprise in semiperipheral counties and the ability of *some* countries to take advantage of what is defined as an acute commodity shortage during such crises: for example oil today, gold today and in

5. This is the basic argument found throughout a long series of articles by Stephen Hymer.
6. The case is made by Meir Merhav, *Technological Dependence, Monopoly and Growth* (London: Pergamon, 1969).

previous downturns, and other commodities yet to be so defined. For such commodity exports show high relative price rises, and in and of themselves may catapult some countries into the semiperipheral category (Saudi Arabian and Iranian oil today, but also South African gold in the 1930s). And here, state policy intervenes at *two* moments, not one: first to ensure and protect the price rise, and secondly to translate the windfall profits into particular kinds of imports. Each additional moment of state intervention represents a benefit for the existing structure of distribution within the world-system, since non-action is on the side of maintaining the status quo.

If the problem were merely one of the confrontation of core *states* and semiperipheral *states*, the interests of both the national bourgeoisie and the professional strata would be basically conservative (albeit including what one might call 'one-shot blackmail programs'). but it is *not* possible, *even* in moments of world contraction, for *all* semiperipheral states to do well, certainly not equally well. Thus there is also a competition *between* semiperipheral states, and it is this fact that may on occasion push the indigenous bourgeoisie and professional strata of a particular country to a more politically 'radical' stance. Fearing that they may lose out in a game of 'each on his own' against the core powers, they may come to favor a strategy of collective transnational syndicalism which inevitably pushes them 'leftward', more in terms of international policy, but with perhaps some carryover in terms of internal redistribution. (A good example might be Algeria's aggressive role in the Group of 77, OPEC, and elsewhere, combined with the moves internally towards 'land reform').

This brings us to the two strata that account for the bulk of the population: the proletariat and the semiproletariat, the two being distinguished not in terms of urban location but in terms of payment leading to family income. Defined in terms of mode of mode of payment, they probably represent in most semiperipheral countries roughly equal proportions of the population. Furthermore, there is one important social complication to bear in mind: the distinction between proletarian and semiproletarian nearly always correlates highly with an ethnic distinction, those in the semiproletariat usually being defined as coming from a 'lower ranking' ethnic stratum. Thus we may speak of working classes, there being roughly *two* main groups, and those classes overlap heavily the ethnic distinction. It is therefore no wonder that a united singular working class represents a political ideal difficult to achieve rather than a description of social reality. Here too we must ask the question, what happens during world-economic contraction? Among 'non-socialist' semiperipheral states, those that succeed in garnering the most collective advantage in such periods may be precisely those who maintain a relatively high wage–labor cost differential with core countries. To obtain such a cost differential they must either be able to hold back the proletariat's demands for real wage increases, using segments of the semiproletariat as 'strike breakers', or if they transfer a portion of the advantage to the proletariat they must obtain the assistance of this group to hold the semiproletariat firmly in check – indeed to expropriate some or all of its land resources. From the outside, states using the first formula may look like right-wing repressive regimes, while the states using the latter seem more difficult to label. These latter may indeed be run by 'progressive military' or 'populist' governments but their 'progressive' quality may in fact be transient (Kemalism in Turkey, Peronism, etc.).

In this economic climate of world contraction, what are the possibilities for revolutionary socialist movements? This is hard to say, since in the modern world to date, there has been no instance of a revolutionary socialist movement arising and coming to power in such a country during such an economic conjuncture. But this does not necessarily predict the future. One of the real difficulties of revolutionary movements in such countries has been a reluctance to openly face and politically deal with the combined economic–ethnic split between the proletariat and the semiproletariat. Movements of the left have tended to be based either in the proletarian sector, which in the long run has pushed them in a reformist direction, or in one wing of the semiproletarian sector, which has pushed them towards subnationalism or 'adventurist' uprisings. Obviously, if a party were to find ways to unite both working-class sectors, the politics of a given semiperipheral country would be transformed. And if several were to be so transformed, the entire face of world politics would be altered.

To summarize the politics of 'non-socialist' semipheral countries during times of world-economic downturn: there tends to be an increase in 'economic nationalism', but most likely the sort that favors the indigenous upper strata, and hence leaves largely intact the cohesion of the capitalist world-economy. However, this view has to be tempered by the effect of the pressures of transnational syndicalism, a subject we shall examine in a moment.

But first we must consider what happens to 'socialist' semiperipheral countries during crises of the capitalist world-economy. The initial economic thrust of those who made the Russian Revolution was that the construction of a socialist society required a withdrawal from the capitalist world-economy to the maximum degree possible. It was a call for autarky, not for its own sake, but to enable the speedy reordering of the whole society. The policies of the Soviet government always envisaged the possibility of some international economic relations with capitalist countries, but this was to be limited in scope and to take place only 'at the frontier', so to speak, via special state agencies. The *de facto* practice of great emphasis on barter arrangements[7] resembled to a considerable extent what in pre-capitalist empires has been called 'administered trade', as described by Polanyi:

Adminstered trade has its firm foundation in treaty relationships that are more or less formal. Since on both sides the import interest is as a rule determinative, trading through government-controlled channels. The export trade is usually organized in a similar way. Consequently, the whole of trade is carried on by administrative methods. This extends to the manner in which business is transacted, including arrangements concerning 'rates' or proportions of the units exchanged; port facilities; weighing; checking of quality; the physical exchange of the goods; storage; safekeeping; the control of the trading personnel; regulation of 'payments'; credits; price differentials. Some of these matters would naturally be linked with the collection of the export goods and the repartition of the imported ones, both belonging to the redistributive sphere of the domestic economy.[8]

7. 'The most distinctive of these [special trade-promoting instruments of socialist countries] is the long-term bilateral trading agreement, or barter agreement, that now covers 50–60 percent of East Europe's – and 90 percent of Russia's – trade with the [Third World]. Normally it sets quantitative targets for the major traded commodities, as 80 percent of Russia's bilateral arrangements do; it stipulates that trade should balance more or less each year and that settlement should be in the currency of the [Third World] partner. In this way the key agreement tends to create fixed, identifiable markets for certain goods while insulating them from world trade.' Michael Kidron, *Pakistan's Trade with Eastern Bloc Countries* (New York: Praeger, 1972), p. 3.
8. Karl Polanyi, 'The Economy as Instituted Process', in K. Polanyi *et al.* (eds.), *Trade and Market in the Early Empires* (Chicago:Henry Regnery, 1971), p. 262.

With the emergence of more than one socialist country, a distinction was made between economic relations among socialist countries, and trade between a socialist country and a capitalist country. The former were seen as involving a new international division of labor, whose organizational expression was the Comecon, whereas the latter proceeded as before. The concept of a second *world-system*, a socialist system, separate and distinct from the capitalist world-economy has been developed more and more explicitly in recent years by Soviet thinkers.[9] The heart of the argument is that capitalist principles do not govern the economic arrangements between socialist states.

The best answer to this point of view, in my estimation, has been given by Comrade Kim Il Sung in 'On Some Theoretical Problems of the Socialist Economy', quoted here *in extenso* because I believe it states the issue with great clarity:

I have heard that some economists are arguing about the questions of whether the means of production are commodities in socialist society and whether the law of value operates in the domain of their production and circulation.

I do not think these questions should be handled indiscriminately. In socialist society the means of production are sometimes commodities and sometimes not, as the case may be. The law of value will operate when they are commodities, and not when they are not. Because the law of value is a law of commodity production.

Then, when are the means of production commodities and when are they not? To find the right solution to this question, I think it necessary, first of all, to have a clear idea of the properties of commodities and the origin of commodity production.

Commodities are produced not for one's own consumption but for sale. In other words, not all products are commodities; only things produced for the putposes of exchange are commodities. As is clear from this, in order for a product to be a commodity there are required: first, the social division of labor through which different kinds of goods are produced; second, the seller and the buyer – the man who gives up the right to possess a thing by selling it, and the man who buys and acquires the right to possess it. That is to say, commodity production presupposes the social division of labour and the differentiation of appropriation of the products. Therefore, where there is no social division of labour and ownership is not differentiated but remains in a unified form, there can be no commodity production.

The continuance of commodity–money relations in socialist society is also due to the existence of the social division of labour and different forms of ownership

9. See for example a recent complete overview by Shalva Sanakoyev, *The World Socialist System: Main Problems, Stages of Development* (Moscow: Progress Publications, 1972). The moment that this system came into existence is left somewhat unclear in Sanakoyev's account: 'The formation of the world socialist system is an intricate and prolonged process which began in October 1917 when the new, socialist world was born' (p. 100).

of the products. As everybody knows, in socialist society the division of labour not only exists but develops day by day. As for ownership, there exist both state and co-operative property of the means of production, and private ownership of consumer goods as well, though in the course of the socialist revolution private property is abolished and different forms of economy that existed early in the transition period are gradually fused into a single, socialist form. Besides, the socialist states must carry on foreign trade while communism has not yet triumphed on a world scale and national frontiers still exist.

All these are conditions that give rise to commodity production in socialist society. It goes without saying that in socialist society commodity production is a production of goods without capitalists and, therefore, the law of value does not operate blindly as in capitalist society but within a limited scope, and the state uses it in a planned way as an economic lever for effective management of the economy. Later, when the transition period is over and co-operative property is transformed into property of the entire people so that a single form of ownership is established, the product of society, leaving aside for a moment the consideration of foreign trade, will not be given the name 'commodity' but simply called 'means of production' or 'consumer goods', or some other names. There the law of value will also cease to operate. Needless to say, even then the social division of labour will continue to develop but there will be no more commodity production.

Scholars, leading economic functionaries and many other people are now committing Right or 'Left' errors both in the domain of theory and in economic management, because they have not fully understood the question of whether or not the means of production are commodities in socialist society. As a result, some fall into the Right tendency to manage the economy in a capitalist way, overrating the importance of commodity production and the law of value in the wake of revisionist theory, while others commit the ultra-left error of failing to streamline management of enterprises and causing great wastage of means of production and labour power by totally ignoring commodity production and the role of the law of value, taking no account of the transitional character of our society. A correct understanding and treatment of this question is of great importance in socialist economic construction. After all, the question of utilizing commodity–money relations is an important one which the working-class state must settle properly in the period of transition from capitalism to socialism. Right or 'Left' mistakes on this question can do serious harm.

The factor determining when the means of production are commodities and when they are not in socialist society, should also be found in the differentiation of ownership. In socialist society the means of production even when shifted from one place to another, are not commodities as long as they do not change hands, and they are commodities when they do change hands. An obvious conclusion follows from this:

First, when means of production made in the state sector are transferred to co-operative ownership or vice versa, they are commodities in both cases and the law of value is therefore operating; second, when means of production are exchanged within the bounds of co-operative ownership – between co-operative farms or between producers' co-operatives, or between the former and the latter – they are just as much commodities and here, too, the law of value is operating; third, when they are exported the means of production are commodities and are traded at the world market price or at the socialist market price. For instance, when countries such as Indonesia or Cambodia ask our country for machine tools, the machine tools sold to these countries are commodities for which we should receive due prices. And when a Confederation of the north and the south, though not yet realized at this time, is established in our country in accordance with our Party's proposal for national reunification, and businessmen in south Korea ask us for machines and equipment, we will have to sell them. In that case the machines and equipment we sell them will be commodities, and the law of value will be bound to come into consideration.

What, then, are the equipment, raw materials and othert supplies that are transferred between the state enterprises? They are not commodities, because means of production such as these are turned out on the basis of socialist co-operation between production enterprises, and even when they are turned over from one enterprise to another they remain under the ownership of the socialist state, and such means of production are supplied not through free trade but under state planning of equipment and material supply. When the state believes it necessary, it provides the enterprises with the means of production, even if the enterprises do not ask for them, just as it provides the army with weapons. Therefore, the machines, equipment, raw materials and other supplies, which are transferred between the state enterprises, cannot be called commodities realized through the operation of the law of value.

Then, what shall we call these means of production transferred between the state enterprises, if not commodities, and what shall we say is being made use of, if not the operation of the law of value, in fixing the prices of the means of production when they are turned over, or in calculating their costs when produced? It would be correct to say that the means of production transferred between state enterprises according to the plans for equipment and material supply and for co-operative production are not commodities, but assume the commodity form and, acordingly, that in this case the law of values does not operate in substance as in the case of commodity production, but only in form.

In other words, such means of production are not commodities in the proper sense of the word, but merely assume the commodity form, and, accordingly, what is made use of here is not the operation of the law of value in the proper sense of the word, but the law of value in its outward form; and in the case of the production and exchange of means of production, it is not value itself but the form of value which is made use of simply as an instrument of economic accounting.

Then, how do you explain that the means of production transferred between state enterprises are not really commodities but only assume the form of commodities? This occurs because the state enterprises are relatively independent in using and managing the means of production and in running the economy, just as if they were under different ownership, when in fact they are all under one and the same state ownership. Though all the cost-acounting enterprises in the state sector are owned by the state, they independently use the means of production received from other enterprises according to unified state plan, and must net a certain profit for the state over and above their production costs...

Why, then, should the enterprises within the state sector be granted independence in management, and, if the means of production are not commodities, why should they be delivered and received under strict accounting, on the principle of equivalence? That has something to do with the specific feature of socialist society, which is a transitional one. In socialist society the productive forces have not developed to such an extent that each person works according to his abilities and each receives according to his needs. And not all people possess so great a collectivist spirit as to value and take responsible care of state properties like their own. In quite a few cases, even those who are educated enough do not care so much about the affairs of other state bodies or enterprises as about their own affairs, nor do they devote themselves to them, to say nothing of those who still harbour such old ideological debris as stodgy departmentalism and parochialism, gnawing away at the interests of the state or other institutions and enterprises, putting the narrow interests of their own institutions and localities above everything else. Further, under socialism labour has become, of course, an honourable and worth-while thing, but not yet life's prime requirement as in communist society. All these things require that under socialism equivalent values be strictly calculated in transactions between the enterprises, though they are all state-owned. If our society had a great affluence of goods and if the managing staffs and working people of all enterprises were free from selfishness, were concerned about all the state properties as about their own, and conducted all the state affairs as devotedly as their own, then there would be no need of keeping accounts on the basis of equivalent exchange.[10]

Let me underline the crucial relevance of this exposition for our analysis. Within a capitalist world-economy, there exists a world market price for any item traded. A socialist country is free to sell an item for a price below the world market price, what Kim Il Sung calls the 'socialist market price', but that is a political decision which amounts to a transfer of surplus for non-economic reasons. No doubt this is frequently done by socialist and capitalist countries; subsidies to friends, allies and clients has long been one of the central interstate political mechanisms of capitalism. But nonetheless, as Kim Il Sung says, 'the law of value will be bound to come into consideration'.[11]

Let us turn to a class analysis of socialist countries. The crucial difference between socialist semiperipheral and 'non-socialist'

10. Kim Il Sung, *On Some Theoretical Problems of the Socialist Economy*, 1 March 1969, placed as an advertisement by the Office of the Permanent Observer of the Democratic People's Republic of Korea to the United Nations, in *The New York Times* (16 March 1975), pp. 6–7.
11. Kidron observes about this pressure: 'However, often what seems to be purely political is so only in the short term and ultimately becomes economic; and even where time does not perform that particular alchemy, both sides would find it punitively expensive to sustain a political association that remained for long at variance with their economic interests. By the early 1960s Russia and the East-European countries were clearly beginning to count, and reject, the cost of purely political trade.' *Pakistan's Trade*, p. 7.

   Kidron's position is that: 'None of this is fortuitous. Faced with the unremitting pressures of world-wide military and economic competition and the growing truculence and power of their own people, the [Socialist bloc] bureaucracies simply cannot afford to forego the technical and organizational advantages of a Western-type economic maturity, no matter how insistent the lobbying from the [Third World].' *Pakistan's Trade*, p. 13.

semiperipheral countries is the absence in the former of an indigenous property-owning bourgeoisie and the exclusion of non-indigenous capitalist enterprises. The latter statement, however, must be modified to the extent that there have existed or may come to exist joint arrangements of socialist state enterprises and multinational corporations. As long as the interstate economic relationships of socialist countries with non-socialist countries is limited largely to the genre of adminstered trade, represented by 'barter deals', and as long as such trade plays a minor role in the overall economic planning of the socialist state, such a socialist state has to some degree 'withdrawn' from the capitalist world-economy. But are there any social forces, internal or external to these states, that would push for more 'normal' integration into the world-economy, towards the transformation of administered trade to simple market trade? The answer is that not only is this so, but one might say that this has been at the heart of a crucial political debate within *all* socialist countries since their respective existences.

Each successive socialist government, starting with the USSR and including the eastern European countries, China, Korea, Vietnam, and Cuba, has sought simultaneously to expand the forces of production and hence total production within its frontiers, and to increase the relative degree of equality of distribution of the social surplus. Furthermore, each has sought to remold the social psychology of its citizens, that is, to create 'socialist man' in one form or another. In the course of pursuing these objectives, each has undergone a debate, often repeatedly, about policy priorities, which in the Chinese literature has been called the issue of 'red and expert'. Obviously, all groups within socialist society say they are for being *both* red *and* expert. The issue is, to the extent that a choice must be made, even momentarily, which takes precedence, and with what frequency? This is a real issue which should not be dusted under the carpet, and as with all real issues it is ultimately a class issue. For there remain today in every socialist country persons who are 'experts', that is, persons having more skill and/or education than others in specific fields, and these persons generally have more organizational responsibility and more income than others. But how much more? And subject to what controls? These are key questions.

Those who lean on the side of expertise naturally tend to draw support from those strata who have this 'expertise'. Their most effective public argument is in terms of efficiency of economic production. That is, they claim that if the policies they propose are pursued by the government, the consequence will be higher productivity. And what is the measure of this efficiency? It can be none other than the scales of the capitalist world market. And what will be the reward of this efficiency? It can be none other than 'national development', precisely the same objective presumably sought by non-socialist nations. Of course, it might be said that 'experts' in socialist countries pursue 'development' more effectively than the indigenous bourgeoisie and state bureaucrats of 'non-socialist' countries; this might even be true. But is this an argument for a socialist to put forward?

Against the technocratic thrust may be found the ideological one. In China, this position is called 'politics in command', but parallel positions have been argued at one time or another in every socialist country. This position reflects different class forces, particularly that of the *semi*proletarianized segments of the working classes. The case for this position is many sided. On the one hand, it is a negative case. 'Politics in command' seeks to prevent the encrustation of the interests of the 'professional strata', minimize the income differentials, and in particular, destroy the persistence and/or growth of a separate style of life and other status group attributes so central to the process of class consolidation in a capitalist mode of production.

On the positive side, 'politics in command' argues that ultimately, given the continuing existence of a capitalist world-economy, de-emphasizing 'expertise' may do more to expand production and productivity during the transitional era than yielding to technocratic priorities. This point has been well articulated in the language of capitalist economics by an American observer:

Individuals may take risks because they are wealthy; poor people rarely become rich by taking risks. From this perspective we can derive some important policy implications. If, for example, market uncertainty must be borne individually, and some individuals are more financially able to bear the risk than others, then a very small percentage of the community will exhibit innovative or entrepreneurial qualities. By distributing the risk inherent in these uncertainties more equally throughout the community, the supply of potential innovators is going to be sharply expanded...Unless collectivization [of land] is accompanied by other policies designed to minimize the withdrawal of innovative behavior by the wealthy and popularize new opportunities for the poor, collectivization may temporarily have a perverse effect on the innovative and risk-taking behavior of a community. The stress on mass technical innovation and mass entrepreneurship by the Chinese elite speaks to this problem as does the effort to cultivate a genuine commitment to the community and the nation among all classes of the people. Indeed, to the extent that egalitarian policies are placed in a group setting, the dynamics of group interaction may lead the community to more innovative and adventurous policies than would be pursued by the individual.[12]

I wish to highlight two points. Since the real issue is that of the proper balance in the politics of 'red and expert', there has been a continual fluctuation in emphasis in *all* socialist countries throughout their respective histories. Secondly, while from the perspective of 'development' within the capitalist world-economy both sides in the debate might be able to put forward cogent arguments, from the perspective of transforming the capitalist world-economy into a socialist system, it is clear that 'politics in command' is the slogan of those giving priority to such efforts, and that this debate is indeed the consequence of a continuing class struggle within socialist countries. The reason this debate has not been *definitively* resolved in any socialist country, nor will be in the near future, is that as long as capitalism is the defining mode of production in the still single world-economy, there are constant benefits for certain powerful strata within the socialist countries to tie economic decisions more closely to the workings of the world market. The internal contradictions of these states express themselves as a continuing strain against pursuing socialism as the objective of state policy, a strain that can only be countered by great political effort, rooted in the poorest strata of the population.

This contradiction, however, expresses itself differently for those socialist countries who, to the extent that they tie themselves to the world-market, do this in the form of core, semiperipheral, or peripheral areas. One key problem of a core country in this era is to find adequate markets for its production. Another is to encourage a deepening of the international division of labor. The USSR shares such interests today with other core capitalist states. To the extent that world economic crisis means a tightening

12. Dennis M. Ray, 'Mao Tse-Tung's Development Strategy: Some Common Criticisms and an Uncommon Defense', *India Quarterly*, 30: 2 (April–June 1974), 118.

of these markets, the USSR is faced with the same world-market squeeze as other major industrial powers. Conversely, some of the smaller and less industrialized socialist states are still playing essentially peripheral roles in the world-economy and must still heavily depend, in terms of annual national income, on exports of basic commodities. To the extent that these commodities are less 'essential', they will face the same difficulties of reduced world demand that will be faced by other peripheral countries in the world-economy.

But the semiperipheral socialist states are our immediate concern here. While it is difficult to determine who they are, they surely include China, Korea, and the German Democratic Republic, and probably several others, especially in eastern Europe. To the extent that world-economic downturn means an improved bargaining position on the world market for semiperipheral states in general, those states should profit from this shift in world terms of trade. How will such states in fact react to the downturn, and in particular to this downturn, which is occurring in a situation involving the end of US world hegemony and a prospective realignment of world politico-military alignments? Obviously, the answer lies there, as well as elsewhere, in the internal *raport de forces* of various social strata and the degree to which external interests can affect internal political decisions. What can be said is that in the 'red versus expert' debate, such a world situation can provide reinforcement for the technocratic element in such states precisely because *short-run* rewards for such state policy may be particularly great.

This brings us to the issue of transnational class alliances and their impact on the internal politics of semiperipheral *states*. We have spoken of the altered *bargaining* possibilities of semiperipheral states *vis-à-vis* core states. Bargaining always raises the issue of syndicalism: 'In union there is strength'. When two interest sectors face each other in a market, one key element in deciding the outcome is the relative internal unity of each sector. Today, interimperialist rivalry is more acute than yesterday – but how much more acute? Today, unity of the semiperipheral nations is unexpectedly vigorous – but how solid is the foundation? We shall concern ourselves primarily with the latter question.

There are two central difficulties in maintaining the unity of the semiperipheral countries of the world today. They can be seen as analogous to the difficulties faced by a group of workers attempting a strike in a nineteenth-century factory. The bosses handled a strike in two ways: first, they tried to divide the strikers by offering attractive bait to the better paid, more efficient workers, thus hoping to sow internal dissension; secondly, they tried to isolate the strikers from external workers' support by bringing in as 'strikebreakers' precisely some economically weaker group of unemployed (often from a different ethnic group). As the attempts to create syndical unity occur today – alliances of key commodity producers, Group of 77, etc. – one danger is that a few of the relatively better off will not go along for 'political' reasons. For example, in 1975 Canada refused to consider joining a prospective cartel of iron producers. The second danger is that the peripheral states will be set against the semiperipheral ones. Recent strains within the Group of 77 and within the Organization of African Unity reflect precisely this possibility.

How these two dangers will be handled is a function of the class consciousness of the syndical group. But here the analogy with nineteenth-century strikers breaks down. The latter were individuals, members of a class, who might or might not have effectively mobilized at a given moment. But semiperipheral states are organizations, not individuals, each itself the meeting point of contradictory internal class forces. How the semiperipheral states act as a collectivity will be a function of two things: the outcomes of the continuing class struggles within each state, and the degree to which the relative strength or victory of socialist forces in one or another of these semiperipheral states will affect the internal balance of power in the others.

Let me put it another way. The semiperipheral states in the coming decades will be a battleground of two major transnational forces. One will be the multinational corporations who will be fighting for the survival of the essentials of the capitalist system: the possibility of continued surplus appropriation on a world scale. The other will be a transnational alignment of socialist forces who will be seeking to undermine the capitalist world-economy, not by 'developing' singly, but by forcing relatively drastic redistributions of world surplus and cutting the long-term present and potential organizational links between multinationals and certain strata internal to each semiperipheral country, including such strata in the socialist semiperipheral states.

It can be predicted that the period of world-economic downturn will be a period of 'low profile' for the multinationals. They will be on their best behavior, particularly *vis-à-vis* the governments of semiperipheral states. They will act in a sophisticated manner and make many concessions. They will even minimize, to the extent possible, their political links with core states, particularly the USA. They will offer the equivalent of a world welfare state for the world's 'middle' strata, provided that they can continue to function and make *real* profits, whatever the channel. They will only be countered by equally sophisticated tactics on the part of socialist forces who remember three points: (1) the internal class struggle continues unabated in the socialist as well as the 'non-socialist' semiperiphery; (2) the professional strata of the *stronger* semiperipheral states will tend to be Trojan horses and can only be effectively neutralized by strong workers' organizations that give due place to the poorest sector of semiproletarianized workers; (3) it will take considerable effort and sacrifice by semiperipheral states to maintain an alliance with peripheral states, *especially* in an era of world-economic downturn.

We are not at Armageddon. But we are at an important turning-point in the historical life of the capitalist world-economy. The next twenty-five years will probably determine the modalities and the speed of the ongoing transition to a socialist world government. We could emerge with a real strengthening of world socialist forces. But there could as well be a setback. One of the critical political arenas is precisely the semiperiphery.

6 ✎ The rural economy in modern world society

The period after the Second World War was one of steady expansion of the world-economy within a framework of US world hegemony at all levels – economic, political, military, and cultural. It is during this period that such ideas as the 'dual economy' and 'economic development' took root, presumably as concepts with which one could formulate a policy that would bring the 'Third World' (another concept of this era) into a more equitable share of this expanding world pie. These concepts were not merely analytic tools; they represented political programs, and popular ones at that. But since about 1967, there have been a series of closely interconnected events – the oil crisis, the food crisis, the defeat of the United States in southeast Asia, Watergate, international monetary fluctuations, and world-economic downturn – the sum of which have been enough to raise great doubts about recent development theory. In particular, one of the key questions is: are there indeed entities suitable for development 'in isolation'?

I would phrase the intellectual questions of our time – which are the moral questions of our time – as follows: (1) Why is there hunger amidst plenty, and poverty amidst prosperity? (2) Why do not the many who are afflicted rise up against the few who are privileged, and smite them? You may note that I have affected the language of the King James edition of the Bible. I have done this to signal two things. At one level our problems are biblical ones, that is eternal ones, ones that confront all of human history. But at a second level, they take on a specifically modern form, of

Originally delivered as the keynote address for Conference on Food and the Rural Economy: Rural Populations in the Industrial Food System, held at Harvard University on 2–3 May 1975, and sponsored by The Center for Ethics and Society, Lutheran Church in America.

a world whose origins in the sixteenth century are heralded precisely by this King James version – a new language for a new era. It is this modern world and its structure we must examine in order to find the causes and the remedies of our present dilemmas.

What was this 'new world'? It was the emergence in the sixteenth century of a capitalist world-economy, whose geographic bounds were initially largely in Europe but which has since come to cover the entire globe. While this world-system is quite different from any of the various systems that existed prior to this time, one of my main themes will be that, despite internal growth of the structures and productive forces of this capitalist world-economy, and despite the fact that this system has been effectively challenged for the first time in the twentieth century, none of its fundamental characteristics has yet changed, and that it will mislead us grievously if we start our search by looking for what is new today rather than for what are the long-term, continuing features of this system.

What distinguishes capitalism from prior systems is the orientation of production to capital accumulation via profit realized on a market – this market is, and has been from the beginning, a *world* market. This makes capitalism into a form of social organization whose prime object is its own perpetuation in an ever-expanding form (the true Promethean myth). The major weapons in this process are increased efficiency of production and the denial of the desires of most people in terms of immediate consumption. Efficiency is translated into plenty and prosperity. Denial is translated into hunger and poverty. The mechanisms by which such a system works and maintains itself in existence as a system are elaborate, subtle, and devious.

Efficiency of production and denial of consumption are a beautiful example of a contradictory symbiosis. In one sense, they work hand in hand; in another, they go in opposite directions. The history of the modern world-system is the history of how this contradiction has been held in check, harnessed to the perpetuation of the system, kept from rending its fabric. This will not be possible forever, but it has been possible for a long time and it will not disappear in one fell swoop for a while yet. Describing how this contradiction works will give us the answer to our second question.

First let us examine the contrary pushes. On the one hand, both more efficient production and the denial of consumption create a larger unconsumed surplus which, if reinvested in capital goods, will expand total production still further. And if part of this surplus is expended on technological invention, the long-term surplus will be magnified still further. Whereupon, if the margin of consumption goes down, remains steady, or even expands more slowly than the rate of production, still more capital is accumulated. And so it goes.

There is one small problem. To accumulate capital, one must realize profit. To realize profit, commodities must be sold on a market. To buy commodities, someone must have money, and once the commodities are bought they are consumed. So it happens that too much denial of consumption interferes with the system every bit as much as too little denial.

The alternation between too much and too little is reflected in the periodic cycles, or crises, of the system, these so-called crises being mechanisms of adjustment. I do not think one can reasonably call them mechanisms of equilibrium because disequilibrium is in fact the true axis of the system. There may still be a few persons surviving who honestly believe there is an unseen hand regulating and harmonizing the system, but magical beliefs need occasional confirmation to renew themselves, and world disharmony has been so giddily obvious for so long that all the imprecations of Milton Friedmann cannot persuade even the most stalwart conservative politicians actually to stand back and let what happens happen.

Not only is the capitalist system not properly described as a system of free enterprise today, but there never was a moment in history when this was a reasonable descriptive label. The capitalist system is and always has been one of state interference with the 'freedom' of the market in the interests of some and against those of others. What has sometimes kept us from seeing this as clearly as we might is that we failed to be very clear about the unit we should analyze.

The scope of an economy is defined by the area within which an effective division of labor exists. And since the beginning of the system, the boundaries of the real division of labor have always been larger than that of any particular sovereign entity. Hence while within a few states, for very brief moments of historical time, it seemed as if the state did not involve itself in the workings of the internal market, the true market has always been the world market, within which some states were always acting to affect the terms under which transactions were made.

Thus we come to the fundamental structural feature of the modern world-system, an economic arena larger than any political unit, within which regions might be classified as performing the roles of core or peripheral areas (and of semiperipheral ones as well). It was this structure that permitted the privileged few to navigate between the shoals of achieving 'too much' versus 'too little' consumption, thereby continually afflicting the many. But the many who were afflicted were not continually the same ones, or at least the degree of affliction varied between afflicted groups over time, which is one of the reasons why the many have not smitten the few.

Not only have different goods been produced in different sectors of the world-economy but the workers who produced these different goods have been paid differential wages, which has been at one and the same time a means of transferring surplus from one area to another (so-called unequal exchange) and a means of becalming social protest in the politically key core areas of the world-economy. We may only have discovered this reality recently, but as a social phenomenon it dates back to the sixteenth century.

While the inequality of the exchange has remained constant, the degree of inequality has varied, in response to the cycles of overall expansion and contraction the world-economy has experienced continually. This variance is what we mean by shifting terms of trade, which is an economist's mode of summarizing in an index world-wide shifts in investment emphases, the response to the permanent disequilibrium of supply and demand in a market economy. Another way to say this is that 'too much' consumption of one good is always 'too little' of another.

Along with the cycles there is a secular trend. The major solution to the contradiction of more efficient production and constraint on consumption is to expand both production and consumption extensively – to 'expand the pie' quite apart from improving the technology. One would think there are limits to such extensive expansion which is a geographic expansion, and indeed there are. But we have not yet reached them! The 'world' has been expanding geographically since the sixteenth century and it is still doing so. What makes us fail to see this sometimes is that the world-economy has long since touched the outer limits of the globe, but it has done so by skipping over interior areas.

Of course, we have not failed to notice this. But the major form of taking notice of this phenomenon has been the theory of the dual economy, that is, the argument that there are some areas included and some not included in the world-economy. The fact is that both areas are included in this world-economy, but in different ways. Furthermore, this dual mode of involvement is neither capricious nor a sign of failure of the system, but is precisely its cornerstone. The slowly developing, slowly eroding, marginal, largely subsistence sector of the world-economy, within which live the largest part of the world's rural populations who are presumably our concern here, do not pose a problem to the capitalist world-economy. These areas are and have been from the beginning one of its major solutions.

Let us see how this 'solution' works. In the sixteenth century, at a moment of overall expansion of the European world-economy, there were two major peripheral areas – eastern Europe, which produced primarily wheat and wood, and Iberian America which produced primarily bullion, but also sugar, indigo, and some other raw materials. As the world-economy expanded, a greater quantity of production of these goods was required. It was obtained by one variant or another of the 'plantation system', using the term loosely and not technically. I mean here by 'plantation system' any form of social organization that grouped relatively large areas of land together with a work force whose legal ability to choose employment was constrained.

Such forms of social organization were low cost, in that the low real wages compensated for the costs of supervision and lack of skill of the work force. They also minimized interruptions of production. The exact social forms varied: the so-called second serfdom in eastern Europe, the *encomienda* system in Hispanic America, slavery, etc. With such a system, the entrepreneur (usually a landowner) could control the total quantity of production, responding (however imperfectly) to the world market. In particular, if further expansion were called for, it was relatively easy to involve a larger land area, as there tended to be a land surplus. Workers in the periphery were in shorter supply and sometimes employers had to go further afield to obtain them.

When world-wide contraction occurred in the middle of the seventeenth century, what happened to these areas of coerced cash-crop production? Since the world market had a lowered demand, it was not rational for the landowners to produce at the same rate, or for some of them to produce at all. We then saw occur what has sometimes been called 'inversion'. Cultivated areas were left untended. The workers were permitted, nay encouraged, to take up a plot of land and feed themselves off it. Trade with the rest of the world diminished. Handicrafts, which had previously died out, were revived. The commercial estate seemed to be reverting to the status of a self-sufficient manor once again. The *encomienda* was transformed into the *hacienda*. The landlord himself moved from the city to the rural area, to partake at least partially in the isolated subsistence economy.

From the point of view of the world-economy, overall production was being brought in line with overall demand. In some cases, new peripheral areas were being opened up, on fresh soil, or under different political control, precisely as old areas were 'inverting'. From the point of view of the landlord of an old area, he eliminated most of his overhead cost of maintenance by 'permitting' subsistence farming. And, which is key, he kept intact a legal title and a work force which made it easier fifty or one hundred years later for his descendants, once the prospects of the world-economy had turned upward, to lay claim once again to re-establishing the plantation system. This is what happened in eastern Europe and the Americas after 1750.

But something else happened. There was extensive (geographic) expansion as well, and also intensive expansion (the industrial revolution). Not only were the 'old' areas and the old work force which had been temporarily withdrawn from the world-economy reinvolved, but additional areas and new work forces were included as well. If then one thinks of inversion therefore not as withdrawal of individuals from a system, but rather a mode of reducing recurrent costs at a moment of slowdown in the system, it is hard not to perceive how important this is to the maintenance of the system and how relatively deliberate is the policy. Nor is this the only way in which those persons seemingly outside the system are in fact inside it. As we move forward in the history of the world-system the overt coercion of coerced cash-crop labor steadily diminished. Slavery was abolished; so was serfdom; so even was peonage. There were several reasons for this.

First, elimination of geographic zones outside the capitalist world-economy (from which slaves, for example were taken) raised the real economic cost of such social forms and made them less plausible. Second, the process of maintaining relative social peace in the core areas required the elaboration of various ideological schemes of 'freedom', which had the inconvenience that the concept spread to realms for which it was not intended. Hence the world 'cultural' ambience took on characteristics that made the more overt forms of coercion more politically costly as well. Third, structural substitutes were evolved which gave virtually the same results. In part the coercion was more hidden. In part, the 'higher' wages of the less coerced labor turned out not to be higher wages.

It is this last point that must be elaborated, for it is crucial. If one reads economic history of the Middle Ages, one finds that carpenters' wages were computed by the day. As the modern factory system emerged in the nineteenth century, we find that workers tended to get a weekly pay envelope. As a mark of status, white-collar workers were and often are paid bimonthly or even monthly. Professionals receive contracts defined in terms of annual salaries. This time variance has something to do with the fact that the lower the true income, the lower the liquidity of the individual, and the more essential it is to have frequent payments. This variation is also a form of mysticism, conferring prestige and even privilege – for the larger the time period of single payment, the greater the possibility for the individual recipient to opt among alternative consumption patterns.

These explanations are from the point of view of the worker – his needs, his preferences. What of the employer? The employer is primarily concerned with the size of the overall wage bill over a long period of time as partly determining his 'costs of production'. The major way an employer can reduce this wage bill is if he can arrange it so that the wages of the employee are not the only source of real income. To the extent that this is so, whoever provides additional sources of real income to the employee (for other than additional productive work) is paying part of the overall wage bill.

The only meaningful way to calculate real income for a worker is real lifetime income – from birth to death. Take a typical wage worker in the contemporary United States. Let us assume, to simplify the matter, that he is married, that he has a non-working wife and non-adult children, that he is steadily employed from entry into the labor market until retirement, and that he did not inherit any money from his parents. His real life income is made up of two parts: his wages, and various government benefits (social security, etc.). The latter in turn are in part merely a disguised savings program, in part employers' contributions, and in some part a redistribution via taxation of someone else's wages. Out of his real life income, he is supposed to sustain himself from entry into the work force until death, sustain his wife from marriage to her death (via life insurance, if she dies after him, etc.), and sustain his children from birth until their entry into the work force. The money he expends on his children may be seen macrocosmically as replacement for the money spent on him and his wife during their childhood by their parents. Therefore it can be said a worker pays for his own childhood costs. What he will consider an absolutely minimum wage must be a wage that will at some bare level cover the above costs for the whole of the periods indicated. His interpretation of a minimum wage must be accepted by the employer if there is not to be acute political conflict. Normally, the employer accepts it.

Let us take a typical wage worker in the peripheral areas of the world. He may be a factory worker in town or in a mine, or more frequently a wage laborer on a cash-crop plantation. If the latter, he will be performing the economic function of the Polish serf or the Indian *encomendado* of the sixteenth century, but now as a 'free man' receiving wages. There will be one key difference between this peripheral wage worker and the one in the United States. He will be far more likely to be a migratory worker. I do not refer to the minor variety of migratory worker who moves domicile seasonally. I mean the one who spends part or even all of his adult working life in cash employment but who spends childhood and probably 'old age' (which may in practice be the period after thirty years of age) in his rural 'subsistence' community.

Let us analyze this man's real income and his expenditures. In childhood, he (and his wife) are sustained by their parents who quite possibly were not wage employees, in which case, his expenditures on his children are not substitutable for his parents on him. During his adult cash-work life, he sustains himself, but quite possibly his wife and non-adult children are sustained in his home village out of village resources. When he ceases cash work and returns to his village, he is unlikely to receive many government benefits, but will rather live on what can be obtained in the village. His real life income is essentially a composite of what his employer has paid and his income from the so-called subsistence economy. Thus, unlike his counterpart in the United States, this semiproletarianized worker is able to claim as a minimum viable income from his employer not what it takes to sustain him and his wife throughout the life cycle but only what it takes to sustain him (and only possibly also his wife) for the number of years he actually works for the employer. The difference in annual or weekly minimum wage will be considerable if this wage is supposed to be allocated over twenty years instead of sixty, and it is the immediate employer and all those who purchase his product who draw the profit from this reduced minimum wage.

From whom do they draw this profit? From the producers in the rural susbistence economy, presumably totally or largely outside the capitalist world-economy. Somewhere in a remote village at this moment a non-wage worker is producing a surplus in which, via multiple intermediaries, each one of us is partaking, if to different degrees. But this particular transfer of surplus is well hidden from view because its traces are swallowed up, in the obscure facts of the life cycle of the non-wage worker's cousin, the wage worker of the peripheral areas.

This is a crudely drawn picture. But we must really stop there and contemplate this central economic reality if we are going to speak meaningfully about the contemporary 'food crisis'. How does this perspective aid us to understand the food crisis? For several years now, there has been an acute famine in a semiarid belt in tropical zones, reaching across Middle America, the Sahelo-Sudanic region of Africa, and south Asia. How do we explain it?

From a short-run perspective we can talk of various minor climatic shifts which reduced output in marginal areas to near zero while reducing total output in the world's lusher areas. This has also some short-run self-reinforcing patterns. For example, when a sedentary farmer abandons his land because of drought, he thereby also reduces the following year's production, because he does not sow. This is a very short-run perspective. We could also mention the fact that during the post-Second World War economic expansion, many of the countries now experiencing acute famine were encouraged to expand non-food cash-crop production at the expense of food growing areas, partly by the lure of profit, partly by the world market uncompetitiveness of their food production in relation to mechanized production in the United States, Canada, Australia, etc., and simultaneously by the political distribution of surplus food by these latter countries. When some of the richer countries began to expand meat production as a result of their increased prosperity, they reduced the margin of 'overproduction', so that when drought struck, there was a sudden world-wide penury of grains.

But the long-run causes are as always the most important. Basically, over two hundred years, the so-called subsistence areas of the peripheral countries have been undertaking to produce a larger and larger food surplus on land which has been unimproved by technology, and this process has led to massive erosion on a world scale. If one throws into the balance the fact that the one indirect benefit of modern technology obtained by the people of such areas has been a lowering of the incidence of endemic disease, the increased burden on the land has been greater still.

Add the fact that immediate climatic conjuncture joined a turn in world-economic cycles, and the pattern of the near future becomes clear. Millions will die of quick starvation. Millions more will die of slow starvation. That is, many will be forced off their land, salvaged by humanitarian agencies, drift to bidonvilles in towns, and die over a ten-year period for lack of employment and because their networks of social security have been disrupted.

And then what? Much land will have been cleared of most of its present population. Such land will be regrouped under new ownership in a plantation form. It will be partially mechanized. The owners will hire wage workers and will sell the commercial products (including food) on a world market. Who will own these plantations? There are several possibilities: the states, cooperatives of small commercial farmers, multinational corporations, or some combination thereof.

On 18 March 1975, *The Wall Street Journal* ran an article whose headline was 'Multinational Firms Help Poorer Nations to Boost Food Output'. The subhead went further: 'By lending their expertise, companies polish image; ultimate motive: profit.' This article describes among other things the role of the Industry Cooperative Program of the Food and Agricultural Organization in bringing together multinationals and the governments of peripheral countries in joint ventures that will be 'mutually profitable': 'Booker McConnell [Ltd, a big British foods company] has a management contract to run a sugar operation in Mumias [Kenya]. "We earn a profit from it," says Mr Bishop, the chairman [of Booker McConnell]. He says it's not as big a profit as might be earned from a 100% company-owned plant, but the capital investment is less, and there aren't any risks of capital loss.'

What we shall probably see in the next fifty years is the last great expansion of the world-economy. The ground will be prepared by world-wide agricultural reorganization during the downward cycle and then, in about 1990 or whenever the world-economy expands again, the shift to wage employment, the proletarianization of the work force, may become virtually universal.

When this happens, the contradiction between greater efficiency and denial of consumption will become far more acute, both because it will no longer be soluble by a further expansion, and because the cash nexus, having become universal, will also become extremely visible. The system will not be able to survive the light of day.

In this coming period, rural areas will not 'develop' any more than they have in the past, although of course some selected areas may improve their relative standing in the world pecking order of surplus extraction. But any such gain will be at someone else's expense. There will however be an important change. The world political conflict will surely have developed along lines that are visible now and perhaps also along some that are unexpected. The conflict will be essentially between those who will try to hold on to a capitalist world-economy that will have exhausted its ability to expand further the forces of production, incapable any longer of holding the contradictions in check, and those who will seek to construct politically a very different kind of world order, a socialist world government.

I shall end on the note of an ethical question: how can we view our own situation in light of this world-system? Suppose I am a strong swimmer swimming at an ocean beach and the sea is choppy. Suppose some motorboats engaged in a race come closer to shore than they should and cause already high waves to become suddenly higher. Suppose a weak swimmer nearby begins to drown.

In analyzing the causes of the dilemma, I could point to the short-term fact that the weak swimmer had failed to get in shape in prior weeks and had thus become exhausted easily. Or I could offer a middle-term explanation that the motorboats recklessly caused already high waves to become even higher. Or I could look at the long-term social roots. The community, though warned, had failed to build breakers to reduce the waves. Or the community had failed to ban motorboat races, or at least police them so that they were less dangerous.

The drowning man would prefer I save his life than analyze the roots of his dilemma. It is thus that the food crisis is often presented to us. There is drought in Ethiopia or earthquake in Brazil: send food, or medicine, or tents, and send them instantly. Who dares say no? Suppose I change the 'givens' slightly. Perhaps I am not in the water myself but on the beach and hence the drowning man is further away. Suppose not one man is drowning but one thousand, but for all the same reasons. Then my ethical dilemma might conceivably be posed as a choice between four courses of action:

(1) I could swim out to save people. I could probably save one or several. What would happen to the rest is uncertain.

(2) I could spend a little time locating a nearby lifeline and toss it into the water. This might save fifty. But the one I might have saved in plan (1) will probably drown in the meantime. What happens to the other 950 is in doubt.

(3) I could do something to stop the speedboats. This might take even more time than locating the lifeline. I probably could save 950, but perhaps the 50 that would have been saved by plan (2) might have drowned in the meantime.

(4) I could seek to change the laws and/or attitudes of the community. Powerful groups would oppose me. I would have to prepare for an organized struggle. Nonetheless, this might save all future swimmers. Meanwhile however, it is conceivable that the present thousand might go under.

It is not easy to decide what to do. You will want more details. You will prefer to do all simultaneously, which is not possible. You may get angry and deny the dilemma, saying no one will drown if they will only swim. Or you may find the moral choice too difficult for mere humans, and leave it to the will of God. My own penchant is to do (3) in the immediate and then move on to (4). I can understand how others might choose differently. I can respect these other choices, if made with clarity of vision and understanding of the consequences and of who it is that will benefit from each of the various solutions to the dilemma. The basic problem is one concerning the structure of inequality of the present world-system. As long as it persists, swimmers will drown. But it is not inevitable that swimmers drown.

Scholars are in the business of doubt. Truth is the objective but one that is never realized, one that is at best momentarily approximated. Churches are in the business of faith. But faith in things sacred implies doubt about things secular. So scholars and churches, and indeed the rest of us, which is most of us, can come together as doubters. For we not only have the right to doubt about the efficacy and the virtue of what is, but we have the moral duty to do so, and to act against what is doubtful. In this fashion, doubt is the beginning of hope and therefore of faith.

7 ❧ Modernization: requiescat in pace

When a concept has died, some try to revive it by invoking it as ritual incantation, some regret its passing wistfully, some pretend it never existed, and some are impatient with any reference to it. But only the American Sociological Association holds a funeral service.

De mortuis nil nisi bonum? A good slogan perhaps for personal matters, but not very helpful in intellectual or political ones. I should like therefore very briefly to review how world social science ever got into this cul-de-sac known as modernization theory and, now that some of us are out of it, what lies on the horizon ahead.

I hesitate to review the history of this idea since it seems to me that this has been done already on a number of occasions. But memorials involve familiar memories. Until 1945 it still seemed reasonable to assume that Europe was the center of the world. Even anti-imperialist movements outside of Europe and against Europe often tended to assume it. But the world moved inexorably on. And everyone's geographical horizons expanded. To cope with this changing world, western scholars invented development, invented the Third World, invented modernization.

Let us start by citing the merits of these inventions. The new terms replaced older, distasteful ones. Backward nations were only underdeveloped. The Yellow Horde became instead the Third World. And progress no longer involved westernization. Now one could antiseptically modernize.

Above all, the new concepts offered hope. No doubt Africa had never invented the wheel, no doubt Asian religions were fatalist, no doubt Islam preached submission, no doubt Latins combined racial miscegenation with a lack of entrepreneurial thrift; but it could now be asserted confidently that these failings were not biological, merely cultural. And if, like the Japanese, the under-developed were clever enough to invent an indigenous version of Calvinism, or if they could be induced to change the content of their children's readers (the children first being taught to read, of course), or if transistors were placed in remote villages, or if farsighted elites mobilized benighted masses with the aid of altruistic outsiders, or if..., then the underdeveloped too would cross the river Jordan and come into a land flowing with milk and honey. This was the hope offered up by the modernization theorists.

It was unquestionably a worthy parable for the times. It would be easy to show how this parable was manipulated by the masters of the world. Let us recognize nonetheless that it served to spur devoted and well-intentioned scholarship and liberal social action. But the time has come to put away childish things, and look reality in its face.

We do not live in a modernizing world but in a capitalist world. What makes this world tick is not the need for achievement but the need for profit. The problem for oppressed strata is not how to communicate within this world but how to overthrow it. Neither Great Britain nor the United States nor the Soviet Union is a model for anyone's future. They are state structures of the present, partial (not total) institutions operating within a singular world-system, which however is and always has been an evolving one.

The last thing we need to do is to make comparative measure-ments of non-comparable and non-autonomous entities when the social system in which we all operate is for the first time in human history a single unit in which the entire game is resumed in the internal relationships to be found within the capitalist world-economy: of core to periphery, of bourgeois to proletarian, of hegemonic culture to cultures of resistance, of dominant strata with their demand for universalistic individual measurement to institutionally oppressed racial and ethnic strata, of the party of order to the party of movement. These relationships can be measured too, but we have not been measuring them.

The first step we must make if we wish to understand our world is radically to reject any and all distinction between history and social science, and to recognize that we are part of a single discipline of study: the study of human societies as they have historically evolved. There are no generalizations that are not historically time bound, because there are no systems and no structures that are unchanging. And there is no set or sequence of social events that is comprehensible without reference to a theoretical construct whose function is to create meaning out of reality.

What was primarily wrong with all the concepts linked to the paradigm of modernization was that they were so ahistorical. After all, the modern world did not come out of nowhere. It involved the *transformation* of a particular variant of the redistributive mode of production, that found in feudal Europe, into a European world-economy based on a capitalist mode of production. It involved the strengthening of state structures in the core areas of this world-economy and the correlative weakening of them in the periphery.

And once capitalism was consolidated as a system and there was no turnback, the internal logic of its functioning, the search for maximum profit, forced it continuously to expand – extensively to cover the globe, and intensively via the constant (if not steady) accumulation of capital, the pressure to mechanize work in order to make possible still further expansion of production, the tendency to facilitate and optimize rapid response to the permutations of the world market by the proletarianization of labor and the commercialization of land. This is what modernization is about if one wants to use such a contentless word.

But whatever word we use, let us remember that the suffix '-ization' in the English language contains an antinomy. It refers both to the state of something and to the process of becoming that something. The capitalist world-economy has not yet, after four to five hundred years of existence, realized a free market, free labor, unentailed land, unbounded flows of capital. Nor do I believe it ever will do so. For I believe that the essence of the capitalist mode of production is the *partial* freedom of the factors of production. It will in fact only be with a socialist world-system that we will realize true freedom (including the free flow of the factors of production). This is indeed what lies behind Marx's phrase about moving from the 'realm of necessity into the realm of freedom'.

I do not intend here to preach a faith. Those who wish will believe. And those who do not will struggle against it. I wish rather to suggest an agenda of intellectual work for those who are seeking to understand the world-systemic transition from capitalism to socialism in which we are living, and thereby to contribute to it.

I think top priority must go to the original concern of the nineteenth-century fathers of social science, the understanding of the capitalist world-economy in which we live as a gestalt. But how do we do that? I see five major arenas of research, each large in scope.

(1) The first arena is the internal functioning of the capitalist world-economy as a system: the institutional ways in which areas get located at the core, the periphery, and the semiperiphery of that system, and how units can and do change their location; the mechanisms of transfers of surplus toward the core; the ways in which classes emerge, consolidate, and disintegrate; the multiple expressions of class struggle; the creation, sustenance, and destruction of all varieties of 'status groups' (ethno-national groups, racial castes, age and sex groups), and the ways these 'status' groupings interweave with class structure; the cultural expressions of conflicting interests; the pattern of interplay between cyclical processes of expansion and contraction and the secular evolutionary processes that undermine the basic stability of the system; the modalities of and resistances to the proletarianization of labor and the commercialization of land; the role of the state in affecting the world market and aiding specific groups within it; the rise of antisystemic revolutionary movements.

This is a long list; but it is only one arena. We must also and simultaneously work in other arenas:

(2) We must reopen the question of how and when the capitalist world-economy was created in the first place; why the transition took place in feudal Europe and not elsewhere; why it took place when it did and not earlier or later; why earlier attempts of transition failed. This is not merely an exercise in archaeological reconstruction; it is rather essential to the full comprehension of the nature of our present system.

(3) Allied with this issue is another on which almost no work has

been done. For at least three centuries (the sixteenth to the eighteenth), the capitalist world-economy functioned side by side with non-capitalist social systems outside it. How did it relate to them? And in particular, what were the processes that made it possible for the capitalist world-economy to incorporate them?

(4) In the light of these interests, it will be clear why we must also turn to a comparative study of the various historical forms of social system, the alternative modes of production. I myself believe there have only been three such modes up to now: the reciprocal (lineage) mode found in minisystems; the redistributive (tributary) mode found in world-empires (either full blown or largely disintegrated); the capitalist (market) mode found in world-economies. But this is a contentious formulation. In any case enormous work has to be done simply to identify properly which historical contructs reflected which modes and to make appropriate comparisons primarily within the systems or modes and secondarily among them.

(5) This then brings me to the fourth system based on a socialist mode of production, our future world government. We are living in the transition to it, which will continue for some time to come. But how are we relating to it? As rational militants contributing to it or as clever obstructors of it (whether of the malicious or cynical variety)? In any case, here too we must look afresh at the various 'socialist' experiences seen as regimes that are seeking both to transform the world-system and partially to prefigure the future one, with greater or lesser success. And we must look to the relationship of revolutionary movements in the various political subdivisions of the world-system to each other.

You may ask whether this agenda is not far wider than the narrow field 'modernization' was to cover. Yes, indeed it is. But that is the point. Modernization theory has served to deflect us from the agenda that would be able to speak to the problems with which it was supposedly concerned. This agenda requires redoing our historical narratives, accumulating new world-systemic quantitative data (almost from scratch), and above all reviewing and refining our conceptual baggage.

There are those who will say that such an agenda is a throwback from the scientific advances of modern social science to the imprecise and ideological musings of the nineteenth century. To such a contention, one can only give the answer of Thomas Kuhn when he discussed the problem of the historical use of measurement in physical science:

Much qualitative research, both empirical and rhetorical, is normally prerequisite to fruitful quantification of a given research field. In the absence of such prior work, the methodological directive, 'Go ye forth and measure', may well prove only an invitation to waste time...

The full and intimate quantification of any science is a consummation devoutly to be wished. Nevertheless, it is not a consummation that can effectively be sought by measuring. As in individual development, so in the scientific group, maturity comes most surely to those who know how to wait.[1]

We have been impatient for the past thirty years. And the wine has turned sour. Let us go back to where we once were: understanding the reality of our world, which is that of a capitalist world-economy in the early stages of its transition to a socialist world government. The road is hard, intellectually and politically. But it is the road both of scholarly integrity and of scientific promise.

1. Thomas S. Kuhn, 'The Function of Measurement in Modern Physical Science', in Harry Woolf (ed.), *Quantification* (Indianapolis: Bobbs-Merrill, 19661), pp. 55, 60.

8 ❧ From feudalism to capitalism: transition or transitions?

The debate on the appropriate definition of terms like feudalism or capitalism is pervasive in discussions of the modern world. I should like to review the nature of this debate and show how it governs what one may mean by a spongy term like 'transition'.

Let me start with capitalism. It seems to me that there have been three perspectives that have governed the use of the term. I associate these respectively with Adam Smith, Werner Sombart, and Karl Marx.

Adam Smith suggests in *The Wealth of Nations*, in an oft-quoted phrase, that the division of labor is a necessary consequence of a 'certain propensity in human nature...to truck, barter, and exchange one thing for another' (p. 13).

It logically follows from this starting point that capitalism is not one of several historically successive social or economic forms but simply 'what comes naturally'. To be sure, there have existed historically many political 'systems' which have interfered with these natural propensities of man, but these interferences are the path of human unwisdom:

It is thus that every system which endeavours, either by extraordinary encouragements to draw towards a particular species of industry a greater share of the capital of the society than what would naturally go to it, or by extraordinary restraints to force from a particular species of industry some share of the capital which would otherwise be employed in it, is in reality subversive of the great purpose which it means to promote. It retards, instead of accelerating, the process of the society towards real wealth and greatness; and diminishes, instead of increasing, the real value of the annual produce of its land and labour.

(Smith, pp. 650–1)

Werner Sombart's approach in *The Quintessence of Capitalism* is strikingly different. Far from capitalism reflecting man's inner

138

nature, Sombart's psychology starts with the opposite presupposition. Capitalism is *un*natural:

The pre-capitalist man was a natural man, man as God made him, man who did not stand on his head or run on all fours (as is the case today in economic activities). The pre-capitalist man stood firmly on his two legs, by the aid of which alone he moved about. His economic outlook is therefore not difficult to ascertain; it springs quite easily from human nature. (p. 13)

Although capitalism is unnatural, it does not necessarily follow that it is good or bad. Capitalism has its virtues and its vices, although it may one day be 'played out'.

And when the capitalist spirit has lost its power of expansion what then? That does not concern us here. Possibly the blind giant may be condemned to draw the wagon of a democratic civilization; possibly it may be the Twilight of the Gods and the gold will have to be restored to the caverns of the Rhine. Who shall say? (Sombart, p. 359)

The key point Sombart was trying to make about capitalism is that it was made possible only by the emergence of a 'capitalist spirit', and all expressions of such a spirit were 'due to personal qualities inherent in the individual'. Sombart thereupon drew two conclusions from a look at empirical reality: '(1) All peoples have the qualities necessary for capitalism...(2) Each nation has the qualities in a varying degree' (p. 210).

Marx had a third standpoint. For him, the issue of whether an entrepreneurial orientation was 'natural' or not was metaphysical mystification.[1] For man's economic behavior *vis-à-vis* other men was a reflection of a particular set of what he called 'relations of production', and these relations evolved historically. In that sense, man's 'nature', as deduced from his economic behavior, changed over time. Of course the change was neither sudden nor capricious, since:

No social order is ever destroyed before all the productive forces for which it is sufficient have been developed, and new superior relations of production never replace older ones before the material conditions for their existence have

1. 'When the economists say that present-day relations – the relations of bourgeois production – are natural, they imply that these are the relations in which wealth is created and productive forces developed in conformity with the laws of nature. These relations therefore are themselves natural laws independent of the influence of time. They are eternal laws which must always govern society. Thus there has been history, but there is no longer any. There has been history, since there were the institutions of feudalism, and in these institutions of feudalism we find quite different relations of production from those of bourgeois society, which the economists try to pass off as natural and, as such, eternal' (Marx, b, p. 121).

matured within the framework of the old society. Mankind thus inevitably sets itself only such tasks as it is able to solve, since closer examination will always show that the problem itself arises only when the material conditions for the solution are already present or at least in the course of formation.   (b, p. 21)

For Marx, therefore, the problem was to explain what was the material base of a capitalist mode of production, precisely as distinguished from other modes of production, and what were the historical circumstances and modalities by which social systems shifted from one mode of production to another.

What is the implication of each of these approaches to the question of transition from feudalism to capitalism? A Smithian approach led logically and inevitably to a total absence of concern for the problem. Capitalism was simply the money economy. The 'transition' was made somewhere in prehistory. Hence our question was an intellectual non-problem or at most a minor footnote in the Whig interpretation of history. Economists were interested in universal formulae, and once the remains of mercantilist thinking were liquidated in the heart of the capitalist world-economy, the problem ceased to be a matter for political polemic. Thereupon Smith's successors, the neoclassical economists, turned away from historical and 'institutional' data and concerns with disdain.

The Marxian critique of the classical economists and liberals in general centered around the argument that their 'universals', whether political (the rights of the individual), economic (the self-regulation of the market), ethical (the categorical imperative) or scientific (empiricism) were in fact all class-bound, the reflections of the perspective of the socially dominant group, the bourgeoisie. Marx accepted much of their analyses *as far as these analyses went*, but insisted that they were historically time-bound and erroneous if expressed as natural laws or eternal truths.

Hence, capitalism *followed* feudalism, both being 'natural', if by that is meant that they occurred and somehow fit into a historical sequence. The 'transition' too was natural, in the sense that it was the culmination of the contradictions inherent in one mode of production that led at a certain point to the qualitative transformation of the social order.

For Sombart, as for Marx, the problem of transition was historically real. But a Marxian perspective, centering on the class conflict, was not to his liking. Sombart was looking for ways to explain (and overcome) 'backwardness' that had less horrendous political implications. However, the power of the Marxian critique was too great to ignore. It had rather to be deflected. The evils of capitalism had to be acknowledged without actually denouncing the perpetrator of the evils. The solution was to make the capitalist system unnatural, but the capitalist heroic.

What was it that was 'unnatural' about capitalism in a Sombartian perspective? It was that men presumably sacrificed the gratification of immediate values (whether of material consumption or 'spiritual' fulfilment) for long-term economic reward. Although such a perspective can lead one to be highly critical of capitalism (viz., Carlyle's denunciation of the 'cash nexus'), it can also lead one conversely to be a great admirer of the 'individual' who stands against the inertia of the masses, Prometheus who steals fire from the gods, in short Schumpeter's entrepreneur.

Since presumably there had always been Promethean men but since also their historic successes had always been momentary, how can we explain success at last, the rise of capitalism in the western world? This is Max Weber's contribution. To put it in crude outline form, for Weber the creation of a capitalist *system* was the consequence of a historically unique conjuncture of a certain level of technology, a particular political framework ('European feudalism'), and the resurrection of an unusual religious tradition (the 'prophetic') in the form of Protestantism, especially Calvinism. This conjuncture enabled the entrepreneurial groups to create protective institutions against the forces that were hostile to them. Thus Sombart's 'unnatural' state of affairs comes into being via Weber's exceptional conjuncture.

It is in this context that we turn to the issue of transition. For who makes a transition, to what, and when? We must begin by distinguishing between three uses of the concept, 'transition', frequently lumped together – not so much by either Marx or Weber, be it said, but by many who claim to be their disciples. For there is enormous confusion in the fact that this same term has in fact covered three rather separate phenomena, and thereby has distorted a historical interpretation of the process of social change.

The first use of 'transition' is to refer to the initial *transformation* of feudal Europe into a capitalist world-economy. The second use of 'transition' is to refer to the subsequent *incorporations* of outside non-capitalist systems into the ongoing and necessarily expanding capitalist world-economy. The third use of transition is to refer to the extension of the *proletarianization* of labor and the *commercialization* of land within the capitalist world-economy to internal regions still utilizing other ways of paying labor or assuring control of land.

Let us start by looking at the 'classical' use of transition, the 'transformation' of feudal Europe into a capitalist world-economy. There has only been one historical moment when a redistributive world-system[2] (in this case based upon a feudal mode of production) was transformed into a capitalist world-economy. This was in Europe (defined as including Iberian America) between 1450 and 1640. There were no doubt other times throughout history when such a transformation seemed to be beginning, such as in the Mediterranean basin between 1150 and 1300. And there were parallel occurrences at other moments in other regions of the world. But for various reasons all the prior transformations were abortive.

A transformation of this kind cannot be located in a day, a month, a year, even a decade. It involved, as we say, a transition. When Weber sought to challenge the basic assumptions of Marx's materialist explanation of history, he chose as his battleground precisely the causes of this singular transition. The debate is familiar and I shall not review it. As for the third school, while the neoclassical economists had buried the whole issue, the realities of an evolving world have led some modern-day Smithians to reconsider the issue. And we now at last have a Smithian interpretation of the singular transformation of feudal Europe into a capitalist world-economy in the book by North and Thomas, *The Rise of the Western World*.

Marx had explained the transformation by arguing that the contradictions of the previous (feudal) mode of production found

2. A redistributive world-system is based on a mode of production wherein a surplus is exacted from agricultural producers, normally in the form of tribute, to sustain an imperial (or state) bureaucracy at a given level of consumption. Samir Amin in fact uses the name 'tributary mode of production' for what I am calling 'redistributive world-systems'. He says that 'the so-called "Asian", "African", and feudal modes [are variants of the tributary mode] which we believe constitute a single family including a central completed variety (China and Egypt) and peripheral varieties notably the West European feudal type and the Japanese feudal type' (pp. 13–14).

their resolution in the emergence of a new (capitalist) mode of production. Weber had explained the transformation by locating a unique conjuncture of historical circumstances in which capitalist values come to prevail. But how can a Smithian who believes that capitalism is natural reconcile this view with the recognition that the modern capitalist world-economy is a 'new and unique phenomenon'?[3] He can only do it by a variant on the Weberian theme. Although capitalism is 'natural', man's nature had always been frustrated until a *unique* conjuncture permitted 'the establishment of institutional arrangements and property rights that create[d] an incentive to channel economic effort into activities that [brought] the private rate of return close to the social rate of return?' (North and Thomas, p. 1). But what was the conjuncture that made this possible? The authors fall back, and with persistence, on a variable they acknowledge to be exogenous to the economy, population. 'In sum a growing population created the basis for trade; the resulting expansion of the market economy caused the medieval economy to react, if slowly, precisely in the manner Adam Smith would have predicted' (p. 26). Why the world benefits from such an efficacious population spurt once and only once in history is not, however, to my mind, adequately explained in turn.[4]

The three points of view on transformation seem rather clear and distinct. Why then has there been so much confusion about transition? It is because many of the disciples of Marx and Weber have transposed the theories of both men from an explanation of a *singular* transformation into a stage theory wherein multiple, individual 'societies', by which these disciples have in fact meant nation-states, each separately become transformed. Whereas both

3. ...casual empiricism suggests that most people prefer more goods to fewer goods and act accordingly. Economic growth requires only that some part of the population be acquisitive...if a society does not grow it is because no incentives are provided for economic initiative' (North and Thomas, pp. 1–2). Note the use of the passive voice: 'are provided'. Adam Smith's unseen hand is his usual busy self. The opening sentence of the book reads: 'The affluence of Western man is a new and unique phenomenon.'

4. See the discussion of this issue in T. S. Brenner (pp. 29–43). The analysis is inconclusive but it suggests the issues to be pursued. The reliance on population growth as a prime mover is to be found also in Emile Durkheim (book II, ch. 2). The key to the transformation from 'mechanical solidarity' to 'organic solidarity' was located in 'population density' which led to 'moral density' which led in turn to the creation of 'noncontractual bases of contract'.

Marx and Weber saw that this transformation of feudal Europe into a capitalist world-economy was a unique happening (although some of the formulations of each might be said to be ambiguous in this regard), their views came to be utilized by many to justify a 'developmentalist' rather than a 'world-systems' perspective.[5] The Weberian functionalists forgot that Weber had not compared Britain with China, but Europe with China.[6] And the Marxian developmentalists forgot that the formula for Marx was 'combined' as well as 'uneven' development. (Although 'stage theory' is more congenial to the Marxian and Sombartian views of capitalism, which see it as a historical phenomenon, there has even been a cautious Smithian variant of the stage theory in 'monetarist' views of national development.[7] North and Thomas, however, explicitly reject stage theory.)[8]

5. I have reviewed the similarities of these two versions of 'developmentalism', as well as their difference from 'world-systems theory' in 'The Present State of the Debate of World Inequality' (above, ch. 3). A good example of what I mean by a Marxist version of 'developmentalism' is Bill Warren.

6. One of the most perceptive Weberian analysts, Guenther Roth, specifically complains of this: 'Weber's studies on the world religions endeavored to explain the rise of Western rationalism. But what was a specific historical question for him has since become a general issue of development and "modernization". The analytical focus has shifted from a unique course of events to the conditions under which cultural borrowing, combined with indigenous mobilization, can lead to similar results. This shift has often involved a reinterpretation, sometimes subtle and sometimes blatant, of Weber's purposes' (p. 111).

7. See for example P. T. Bauer's formulation: 'Neither formal growth models nor stages-of-growth theories help to *explain* or predict the long-term development of entire societies. But this does not preclude the possibility of specific generalizations about some of the major aspects or determinants of material progress. Indeed, some specific generalizations about these matters, rather than the framing of complete systems, are in the tradition of the literature, even though they may not be expressed in terms of conventional or formal analysis. Examples include the relationship between the extent of the market specialization and productivity, and the importance for development on the habits of "order, economy, and attention, to which mercantile business naturally forms a merchant".' (The internal quote is from Adam Smith, *Wealth of Nations*, book III, ch. 4) (Bauer, b, pp. 296–7).

In a review Bauer and Charles Wilson did of Walt W. Rostow, *The Stages of Economic Growth*, in *Economica*, May 1962, they say: 'The market, specialization and productivity, and the importance for development into a model with explanations or predictive powers, may nevertheless be illuminating if it succeeds in focusing attention on revealing differences, and especially on real turning points in the course of history' (as reprinted in Bauer, a, p. 489).

How Bauer himself conducts affirmatively the comparison of development in Britain and Western Europe with Third World countries may be found in P. T. Bauer (a, pp. 44–84).

8. 'That the Middle Ages were an unchanging economic plateau was once the prevailing opinion of historians. Along with its theoretical underpinning, the stage theory of history, this view has now been assigned to the intellectual rubbish heap.'

It is because of the confusion caused by stage theory that we must analyze the other two processes that seem to involve transitions, that is, 'incorporation' on the one hand, and 'proletarianization of labor' and 'commercialization of land' on the other. In fact, these two processes do *not* involve the transformation of feudalism into capitalism but are aspects of the development of the capitalist world-economy which, over historical time, has expanded extensively (incorporation) and intensively (the progressive proletarianization of labor and commercialization of land).

We use the term incorporation only to refer to the addition of new geographic areas to the capitalist world-economy at points of time posterior to the 'initial' expansion of the sixteenth century which had been an integral part of the transformation of feudal Europe into a capitalist world-economy. We should remember that these subsequent expansions were not continuous but occurred in historical spurts. Furthermore, by about 1900, these expansions had more or less come to an end, as the capitalist world-economy could be said by that point to cover the entire globe.

Areas that were incorporated entered the capitalist world-economy as territorial units, sometimes sovereign, sometimes colonized. These incorporations were seen for the most part as historically dramatic, since they usually involved a derogation, at least partial, of previously existing sovereignties. In fact the dramatic changes noticed by historians were often preceded by a less dramatic incorporation which took the form of 'informal empire'. Some of the newly incorporated areas had previously been economically autonomous world-empires, like the Russian, the Ottoman, and the Chinese. Other areas had been separate proto-world-economies, like the Indian Ocean or the western Sudan. And there were of course in addition isolated minisystems in various parts of the world, especially in Africa and Oceania. The territorial units constituted in these incorporated areas were sometimes similar to and sometimes radically different from the previous political boundaries. In economic terms, such areas were normally incorporated as peripheral areas of the world-economy. But occasionally, because of the strength of a particular state structure, they could enter as semiperipheral areas (as did Russia) or could rapidly become such (as in the case of Japan).

Incorporation, as we are using the term, involved the outward expansion of the capitalist world-economy and thus inevitably it came to an historical end when the geographic limits of the globe were reached. Proletarianization of labor and commercialization of land refer however to processes *internal* to the capitalist world-economy and therefore have been less historically dramatic or discontinuous, and have still not exhausted their historical potential. It is in this connection that confusion in the use of the term 'feudalism' has had the most deleterious impact on clarity of analysis concerning the functioning of the capitalist world-economy, and most particularly, in Marxian analyses. For the Smithians and the Weberians have tended to use the term 'traditionalism' rather than 'feudalism' to englobe all non-'modern', that is non-capitalist, arenas of activity.[9] Marxian 'developmentalists' have however frequently taken the term feudalism, fairly clear when referring to a particular historical 'system' of medieval Europe, and used it in the same way as others have used 'traditionalism'. Feudalism has been applied either to almost all non-capitalist structures encountered by capitalist institutions when new areas were incorporated into the capitalist world-economy, or to entities, groups, or units resistant to the processes of the proletarianization of labor and the commercialization of land.[10]

This is an aberrant and antihistorical reification of Marxian categories. Far from being denied, however, it is curiously vaunted by some self-styled Marxists. For example, John Taylor in a denunciation of the theories of Paul Baran and André Gunder Frank speaks of 'Marx's profoundly antihistoricist problematic in Capital' (p. 18). Thus some 'Marxists' return to the Proudhonian universals Marx took such energy to denounce in *The Poverty of Philosophy*:

Economic categories are only the theoretical expressions, the abstractions of the social relations of production...

The same men who establish their social relations in conformity with their material productivity, produce also principles, ideas and categories, in conformity with their social relations.

Thus these ideas, these categories, are as little external as the relations they express. They are *historical and transitory products*.

There is a continual movement of growth in productive forces, of destruction

9. For a devastating attack on the misleading quality of the concept of 'traditionalism' see Abdallah Laroui (pp. 45–54).
10. This has been intelligently denounced by Perry Anderson (pp. 397–412).

in social relations, of formation in ideas; the only immutable thing is the abstraction of movement – *mors immortalis.*   (a, pp. 109–10)

This clarification is essential to understanding why the progressive proletarianization of labor and commercialization of land should in no sense be confused with the historically unique 'transition from feudalism to capitalism'. If we utilize a 'formal' definition of feudalism, we can believe that areas within a capitalist world-economy still exhibit a feudal 'mode of production'. However, the *formal* relations of land controller to productive worker are not in fact what matters. The so-called reciprocal nexus we identify with feudalism, the exchange of protection for labor services, constitutes a feudal *mode of production* only when it *is determinative of other social relations*. But once such a 'nexus' is contained *within* a capitalist world-economy, its autonomous reality disappears. It becomes rather one of the many *forms* of bourgeois employment of proletarian labor to be found in a *capitalist* mode of production, a form that is maintained, expanded or diminished in relation to its profitability on the market.

It is bizarre to cite against this view Marx, the Marx who said in 1847: 'Direct slavery is just as much a pivot of bourgeois industry as machinery, credits, etc. Without slavery you have no cotton; without cotton you have no modern industry. It is slavery that gave the colonies their value; it is the colonies that created world trade, and it is world trade that is the pre-condition of large-scale industry' (a, p. 111). And it is even more bizarre to claim that such a view ignores the relations of production in favor of so-called relations of exchange, also in the name of Marx who in fact said:

When [Proudhon] talks about division of labour he does not feel it necessary to mention the word *market*. Yet must not the division of labour in the fourteenth and fifteenth centuries, when there were still no colonies, when America did not as yet exist for Europe and Eastern Asia only existed for her through the medium of Constantinople, have been fundamentally different from what it was in the seventeenth century when colonies were already developed?   (Letter to D. V. Annenkov, Brussels, 28 December 1846, reprinted in Marx, a, p. 183)

A capitalist mode of production is not based on free labor and land. Rather, it is a mode of production that *combines* proletarian labor and commercialized land with other forms of wage payment and land ownership. The existence of non-proletarianized labor and non-commercialized land is quite essential for the optimization of opportunities for overall profit in a capitalist world market for several reasons. One is that such a combination maintains land areas in reserve for expansion of primary production at low overhead costs, able to respond to significant shifts of demand in the world market. A second is that it preserves a reserve pool of labor even in moments of 'prosperity'. When additional labor is needed, it is remarkable how fast the 'traditional' restraints disappear. Third, it reduces the global cost of labor by allowing the traditional sectors to bear the lifetime costs of childhood and old-age maintenance of large sectors of cash-crop or urban workers. This has always been especially true in the peripheral areas of the world-economy and, as Samir Amin says, 'is not truly antiquated even today' (p. 52) as an integral part of the system. To be sure, the continuing long-term secular expansion of the world-economy (even taking the continual crises of accumulation that appear as contractions) has involved the utilization of ever more land area ever more intensively. Over time, it has steadily become less profitable to use non-wage modes of remuneration. But they still continue to be used in part. As Marx said, 'The point at issue is not the role that various economic relations have played in the succession of various social formations appearing in the course of history; even less is it their sequence "as concepts" (Proudhon) (a nebulous notion of the historical process), but their position within modern bourgeois society' (b, p. 213). Or we may put it in the somewhat more metaphorical terms of Fernand Braudel, and see the modern world as a house with three stories: material life, economy, and capitalism:

With economic life we will emerge from the routine, from the unconscious daily round. However, in economic life, the regularities are still with us; an old and progressive division of labour causes inevitable partings and meetings, on which active and conscious daily life feeds, with its tiny profits, its micro-capitalism, which is not unattractive, barely distinguishable from ordinary work. Higher still on the top floor we will place capitalism and its vast ramifications, with its games that already seem evil to the common run of mortals. What, we will be asked, has this sophistication to do with the humble lives at the bottom of the ladder? Everything perhaps, because it incorporates them in its game.[11]

We cannot understand the issue of the progressive proletarianization of labor and the commercialization of land if we adopt

11. Braudel, p. 445. I have taken the liberty of changing the translation slightly.

a definition of capitalism that derives from the doctrines of Adam Smith. No free market ever has existed, or could have existed, within a capitalist world-economy. The hypothetical free market is an intellectual construct which serves the same intellectual function as frictionless movement, as a standard from which to measure the degree of deviation. Rather, capitalists seek to maximize profit on the world market, utilizing whenever it is profitable, and whenever they are able to create them, legal monopolies and/or other forms of constraint of trade.

Capitalism has been developed by the extension in space of its basic framework and within that by the progressive 'mechanization' of productive activity. Increasingly, the producers of surplus have been remunerated in the form of wages (exclusively or in combination with commodities for which exact market computations of value are available). Many have argued that the *typical* features of capitalism are the total availability of all labor and land as commodities, the orientation of all productive activity to the creation and appropriation of surplus value. But at no point up to now have these *typical* features in fact been *exclusive* features. They have to be sure become steadily more predominant, but it is the *combination* of free and 'unfree' labor and land that in fact characterizes the capitalist world-economy.

As the capitalist world-economy approaches the asymptote of the total extension of the market principle, so it accentuates the social, economic, and above all political contradictions of the system. Capitalism thereby finally destroys its 'protecting strata' (in Schumpeter's terms), renders perfectly clear the nature of its exploitative system, and in so doing, provides the social basis for the termination of the process, of the supercession of capitalism as a system. This is not an automatic process. It is brought about by the organized opposition of oppressed strata. The point, however, is that the processes of capitalism themselves undermine the political strength of the system.

I would end on this note from Schumpeter, whom I regard as the most sophisticated of the defenders of capitalism, the one who grappled hardest with the key arguments of Marx:

We have rediscovered what from different standpoints and, so I believe, on inadequate grounds has often been discovered before; there is inherent in the capitalist system a tendency toward self-destruction which, in its earlier stages, may well assert itself in the form of a tendency toward retardation of progress.

I shall not stay to repeat how objective and subjective, economic and extra-economic factors, reinforcing each other in imposing accord, contribute to that result. Nor shall I stay to show what should be obvious and in subsequent chapters will become more obvious still, viz., that those factors make not only for the destruction of the capitalist but for the emergence of a socialist civilization. They all point in that direction. The capitalist process not only destroys its own institutional framework but it also creates the conditions for another. Destruction may not be the right word after all. Perhaps I should have spoken of transformation. The outcome of the process is not simply a void that could be filled by whatever might happen to turn up; things and souls are transformed in such a way as to become increasingly amenable to the socialist form of life. With every peg from under the capitalist structure vanishes an impossibility of the socialist plan. In both these respects Marx's vision was right. We can also agree with him in linking the particular social transformation that goes on under our eyes with an economic process as its prime mover. What our analysis, if correct, disproves is after all of secondary importance, however essential the role may be which it plays in the socialist credo. In the end there is not so much difference as one might think between saying that the decay of capitalism is due to its success and saying that it is due to its failure.   (p. 162)

I believe, as did Schumpeter, that we are living in the early stages of the transition from capitalism to socialism, which is going on 'under our eyes'. One of the reasons we are interested in analyzing the 'transition from feudalism to capitalism' is to understand how these relatively rare singular transformations work. With this in view, it is important to underline that it is not 'national societies' or such-like constructs that undergo these transitions. It is world-systems. To be sure, I repeat, a transformation of this magnitude cannot be located in a day, a month, or a year. It is a transition. That means that the transformation is composed of a multitude of partial changes, major and minor, which include of course the coming to power in existing state structures of socialist regimes who implement as best they can within the still existing capitalist world-economy socialist forms and socialist values. Such efforts are part of the process of transition. They do not necessarily exemplify the ultimate product of qualitative change. 'Marx's vision was right', said Schumpeter. But Marx himself warned us not to take a vision as a detailed prophecy. The future will unfold as we make it unfold, within the constraints of the world as it is.

References

Amin, S. 1974. 'Le capitalisme et la rente foncière'. In Samir Amin and Kosta Vergopoulos, *La question paysanne et le capitalisme*. Paris: Anthropos-IDEP

Anderson, Perry. 1974. *Lineages of the Absolutist State*. London: New Left Books

Bauer, P. T. a: 1957. *Economic Analysis and Policy in Underdeveloped Countries*. Durham: Duke University Press

   b: 1971. *Dissent on Development*. London: Weidenfeld & Nicolson

Braudel, Fernand. 1967. *Capitalism and Material Life*. New York: Harper & Row, 1973

Brenner, Y. S. 1971. *Agriculture and the Economic Development of Low Income Countries*. The Hague: Mouton

Durkheim, Emile. 1893. *On the Division of Labor in Society*. New York: Free Press, 1964

Laroui, Abdallah. 1974. *La crise des intellectuels arabes*. Paris: Maspéro

Marx, Karl. a: 1847. *The Poverty of Philosophy*. New York: International Publishers, 1963

   b: 1859. *A Contribution to the Critique of Political Economy*. Moscow: Progress Publications, 1970

North, Douglass, and Robert Paul Thomas. 1973. *The Rise of the Western World*. Cambridge: University Press

Roth, G. 1971. 'Sociological Typology and Historical Explanation'. In Reinhard Bendix and Guenther Roth, *Scholarship and Partisanship: Essays on Max Weber*. Berkeley: University of California Press

Schumpeter, Joseph. 1942. *Capitalism, Socialism and Democracy*. London: Allen & Unwin, 1943

Smith, Adam. 1776. *The Wealth of Nations*. New York: Modern Library, 1937

Sombart, Werner. 1913. *The Quintessence of Capitalism. A Study of the History and Psychology of the Modern Business Man*. New York: Fertig, 1967

Taylor, J. 1974. 'Neo-Marxism and Underdevelopment – A Sociological Phantasy'. *Journal of Contemporary Asia*, 4: 1

   Wallerstein (ed.), *World Inequality*. Montreal: Black Rose Books and above, ch. 3

Warren, B. 1973. 'Imperialism and Capitalist Industrialization'. *New Left Review*, 81 (September–October), 3–44

9 ❧ A world-system perspective on the social sciences

It was in the nineteenth century and the early twentieth that the organizational structures of the sciences of man which we use today became fixed. In 1800 the categories (or 'disciplines') which today are standard – history, economics, sociology, anthropology, political science – did not for the most part exist as concepts, and certainly were not the basis of sharply differentiated groups of teachers and researchers. The somewhat tortuous process by which certain combinations of concerns and concepts took particular forms resulted in major 'methodological' debates, which we sometimes still hear about under the rubric, 'philosophy of history'. Among the debates, one of the most influential was that between so-called nomothetic and idiographic knowledge, between the possibility and impossibility of generalizations about human behavior, between the universalizers and the particularizers.

The universalizers spoke of themselves as 'scientists'. They tended to argue that human behavior was a natural phenomenon like any other, and could therefore be studied on the same basis as any other natural phenomenon, using the same rules of logic ('the scientific method') and capable eventually of yielding precise results comparable to those achieved in the natural sciences. The particularists, in contrast, often termed themselves 'humanists'. They tended to argue that human life, being thinking life, could not be viewed in the same way as other natural phenomenon, for one of two reasons. Either it was because, said some, humans have souls and are therefore resistant to arbitrary uniformities, or it was because, said others, the human researcher inevitably distorted the human subject of analysis in the very process of observing him and therefore the generalizations would never be valid.

Like all such grand debates there is just so much that can be said on the subject, and it has largely been said. This does not mean that the debate is over or forgotten but simply that the divisions have been institutionalized and thereby contained. *Grosso modo*, the universalizers were assigned the departments of economics, sociology, and political science, and the particularizers the departments of history and anthropology. Obviously, given the high capriciousness of the organizational dividing lines, there were dissidents in each 'disciplinary' structure (such as political 'theorists' in political science, and linguists in anthropology). But no matter! Spheres of influence had been demarcated, and the status quo enshrined.

This crude picture has to be qualified by taking into account regional variation. My description works best for the Anglo-American core of the world-system. The Germans chafed at British definitions of social knowledge and gave birth to an uncertain crossbreed, *Staatswissenschaft*. Some French chafed at the failure of other Frenchmen to chafe, which led to the birth of the *Annales* school. And the Western European working classes chafed at the system in general, and nourished outside the academy a critical perspective, Marxism, which challenged the universality of the 'universals'.

Underlying the dominant institutionalization of the great methodological split, universalizer versus particularizer, there turned out to be, as there usually is, a hidden but very important consensus, the concept of the individual society as the basic unit of analysis. Everyone seemed to agree that the world was composed of multiple 'societies'. They disagreed about whether it was the case that all societies pursued *similar* paths down the road of history (albeit at differing rates) or that each society went its own historic way. They disagreed whether society in question took the form of a 'state' or a 'nation' or a 'people', but in any case it was some politico-cultural unit.

The period after the Second World War saw in this field, as in so many others, the culmination of these intellectual tendencies in the elaboration of a perspective we may call 'developmentalism', which for most of its devotees went hand in hand with 'behaviorism'. This perspective assumed that all states were engaged in 'developing' (which for many meant 'becoming nations'), that their progress along this path could be measured quantitatively and synchronically, and that on the basis of knowledge derived from such measurements, governments could in fact hasten the process, which was a highly commendable thing to do. Since these states were proceeding down parallel paths, *all* states were intrinsically capable of achieving the desired results. The only serious intellectual question was why many resisted doing so.

This viewpoint swept the scholarly world – not only of the hegemonic power, the United States, and its allies, old Europe, but also of its chief antagonist, the USSR. The theories of what governmental actions would promote development, and what social forces impeded it varied widely, but the plausibility of 'development' as a matrix of analysis reigned supreme until the mid-1960s, when it foundered on one economic reality and two political developments.

The economic reality was that, despite all the theories, and all the presumed effort (aid, technical assistance, human investment), the so-called 'gap' between the 'developed' and the 'developing' countries was growing bigger, not smaller.

The two political developments were in fact ultimately a reflection of this economic reality. One was the emergence of national liberation movements throughout the world which engaged in armed struggle with more or less success – Vietnam, Algeria, Cuba. Their struggle had a resonance within the United States and western Europe – among students, professors, and the 'Third World within' – which in fact shook the up-to-then facile dominance of the developmentalists in the academy.

But this same political upheaval affected the communist countries as well, where a long series of interrelated crises – the xxth Party Congress of the CPSU, the 'upheavals' in eastern Europe, the split between the Chinese and the Russians, the Cultural Revolution, the rise of 'Euro-communism' – similarly has undermined the internal credibility of the Stalinist version of developmentalism, the crude sequence through which each state was destined to 'pass'.

When a theory no longer seems to serve an adequate *social* function, scholars usually begin to question its intellectual credentials. As 'developmentalism' seemed less and less to explain the social reality through which we are living, various authors criticized one or another of its premises, groping towards an alternative framework of explanation, which I shall call a 'world-system perspective'.

The key difference between a developmentalist and a world-system perspective is in the point of departure, the unit of analysis. A developmentalist perspective assumes that the unit within which social action principally occurs is a politico-cultural unit – the state, or nation, or people – and seeks to explain differences between these units, including why their economies are different. A world-system perspective assumes, by contrast, that social action takes place in an entity within which there is an ongoing division of labor, and seeks to discover *empirically* whether such an entity is or is not unified politically or culturally, asking *theoretically* what are the consequences of the existence or non-existence of such unity.

By throwing overboard the *presupposition* that there is a 'society' we are forced to look at the alternative possibilities of organizing the material world. We in fact rapidly discover that there are a limited number of possibilities, which we may call varying 'modes of production', meanming by that something very close to what the phrase seems on the surface to convey: the way in which decisions are made about dividing up productive tasks, about quantities of goods to be produced and labor time to be invested, about quantities of goods to be consumed or accumulated, about the distribution of the goods produced.

One mode, historically the earliest, we may call the reciprocal-lineage mode. It is based on limited and elementary specialization of tasks in which the products are reciprocally exchanged among producers. In this mode the chief productive resource is human labor and therefore the chief guarantee of subgroup survival the control of reproduction (via the control of women and their offspring). Production over a certain level is politically unsettling by enabling younger persons to escape the control of elders and therefore inequalities though real are limited.

Empirically, it is the case (and I think it could be established that theoretically it must be the case) that such systems are small in physical scope, and that the economic boundaries are largely identical with political and cultural boundaries. Minisystems seem a reasonable name. I believe it is the case that such minisystems are not only small in physical scope but short lived historically (meaning a life of say six generations or so). This short life can be accounted for in various ways: the dangers for such a technologically primitive group of physical extinction (through warfare or natural calamity); the possibility of conquest; fission of the group as the result of slow growth in accumulated stock; reorganization of the division of labor resulting from physical flight and consequent ecological adjustment.

If this is an accurate description, the world has known countless such groups over historical time and has virtually no historical records of how they functioned. Some ethnologists claim to have recorded such groups, but for the most part I am sceptical that the units studied were truly autonomous systems, since one of the preconditions of most such study has in fact been imperial control of the area studied by a larger political entity which in turn existed within a far wider division of labor.

Our empirical knowledge is largely limited to larger divisions of labor which I shall term world-systems, using the word 'world' to signify larger space and longer time than minisystems, and operationally to mean an arena, or division of labor, within which more than one 'cultural' grouping exists, but which may or *may not* be politically unified.

There have in fact, up to now, been two basic forms of world-systems. Since in one form the prototype is the unified political system, we shall call this type the 'world-empire', by contrast with the other type which is precisely defined by the continuing absence of such political unity, the 'world-economy'.

The 'world-empire' has many variations in terms of the political superstructure and the cultural consequences. A large part of Weber's *Economy and Society* is a morphology of these variations. But the mode of production is common to these variant forms. It is a mode of production which creates enough of an agricultural surplus (based therefore on a more advanced technology than the reciprocal-lineage mode) sufficient to maintain both the artisans who produce non-agricultural goods and, in the widest sense, an 'administrative' stratum. Whereas the agricultural and artisanal producers in some sense 'exchange' goods, either reciprocally or in local markets, goods are transferred from producers to 'administrators' by a forced appropriation, 'tribute', which is centralized by someone or some institution – how remote this institution is from the producer is one of the major variables of the differing forms – and thereupon 'redistributed' to the 'administrative bureaucracy'.

The principal difference in this mode of production from the reciprocal-lineage mode was the fact that a class which did not produce 'goods' was supported (and indeed supported well). But there was a major similarity common to both pre-modern forms. In neither mode of production was maximal production desirable or desired. The reason is clear. Since the channel upward of the surplus appropriation in the redistributive-tributary form was the same 'bureaucracy' to whom the top of the structure 'redistributed' this surplus, too large a surplus created a strong temptation for 'pre-emption' of this surplus on the way upward. This of course constantly happened. But it meant that the ruling groups were always caught in the contradiction of wanting more, but not 'too much'.

The consequences were manifold. Technological advance was not desirable *per se*. It no doubt occurred, but it was probably less the desire to expand production than the need, when it occurred, to *stem a decline* in real production that served as its spur. Secondly, the contradictory needs of the ruling groups (more, but not too much) were communicated to the direct producers in terms of socially fixed as opposed to socially open quotas of appropriation. That is not to say that these quotas never changed. They changed constantly, but discontinuously, and the myth of the constant rate was a central ideological motif of the social structure.

In this mode of production, inequalities were enormous in comparison to the reciprocal-lineage mode, but there were some inbuilt limits. The ruling groups might have the power of life and death by the sword over the direct producers, but they were normally concerned to prevent starvation, since the 'fixed' income of the ruling groups was dependent on a 'fixed' level of appropriation from a 'fixed' estimated total production. Starvation might occur despite the efforts of the local ruling groups but seldom amidst their indifference.

Empirically it is the case (and again I think it could be established that theoretically it must be the case) that such systems were larger in physical size than the reciprocal-lineage forms (and occasionally very large, as for example the Roman Empire at its height). Within the economic division of labor, multiple 'cultures' flourished – parallel groups of agricultural producers, 'world'-wide trading groups, endogamous translocal 'administrative' groups. But the keynote of this mode of production was the political unity of the economy, whether this 'unity' involved extreme administrative decentralization (the 'feudal' form) or relatively high centralization (an 'empire' proper).

Such 'world-empires' have existed ever since the Neolithic Revolution, and right up to very recent times. The number was large, but not 'countless'. The life of such systems varied according to their size, their isolation, their ecological base, and so forth. But the *pattern* of such systems was a cyclical one – expansion of size and hence total surplus appropriation to the point where the bureaucratic costs of appropriating the surplus outweighed the surplus that could, in socio-political terms, be effectively appropriated, at which point decline and retraction set in.

The cycle of expansion and contraction involved the perpetual incorporation and releasing of 'units' which, when outside the 'world-empire', formed reciprocal-lineage minisystems, but which when incorporated within it, formed merely one more *situs* out of which tribute was drawn and whose socio-economic autonomy was thereby eliminated. Thus these two modes of production coexisted on the earth for thousands of years.

'Civilization' is a term which is often used to mean the patterns of 'high culture' developed by the ruling and 'administrative' strata in such 'world-empires'. And since there was a certain 'revival' of the forms of a particular culture each time a new world-empire was created in the same geographic zone, we can also use the concept 'civilization' to connote those cultural forms that are common to *successive* world-empires in the same zone. (China is the model case of a long series of such successive world-empires.)

Since the needs of world-empires were facilitated by 'rationality' in administration, the development of 'records' was normal and we have considerable 'documentation' from which to reconstruct the workings of such systems, which we may thus 'observe' across historical time (or rather reconstruct in terms of our contemporary needs).

The 'world-economy' is a fundamentally different kind of social system from a 'world-empire' and *a fortiori* from a minisystem – both in formal structure and as a mode of production. As a formal structure, a world-economy is defined as a single division of labor within which are located multiple cultures – hence it is a *world*-system like the world-empire – but which has no over-arching political structure. Without a political structure to re-distribute the appropriated surplus, the surplus can only be redistributed via the 'market', however frequently states located within the world-economy intervene to distort the market. Hence the mode of production is capitalist.

A capitalist mode is one in which production is for exchange; that is, it is determined by its profitability on a market, a market in which each buyer wishes to buy cheap (and therefore that which is, in the long run, most efficiently produced and marketed) but in which each seller wishes to sell dear (and therefore is concerned that the efficiencies of others are not permitted to reduce his sales). Thus the individual as buyer rewards efficiency and as seller uses his political power to thwart it.

The basic contradiction that informs capitalism as a social system results from the simultaneous desirability of freedom for the buyer and its undesirability for the seller – freedom of labor, freedom of the flow of the factors of production, freedom of the market. The combination of freedom and unfreedom that results is the defining characteristic of a capitalist world-economy. This ambi-valence about freedom pervades its politics, its culture, its social relations.

Whereas the quantities of production in a redistributive-tributary mode were more or less socially 'fixed', precisely the opposite is true of a capitalist mode. There is no social limit to profit, only the limit of the market: of competitive sellers and inadequate numbers of buyers. An individual producer produces not a fixed amount but as much as he can, and anything that can aid him to produce more, and more efficiently – science and technology – is welcome. But once produced, it must be sold, or no profit is realized. And once profit is realized, the less that is consumed immediately, the more future profit will be possible.

But as everyone proceeds this way – the 'anarchy of production' – there will soon come a point where additional production offers not profit but loss. Hence there are cycles here too – not the political cycles of the world-empires but the economic cycles of the world-economies.

There are to be sure profound inequalities of distribution too, and probably *greater* inequalities than in world-empires (although liberal social science has always argued the opposite). The reason has to do with the greater wealth to be maldistributed (as a result of technological advance) and the technique by which the maldistribution is enforced.

In a redistributive system, the primary weapon of the powerful is the sword. Thus death to the political resistant, but minimal life for the acquiescent producer is the basic law of political life. But in a capitalist mode, with *economic* cycles, the life of the producer can be more unprofitable as consumer of surplus than profitable as producer of surplus. Thus the politico-military machinery can frequently best serve to maximize profit by permitting starvation, both literally and figuratively.

Historically, world-economies were very fragile institutions whose life spans were probably less than a century and hence had little opportunity to become an ongoing, capital expanding system. They lacked the political structures to prevent withdrawl of regions from the system and hence the world-economies that emerged from time to time often disintegrated. Or, if they did not, it was because a member state expanded to fill the boundaries of the division of labor, the world-economy thus being transformed into a world-empire, and the beginnings of a capitalist mode rapidly reverting to a redistributive-tributary mode of production.

What is remarkable then about the modern world is the emergence of a capitalist world-economy *that survived*. Indeed it did more than survive: it has flourished, expanded to cover the entire earth (and thereby eliminated all remaining minisystems and world-empires), and brought about a technological and ecological 'explosion' in the use of natural resources.

There are three separate intellectual questions that may be asked about this modern world-system. The first is the explanation of its genesis: how is it that the sixteenth-century European world-economy survived, unlike previous such systems. The second question is how such a system, once consolidated, operates. The third is what are the basic secular trends of a capitalist system, and therefore what will account for its eventual decline as a social system.

Each of these three questions is a long and complex one and cannot be answered briefly with any degree of satisfaction. Since, however, I have attempted longer answers to these questions elsewhere, I will merely outline my position on these three issues here in the most summary of fashions.

The genesis is to be located in the process of 'decline' of a particular redistributive world-system, that of feudal Europe, which seems to have 'exhausted its potential' in its great socio-economic spurt of 1100–1250. In the 'crisis' of contraction of the following two centuries, the real income of the ruling strata seemed to take a real fall. One reason was the rising real wages of the producers, the result of demographic disasters. A second was the destruction that occurred because of widespread peasant revolts (consequence of the previous exaggerated level of ex-ploitation) and the internecine warfare of the ruling strata (conse-quence of their long-term proportional expansion, reaching the conjuncture of economic decline). The prospect was collapse.

Had there been a world-empire on the edges capable of conquering the core of the system (the old 'dorsal spine' of Europe), or had feudal Europe itself been more centralized, there might have been a more traditional political reorganization of 'empire'. But there wasn't. Instead there was a sort of creative leap of imagination on the part of the ruling strata. It involved trying an alternative mode of surplus appropriation, that of the market, to see whether it might serve to restore the declining real income of the ruling groups. This involved geographical expan-sion, spatial economic specialization, the rise of the 'absolutist' state – in short, the creation of a capitalist world-economy.

The genesis of capitalism was not in the triumph of a new group, the urban burghers, over the landed feudal nobility. Rather it should be seen as the reconversion of seignior into capitalist producer, an essential *continuity* of the ruling families. Further-more, it worked magnificently, as any look backward from say 1800 to 1450 can show. The 'crisis of seigniorial revenues' was no more.

The crisis was now located in the revenues of the producers. The 'poor' had been created as a major social category.

The operation of the system, once established, revolved around two basic dichotomies. One was the dichotomy of class, bourgeois versus proletarian, in which control by ruling groups operated primarily not through lineage rights (as in the minisystems) nor through weapons of force (as in the world-empires), but through access to decisions about the nature and quantity of the production of goods (via property rights, accumulated capital, control over technology, etc.).

The other basic dichotomy was the spatial hierarchy of economic specialization, core versus periphery, in which there was an appropriation of surplus from the producers of low-wage (but high supervision), low-profit, low-capital intensive goods by the producers of high-wage (but low supervision), high-profit, high-capital intensive, so-called 'unequal exchange'.

The genius, if you will, of the capitalist system, is the interweaving of these two channels of exploitation which overlap but are not identical and create the cultural and political complexities (and obscurities) of the system. Among other things, it has made it possible to respond to the politico-economic pressures of cyclical economic crises by rearranging spatial hierarchies without significantly impairing class hierarchies.

The mechanism by which the capitalist system ultimately resolves its recurrent cyclical downturns is expansion: outward spatially, and internally in terms of the 'freeing' of the market – remember the basic ambivalence about the free market, good for the buyer and bad for the seller – via the steady proletarianization of semiproletarian labor and the steady commercialization of semi-market oriented land.

Both of these processes have logical limits. In the case of geographical expansion, these limits were largely reached by the beginning of the twentieth century. In the case of internal expansion, there is still much room. The world is probably halfway, more or less, in the process of freeing the factors of production. But here too the world eventually approaches an asymptote, at which point the possibility of resolving economic crises will largely disappear, and thereby we will enter into a true crisis of the system as such.

Linked to these structural limits are the curves of political repression. A system of unequal distribution (all known systems hitherto) is only possible by repression, which is a function of the relation of two curves, the ability and willingness of the upper strata to repress, the ability and willingness of the lower strata to rebel.

But over historical time, within the capitalist world-economy, the first curve is continually going down in strength and the second curve is continually rising. The reason is simple. The 'cost' of repression is the partial redistribution of the surplus to the repressors, who are in fact the intermediate strata. The process is called 'cooptation'. But each cooptation is less 'worthwhile' than the previous one, since it involves further deductions from a *declining percentage* of the surplus controlled by the top strata, in order to buy off once again the intermediate strata. (One does not 'buy off' lower strata. The whole point is to exploit them, whence comes the money with which one 'buys off' others, that is, shares the spoils.)

Let us be clear what we are saying. Even if the *world-wide* appropriation of the producers has remained about as high in recent decades as in earlier periods of the capitalist world-economy, the distribution of this surplus has begun to shift from the top to the intermediate strata. This is politically crucial. The so-called 'rise of the middle classes' is often seen as politically stabilizing, because it is alleged this is depriving the lower strata of their leadership. I see it quite differently. It is politically *de*stabilizing because it is depriving the top strata of a prize high enough to be worth struggling for. This is the 'failure of nerve' that is setting in.

Conversely, the lower strata are in fact becoming ever better organized, not *despite* but *because* of the 'rise of the middle clases'. This rise has in fact made it ever clearer that the interests of the producers are *not* tied to the needs and demands of the inter-mediate strata (as expressed historically in reform movements and ethno-national demands for *spatial* reorganization of the distribu-tion of profits).

However the continuing technological advances of the capitalist economy are creating possibilities of *political* organization of direct producers unknown in previous eras. Furthermore, in rebellion, success leads to success in the sense of revealing its potentials.

To resume this simple and simplified picture, the transition from a capitalist world-economy to a socialist world government in which we are living and which will take a long time to complete, is theoretically the consequence of two secular trends: the potential exhaustion of the limits of structural expansion which is required to maintain the economic viability of the capitalist system; the closing of the gap between the two political curves of the will to fight of the ruling groups and the direct producers *on a world level.*

What is crippling about a developmentalist perspective is the fact that these large-scale historical processes are not even discussable, if one uses the politico-cultural entity (the 'state') as the unit of analysis. It is only by recognizing that it is world-systems we muct study that we can begin to locate the data of modern history, both those that are 'universal' and those that are 'particular', within the process of the social structures the world has seen over historical time.

It is only then, too, that we can begin to be 'scientific' about a central natural phenomenon, the human group, and 'humane' in opting for the possible choices that will in fact enable us, all of us, to reach our potentials and create our worlds within our limits.

Part II

The inequalities of class, race and ethnicity

10 ❧ Social conflict in post-independence Black Africa: the concepts of race and status group reconsidered

The theoretical confusion

Everyone 'knows' that something called 'racial tensions' exists in South Africa, in the United States, in Great Britain. Some people think it exists in parts of Latin America, in the Caribbean, in various countries of south and southeast Asia. But is there such a thing as 'racial tension' to be found in the independent states of Black Africa? Conversely, everyone 'knows' that 'tribalism' exists in Black Africa. Is 'tribalism' a phenomenon only of Africa or is it also known in industrialized, capitalist states?

The problem arises from some conceptual difficulties. The categories of social strata or social groupings in everyday scientific use are many, overlapping, and unclear. One can find such terms as class, caste, nationality, citizenship, ethnic group, tribe, religion, party, generation, estate, and race. There are no standard definitions – quite the contrary. Few authors even try to put the terms into relation with each other.

One famous attempt was that of Max Weber who distinguished three basic categories: class, status group (*stand*), and party (see

Weber 1968, pp. 302–7, 385–98, 926–40). One trouble with Weber's categorization is that it is not logically rigorous, but is in many ways constructed out of examples. And he draws these examples largely from nineteenth-century Europe, the European Middle Ages, and classical antiquity. Fair enough for Weber, but for those who deal with the empirical reality of the twentieth-century non-European world, it may be difficult to find an appropriate reflection in Weber's distinctions. Weber defines class more or less in the Marxist tradition, as a group of persons who relate in similar ways to the economic system. He defines party as a group who are associated together within a corporate group to affect the allocation and exercise of power. Status group, however, is in many ways a residual category. There seem to be positive criteria, to be sure. Status groups are primordial[1] groups into which persons are born, fictitious families presumably tied together by loyalties which are not based on calculated goal-oriented associations, groups encrusted with traditional privileges or lack of them, groups which share honor, prestige rank, and, above all, style of life (often including a common occupation) but which do not necessarily share a common income level or class membership.[2]

Does not the nation, the nation towards which we have 'nationalist' sentiments, fit this definition very closely? It would seem so. Yet it is not national affiliation which is usually first thought of when use is made of the concept of status group. Weber's concept was inspired primarily by medieval estates, a category of rather limited applicability to contemporary Africa. Much of the literature of modern Africa, rather, talks of a 'tribe' and/or 'ethnic group'. Most writers would take 'ethnic group' as the most

1. To use the term added by Shils (cf. Shils 1957, pp. 130–45). For Shils, primordial qualities are 'significant relational' ones, more than just a 'function of interaction'. Their significance (p. 142) is 'ineffable' (cf. Geertz 1963).
2. Weber's (1968, p. 932) definition emphasizes honor:
    In contrast to classes, *Stände* (*status-groups*) are normally groups. They are, however, often of an amorphous kind. In contrast to the purely economically determined 'class situation', we wish to designate as *status situation* every typical component of the life of man that is determined by a specific, positive or negative, social estimation of *honor*...
    Both propertied and propertyless people can belong to the same status-group, and frequently they do with very tangible consequences...
    In content, status honor is normally expressed by the fact that above all else a specific *style of life* is expected from all those who wish to belong to the circle.

meaningful empirical referent of status group, and there is no doubt it fits the spirit of Weber's concept. The term *race* is often used, though its relation, in the spirit of most authors, to status group is left inexplicit. *Race* is used in studies of Africa primarily with reference to conflicts between white persons of European descent and black persons indigenous to the continent (a third category in some areas being persons coming from or descended from immigrants from the Indian subcontinent). But the term is seldom used to distinguish varieties among the indigenous Black population.

Are *race* and *ethnic group* then two different phenomena, or two variations of the same theme? Given the terminological confusion,[3] it might be best to describe first the empirical reality and see what might follow theoretically rather than to lay out in advance a theoretical framework within which to explain the empirical reality.

The empirical data: how many kinds of status groups?

Precolonial Africa included many societies that were complex and hierarchical. No one has ever estimated what percentage of Africa's land area or population was in such groups, as opposed to segmentary societies, but surely at least two-thirds of it was. Some of these states had 'estates' – that is, categories of people with hereditary status: nobles, commoners, artisans, slaves, etc. Some of these states had 'ethnic groups' – categories of people with separate designations indicating presumed separate ancestry. These were usually the outcome of conquest situations.[4] Many

3. The French-language literature is even more confusing, since the French word *race* is used by many writers where English writers would use 'tribe'.
4. Jean Suret-Canale (1969, p. 112) argues that both phenomena derive from conquest situations, but that for some unexplained reason assimilation proceeds faster in some areas than in others:

> As long as class antagonisms remained almost non-existent within a tribe...no state superstructure emerged...Where class antagonisms developed with the extension of slavery and the creation of a tribal aristocracy, various kinds of states... emerged...
>
> When the creation of these states involved the domination and incorporation of other tribal groups, and the creation within the framework of the state of a new cultural and linguistic unity, the vestiges of tribal organization more or less disappeared...for example, in Zululand...It could happen that the division into classes retained the appearance of a tribal conflict: this was the case in the monarchies of the interlacustrian zone of eastern Africa (Rwanda, Burundi, etc.) where the conquerors, the pastoral Tutsi, constituted the aristocracy, dominating the indigenous peasants, the Hutu.

states had, in addition, a recognized category of 'non-citizens' or 'strangers' (see Skinner 1963). Finally, even the nonhierarchical societies usually had a division of persons according to some specified principle of classification which created a fictitious descent group, often called a 'clan' by anthropologists, or according to generation, that is, an 'age set'.[5]

The establishment of colonial rule changed none of these categorizations immediately. It did, however, impose at least one new one – that of colonial nationality, which was double or even triple (for example, Nigerian, British West African, British imperial).

In addition, in many instances, religious categories took on a new salience under colonial rule. Christians emerged as a significant subgroup, both within the 'tribe'[6] and within the 'territory'.[7] Although Islam predates European colonial rule almost everywhere, it is probable that Moslems became in many areas a more self-conscious category in counterpoise to Christians. The sudden spread of Islam in some areas seems to indicate this (see Hodgkin 1962; also Froelich 1962, ch. 3). And everywhere, new 'ethnic groups' came into existence.[8] Finally, *race* was a primary category of the colonial world, accounting for political rights, occupational allocation, and income.[9]

The rise of the nationalist movements and the coming of independence created still more categories. Territorial identification – that is, nationalism – became widespread and important. Along with such territorial identification came as a new devotion to ethnic identification, often called tribalism. As Elizabeth Colson (1967, p. 205) said:

Probably many youths found their explicit allegiance to particular ethnic traditions at the same time that they made their commitment to African independence...in Africa it has been the school man, the intellectual, who has been most eager to advance his own language and culture and who has seen himself as vulnerable to any advantages given to the language and culture of any other groups within the country.

5. See the excellent discussion of the social organization of such non-hierarchical societies in Horton (1971).
6. See Busia (1951). Busia describes in some detail the causes and consequences of a Christian–non-Christian split among the Ashanti.
7. Uganda is a prime case, where politics crystallized to some extent along a religious trichotomy: Protestants, Catholics and Moslems.
8. I have argued this in Wallerstein (1960).
9. This point is argued throughout the works of Georges Balandier and Frantz Fanon.

The economic dilemmas of the educated classes in the post-independence era exacerbated this tendency to 'tribalism' (see Wallerstein 1971). Finally, nationalism also involved pan-Africanism. That is, there came to be a category of 'Africans' corresponding to its opposite, the 'Europeans'. At first, this dichotomy seemed to correlate with skin color. However, beginning with 1958, Africa as a concept began to include, for many, northern (Arab) Africa (but still did not include white settlers in North, East, or southern Africa).[10]

Independence also intruded one other significant variable: a rather rigid juridical definition of first-class membership in the larger moral community, that of citizenship. The lines drawn by this concept were different not only from those of pre-colonial Africa but also from those of the colonial era. During the colonial era, for example, a Nigerian could vote in a Gold Coast election, if he had transferred residence, since both territories were part of British West Africa, and the individual was a British subject. After independence, however, although colonial-era federal administrative units often survived as units of national aspiration, membership in them no longer conferred rights of equal participation in each territorial subunit, now a sovereign nation-state, as many a politician and civil servant came to learn in the early post-independence years.

It is clear from even the briefest glance at the literature that there is no independent country in Africa in which the indigenous population is not divided into subgroups which emerge as significant elements in the political divisions of the country. That is to say, 'tribal' or ethnic affiliations are linked to political groupings or factions or positions, are often linked to occupational categories, and are surely linked to job allocation. When foreign journalists comment on this, African politicians often deny the truth of such analysis. Such denials, however, as well as the contradictory assertions by outside observers, serve ideological rather than analytic ends. Thus, there are a long list of well-known ethno-political rivalries in African states (for example, Kikuyu versus Luo in Kenya; Bemba versus Lozi in Zambia; Sab versus Samaale in Somalia). In each of these cases, often despite presumed efforts

10. Why this came to be so, and what were the consequences of this non skin-color definition of 'African-ness', I have discussed in Wallerstein (1967).

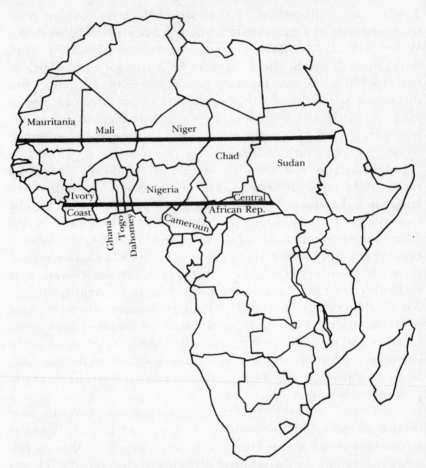

Dividing points. Several factors in addition to tribal insularity reinforce the division of Africa's indigenous population into subgroups. A continuous imaginary line drawn through Mauritania, Mali, Niger, Chad and Sudan indicates for the Sudanic belt a general dividing point. Peoples to the north of the line are lighter-skinned, Arabized, and Moslem; peoples to the south are generally darker-skinned and Christian/animist. A similar line, running from the West Coast into Central Africa through the Ivory Coast, Ghana, Togo, Dahomey, Nigeria, Cameroun, and the Central African Republic, indicates the same sort of division: peoples to the north and south of the line tend toward the opposite in mode of life, culture-family, religion, and education.

of the government or a nationalist political movement to prevent it, individuals have been aligned and/or mobilized on 'tribal' lines for political ends (cf. Rothschild 1969; Rotberg 1967; Lewis 1958).

In some countries, these so-called tribal divisions have been reinforced by some additional factors. In Ethiopia, for example, the divisions between the Amhara or Amhara-Tigre and the Eritreans coincides more or less with a religious division between Christians and Moslems, of which the participants are fully conscious, all the more since such a conflict has a long historical tradition behind it (see Jesman 1963).

Along the West African coast and into central Africa, there are seven contiguous states (the Ivory Coast, Ghana, Togo, Dahomey, Nigeria, Cameroun, and Central African Republic) through which a continuous horizontal line could be drawn. The peoples to the north and south of this line tend to be opposite in a series of features: savannah versus forest in soil conditions and corresponding large culture-family; Moslem/animist versus Christian/animist in religion; less modern education versus more modern education (largely the result of more Christian missionaries in the southern halves during the colonial era (see Milcent 1967; also Schwartz 1968). A similar line might be drawn in Uganda between the non-Bantu, less educated north and the Bantu, more educated (and more Christianized) south (see Hopkins 1967; also Edel 1965).

Further to the north, in the so-called Sudanic belt, an analogous line might be drawn through Mauritania, Mali, Niger, Chad, and Sudan. In the north of Mauritania, Chad, and Sudan, the people are lighter skinned, Arabized, and Moslem. To the south, they are darker skinned and Christian/animist. In Mali and Niger, however, those to the south are Moslem, as well. In all these states except the Sudan, those to the north are more likely to be nomadic and less educated. In Mauritania and the Sudan, those to the north are in the majority and in power. In Mali, Niger, and Chad, the reverse is true (see Watson 1963; Paques 1967; Shepherd 1966). Because these cultural distinctions in the Sudanic belt countries correlate with skin-color differences, these divisions are sometimes spoken of as 'racial'.

There is a further group of countries interesting to note. These are states which existed as political entities in precolonial times and have survived as such through the colonial and post-independence era, and in which there were clear pre-colonial 'tribal' stratification. These are Zanzibar (Arabs and Afro-Shirazis), Rwanda (Tutsi and Hutu), Burundi (Tutsi and Hutu), Madagascar (Merina and others). In all of these cases (except Burundi) the pre-colonial majoritarian lower stratum has now achieved political top status (see Lofchie 1963; Kuper 1970; Ziegler 1967; Kent 1962). Where similar pre-colonial stratification systems existed within larger colonial and post-colonial units, the political outcome has been far more ambiguous (Fulani sultanates in Nigeria and Cameroun, Hima kingdoms in Uganda and Tanganyika).

Since self-rule and independence, there have been a large number of 'repatriations' of Africans to their 'home' countries. Empires are notoriously liberal in the movement of peoples. It serves the purpose of optimal utilization of personnel. Nation-states, on the other hand, are trying precisely to demonstrate that privileges accrue to the status of citizen.

The first group to feel this pressure were politicians. As independence approached, the category of French West African or British East African tended to disappear. Malians who had made their political career in Upper Volta, or Ugandans who had made theirs in Kenya, found it prudent to go back to their home base. In addition to these discrete recognitions of a new political reality, there were the public and semipublic expulsions of large categories of persons: Dahomeans (and Togolese) from the Ivory Coast, Niger, and elsewhere; Nigerians and Togolese from Ghana; Malians from Zaïre. In each of these cases, those expelled had occupied positions in the money economy at a time of growing unemployment. The groups in question found themselves suddenly defined as non-nationals rather than as Africans. This was *a fortiori* true of categories of non-Africans, even where they had in some cases taken out formal citizenship: Arabs in Zanzibar, Asians in Kenya, sporadic expulsions of Lebanese in Ghana. Thus far, no major wholesale expulsion of Europeans has taken place in Black Africa, although there was an exodus of Belgians from Zaïre at one point.

This rapid sketch of the African scene is meant to underline one point: there is no useful distinction among the presumed varieties of status groups, such as ethnic groups, religious groups, races, castes. They are all variations of a single theme: grouping people by an affinity that mythically predates the current economic and political scene and which is a claim to a solidarity overriding those defined in class or ideological terms. As such, they appear, as Akiwowo (1964, p. 162) says of tribalism, as 'a set of patterned responses, adaptive adjustments if you will, to the unanticipated consequences of the processes of nation-building'. Or, in the more blunt words of Skinner (1967, p. 173), their central function is 'to permit people to organize into social, cultural or political entities able to compete with others for whatever goods and services [are] viewed as valuable in their environment'.

Insofar as this function is inherent to the concept, then by definition status groups cannot exist prior to some larger society of which they are a part, even when groups claim to be organized or to exist in more than one societal system.[11] What Fried (1967, p. 15) states cautiously of 'tribes' is true of all status groups:

> Most tribes seem to be secondary phenomena in a very specific sense: they may well be the product of processes stimulated by the appearance of relatively highly organized societies amidst other societies which are organized much more simply. If this can be demonstrated, tribalism can be viewed as a reaction to the creation of complex political structure rather than as a necessary preliminary stage in its evolution.

In the modern world situation, a status group is a collective claim to power and allocation of goods and services within a nation-state on grounds that are formally illegitimate.

The relationship of class and status group

How then do such claims stand in relation to the claims of class solidarity? Marx, in using the concept of class, distinguished between classes *an sich* and *für sich*. Weber (1968, p. 930) repeated this distinction when he said: 'Thus every class may be the carrier of any one of the innumerable possible forms of class action, but this is not necessarily so. In any case, a class does not in itself constitute a group (*Gemeinschaft*).'

Why is it that classes are not always *für sich*? Indeed, why is it they are so seldom *für sich*? Or to put the question another way,

11. Cf. Weber (1968, p. 939): 'we should add one more general observation about classes, status groups and parties: the fact that they presuppose a larger association, especially the framework of a polity, does not mean that they are confined to it. On the contrary, at all times it has been the order of the day that such association...reaches beyond the state boundaries...But their aim is not necessarily the establishment of a new territorial dominion. In the main they aim to influence the existing polity.' Except, I should add, insofar as one considers loyalty to a nation-state in a world-system as an expression of status group consciousness.

how do we explain that status group consciousness is so pervasive and powerful a political force, in Africa and throughout the world, today and throughout history? To answer that it is false consciousness is simply to push the question one step logically back, for then we should have to ask how it is that most people most of the time exhibit false consciousness?

Weber (1968, p. 938) has a theory to account for this. He states:

As to the general economic conditions making for the predominance of stratification by status, only the following can be said. When the bases of the acquisition and distribution of goods are relatively stable, stratification by status is favored. Every technological repercussion and economic transformation threatens stratification by status and pushes the class situation into the foreground. Epochs and countries in which the naked class situation is of predominant significance are regularly the periods of technical and economic transformations. And every slowing down of the change in economic stratification leads, in due course, to the growth of status structure and makes for a resuscitation of the important role of social honor.

Weber's explanation seems very simple and makes class consciousness the correlate of progress and social change, stratification by status the expression of retrograde forces – a sort of vulgar Marxism. While one may agree with the moral thrust of the theorem, it is not very predictive of the smaller shifts in historical reality nor does it explain why one can find modern economic thrusts in status group garb (see Favret 1967), as well as mechanisms of the preservation of traditional privilege in class consciousness (see Geertz 1967).

Favret (1967, p. 73) gives us a clue in her discussion of a Berber rebellion in Algeria:

[In Algeria] primordial groups do not exist substantively, unaware of their archaism, but reactively. The anthropologist tempted by collecting traditional political phenomena is in danger therefore of a colossal misunderstanding in interpreting them naively, for their context is today inverted. The choice for the descendants of the segmentary tribes of the nineteenth century is no longer among ends – to co-operate with the central government or to institutionalize dissidence – for only the former choice is henceforth possible. The choice – or the fate – of the peasants of the underdeveloped agricultural sector is in the means of attaining this end; among which, paradoxically, is dissidence.

Favret pushes us to look at claims based on status group affiliation not in the intellectual terms of the actors in the situation, but in terms of the actual functions such claims perform in the social system. Moerman makes a similar appeal in an analysis of the Lue, a tribe in Thailand, about whom he asks three trenchant questions:

What are the Lue? Why are the Lue? When are the Lue? He concludes (1967, p. 167):

Ethnic identification devices – with their important potential of making each ethnic set of living persons a joint enterprise with countless generations of unexamined history – seem to be universal. Social scientists should therefore describe and analyse the ways in which they are used, and not merely – as natives do – use them as explanations...It is quite possible that ethnic categories are rarely appropriate subjects for the interesting human predicates.

Perhaps then we could reconceive the Weberian trinity of class, status group, and party not as three different and cross-cutting groups but as three different existential forms of the same essential reality. In which case, the question shifts from Weber's one of the conditions under which stratification by status takes precedence over class consciousness to the conditions under which a stratum embodies itself as a class, as a status group, or as a party. For such a conceptualization, it would not be necessary to argue that the boundary lines of the group in its successive embodiments would be identical – quite the contrary, or there would be no function to having different outer clothing – but rather that there exist a limited set of groups in any social structure at any given time in relation to, in conflict with, each other.

One approach, suggested by Rodolfo Stavenhagen, is to see status groups as 'fossils' of social classes. He argues (1962, pp. 99–101) that:

Stratifications [i.e., status groups] represent, in the majority of cases, what we call social *fixations*, frequently by juridical means, certainly subjectively, of specific social relations of production, represented by class relations. Into these social *fixations* intrude other secondary, accessory factors (for example, religious, ethnic) which reinforce the stratification and which have, at the same time, the function of 'liberating' it of its links with its economic base; in other words, of maintaining its strength even if its economic base changes. Consequently, stratifications can be thought of as justifications or rationalizations of the established economic system, that is to say, as ideologies. Like all phenomena of the social superstructure, stratification has a quality of inertia which maintains it even when the conditions which gave it birth have changed. As the relations between classes are modified...stratifications turn themselves into *fossils* of the class relations on which they were originally based...[Furthermore], it seems that the two types of groupings (dominant class and higher stratum) can coexist for some time and be encrusted in the social structure, according to the particular historical circumstances. But sooner or later a new stratification system arises which corresponds more exactly to the current class system.

In a later analysis, using Central American data, Stavenhagen spells out how, in a colonial situation, two caste-like lower status groups (in that case, *indios* and *ladinos*) could emerge, become encrusted, and survive the various pressures at what he called class clarification. He argues that two forms of dependence (a colonial form, based on ethnic discrimination and political subordination) and a class form (based on work relations) grew up side by side and reflected a parallel ranking system. After independence, and despite economic development, the dichotomy between *indios* and *ladinos*, 'profoundly ensconced in the values of the members of society', remained as 'an essentially conservative force' in the social structure. 'Reflecting a situation of the past...[this dichotomy] acts as a constraint on the development of the new class relations' (1963, p. 94). In this version, present stratification is still a fossil of the past, but it is not so simply a fossil of class relations *per se*.

Another approach would be to see class or status affiliation as options open to various members of the society. This is the approach of Peter Carstens. In two recent papers, one by Carstens (1970) and one by Allen (1970), there is agreement that Africans working on the land in the rural areas should be thought of as 'peasants' who are members of the 'working class', that is who sell their labor power even when they are technically self-employed cash-crop farmers. But while Allen is concerned with emphasizing the pattern of tied alternation between cash-crop farming and wage-earning,[12] Carstens is more concerned with explaining the status group apparatus of peasant class organization, or what he calls 'peasant status systems'.

Carstens (1970, p. 9) starts with the argument that 'the retention or revival of tenuous tribal loyalties are resources available to persons to establish prestige or esteem'. He reminds us (1970, p. 10) that 'the same institutions that effected the hidden force that produced a peasant *class*, also created peasant *status* systems.

12. 'Wage-earners experience fluctuations in their living standards and employment whereas the peasant producers experience fluctuations in their living standards and the intensity of work. A depression in the living standards of wage-earners or in increase in unemployment, however, produces a movement of labour back to peasant production or is borne because the resources of peasant production exist as an insurance cover' (Allen 1970). Cf. a similar argument made by Arrighi (1969). An English version under the title 'Labor Supplies in Historical Perspective: A Study of the Proletarianization of the African Peasantry in Rhodesia' in Giovanni Arrighi and John S. Saul, *Essays on the Political Economy of Africa* (New York: Monthly Review Press, 1973), 180–234.

For example...the surest way to achieve recognition, prestige, and esteem in the eyes of the ruling class as well as from the local peasants is to participate in the externally imposed educational and religious institutions.' It therefore follows that 'it is only by the manipulation of their internal status systems that they are able to gain access to other status systems which are located in the higher class. The strategy of status manipulation is best seen then as a means for crossing class boundaries' (1970, p. 8).

The strength of stratification by status can be seen in this light. Status honor is not only a mechanism for the achievers of yore to maintain their advantages in the contemporary market, the retrograde force described by Weber; it is also the mechanism whereby the upward strivers obtain their ends within the system (hence the correlation of high ethnic consciousness and education, to which Colson called attention). With support from two such important groups, the ideological primacy of status group is easy to understand. It takes an unusual organizational situation to break through this combination of elements interested in preserving this veil (or this reality – it makes no difference).

Weber was wrong. Class consciousness does not come to the fore when technological change or social transformation is occurring. All of modern history gives this the lie. Class consciousness only comes to the fore in a far rarer circumstance, in a 'revolutionary' situation, of which class consciousness is both the ideological expression and the ideological pillar. In this sense, the basic Marxian conceptual instinct was correct.

The African data reanalyzed

Let us now return to the empirical reality of contemporary independent Africa in the light of this theoretical excursus. Independent Black Africa is today composed of a series of nation-states, members of the United Nations, almost none of which can be considered a national society, in the sense of having a relatively autonomous and centralized polity, economy, and culture. All of these states are part of the world social system and most are well integrated into particular imperial economic networks. Their economic outlines are basically similar. The majority of the population works on the land, producing both crops for a world market and food for their subsistence. Most are workers, either in the sense of receiving wages from the owner of the land or in the sense of being self-employed in a situation in which they are obliged to earn cash (and see farming as an economic alternative to other kinds of wage employment). There are others who work as laborers in urban areas, often as part of a pattern of circulatory migration.

In each country, working for the most part for the government, there is a bureaucratic class which is educated and seeking to transform some of their wealth into property. In every case, there are certain groups (one of several) who are disproportionately represented in the bureaucratic class, as there are other groups disproportionately represented among urban laborers. Almost everywhere, a group of whites lives, holding high status and filling technical positions. Their prestige rank has scarcely changed since colonial rule. The local high rank of whites reflects the position of these countries in the world economic system where they are 'proletarian' nations, suffering the effects of 'unequal exchange'.[13]

The degree of political autonomy represented by formal sovereignty enabled the local elites or elite groups to seek their upward mobility in the world-system by a rapid expansion of the educational system of their countries. What is individually functional in terms of the world-system is collectively dysfunctional. The workings of the world-system do not provide sufficient job outlets at the national level. This forces elite groups to find criteria by which to reward parts of themselves and to reject others. The particular lines of division are arbitrary and changeable in details. In some places, the division is along ethnic lines; in others, along religious; in others, along racial lines; in most, in some implicit combination of all of these.

These status group tensions are the inefficacious and self-defeating expression of class frustrations. They are the daily stuff of contemporary African politics and social life. The journalists, who are usually closer to popular perceptions than the social scientists, tend to call this phenomenon 'tribalism' when they write of Black Africa. Tribal, or ethnic, conflicts are very real things,

13. For an elaboration of the concept and an explanation of its social consequences, see Emanuel (1969).

as the civil wars in the Sudan and Nigeria attest most eloquently. They are ethnic conflicts in the sense that persons involved in these conflicts are commonly motivated by analyses which use ethnic (or comparable status group) categories; furthermore, they usually exhibit strong ethnic loyalties. Nonetheless, behind the ethnic 'reality' lies a class conflict, not very far from the surface. By this I mean the following straightforward and empirically testable proposition (not one, however, that has been definitively so tested): were the class differences that correlate (or coincide) with the status group differences to disappear, as a result of changing social circumstances, the status group conflicts would eventually disappear (no doubt to be replaced by others). The status group loyalties are binding and affective, in a way that it seems difficult for class loyalties to be other than in moments of crisis, but they are also more transient from the perspective of the analyst. If the society were to become ethnically 'integrated', class antagonisms would not abate; the opposite in fact is true. One of the functions of the network of status group affiliations is to conceal the realities of class differentials. To the extent, however, that particular class antagonisms or differentials abate or disappear, status group antagonisms (if not differentials, but even differentials) also abate and disappear.

The usefulness of the concept of race

In Black Africa, one speaks of 'ethnic' conflict. In the United States or in South Africa, one speaks of 'racial' conflict. Is there any point in having a special word, *race*, to describe status groupings that are the most salient in some countries but not in others (like Black African states)? If we were to regard each national case as discrete and logically separate, there would not be, since stratification by status serves the same purpose in each.

But the national cases are not discrete and logically separate. They are part of a world-system. Status and prestige in the national system cannot be divorced from status and rank in the world-system, as we have already mentioned in discussing the role of expatriate white Europeans in Black Africa today. There are international status groups as well as national ones. What we mean by race is essentially such an international status group. There is a basic division between whites and non-whites. (Of course, there are varieties of non-whites, and the categorization differs according to time and place. One grouping is by skin color but it is not in fact very prevalent. Another more common one is by continent, although the Arabs often lay claim to being counted separately.)

In terms of this international dichotomy, skin color is irrelevant. 'White' and 'non-white' have very little to do with skin color. 'What is a black? And first of all, what color is he?' asked Jean Genêt. When Africans deny, as most do deny, that the conflict between the lighter-skinned Arabs of northern Sudan and the dark-skinned Nilotes of southern Sudan is a racial conflict, they are not being hypocritical. They are reserving the term *race* for a particular international social tension. It is not that the conflict in the Sudan is not real and is not expressed in status group terms. It is. But it is a conflict which, though formally similar to, is politically different from, that between blacks and whites in the United States, or Africans and Europeans in South Africa. The political difference lies in its meaning in and for the world-system.

Race is, in the contemporary world, the only international status group category. It has replaced religion, which played that role since at least the eighth century AD. Rank in this system, rather than color, determines membership in the status group. Thus, in Trinidad, there can be a 'Black Power' movement, directed against an all-black government, on the grounds that this government functions as an ally of North American imperialism. Thus, Quebec separatists can call themselves the 'white Niggers' of North America. Thus, pan-Africanism can include white-skinned Arabs of North Africa, but exclude white-skinned Afrikaners of South Africa. Thus, Cyprus and Yugoslavia can be invited to tricontinental conferences (Asia, Africa, and Latin America) but Israel and Japan are excluded. As a status group category, race is a blurred collective representation for an international class category, that of the proletarian nations. Racism, therefore, is simply the act of maintaining the existing international social structure, and is not a neologism for racial discrimination. It is not that they are separate phenomena. Racism obviously utilizes discrimination as part of its armory of tactics, a central weapon, to be sure. But there are many possible situations in which there can be racism without discrimination, in any immediate sense. Perhaps there can even be discrimination without racism, though this seems harder. What is important to see is that these concepts refer to actions at different levels of social organization: racism refers to action within the world arena; discrimination refers to actions within relatively small-scale social organizations.

Summary

In summary, my main point is that status groups (as well as parties) are blurred collective representation of classes. The blurred (and hence incorrect) lines serve the interests of many different elements in most social situations. As social conflict becomes more acute, status group lines approach class lines asymptotically, at which point we may see the phenomenon of 'class consciousness'. But the asymptote is never reached. Indeed, it is almost as though there were a magnetic field around the asymptote which pushed the approaching curve away. Race, finally, is a particular form of status group in the contemporary world, the one which indicates rank in the world social system. In this sense, there are no racial tensions today within independent Black African states. One of the expressions of national identity, however, as it will be achieved, will be increasing international status group consciousness, or racial identification, which would then only be overcome or surpassed as one approached the asymptote of international class consciousness.

References

Akiwowo, Akinsola A. 1964. 'The Sociology of Nigerian Tribalism'. *Phylon*, 25: 2 (Summer), 155–63

Allen, V. L. 1970. 'The Meaning and Differentiation of the Working Class in Tropical Africa'. Presented at the Seventh World Congress of Sociology, Varna, Bulgaria (13–19 September)

Arrighi, Giovanni. 1969. 'L'offertà di lavoro in una perspettiva storica'. In *Sviluppo economico e sovrastrutture in Africa*, pp. 89–162. Turin: Einaudi

Arrighi, Giovanni and John S. Saul. Forthcoming, 1973. *Essays on the Political Economy of Africa*. New York: Monthly Review Press

Busia, K. A. 1951. *The Position of the Chief in the Modern Political System of Ashanti*. London: Oxford University Press

Carstens, Peter. 1970. 'Problems of Peasantry and Social Class in Southern Africa'. Presented at the Seventh World Congress of Sociology, Varna, Bulgaria (13–19 September)

Colson, Elizabeth. 1967. 'Contemporary Tribes and the Development of Nationalism'. In June Helm (ed.), *Essays on the Problem of Tribe*, pp. 201–6. Proceedings of the 1967 Annual Spring Meeting Of the American Ethnological Society

Edel, May. 1965. 'African Tribalism: Some Reflections on Uganda'. *Political Science Quarterly*, 80: 3 (September), 357–72

Emanuel, Arghiri. 1969. *L'échange inégal*. Paris: Maspéro

Favret, Jeanne. 1967. 'Le traditionalisme par excès de modernité'. *Archives européennes de sociologie*, 8: 1, 71–93

Fried, Morton H. 1967. 'On the Concept of "Tribe" and "Tribal Society".' In June Helm (ed.), *Essays on the Problem of Tribe*, pp. 3–20. Proceedings of 1967 Annual Spring Meeting of the American Ethnological Society

Froelich, J.-C. 1962. *Les musulmans d'Afrique Noire*. Paris: Ed. de l'Orante

Geertz, Clifford. 1963. 'The Integrative Revolution, Primordial Sentiments and Civil Politics in the New States'. In C. Geertz (ed.), *Old Societies and New States*, pp. 105–57. Glencoe: Free Press

  1967. 'Politics Past, Politics Present'. *Archives européennes de sociologie*, 8: 1, 1–14

Hodgkin, Thomas. 1962. 'Islam and National Movements in West Africa'. *Journal of African History*, 3: 1, 323–7

Hopkins, Terence K. 1967. 'Politics in Uganda: the Buganda Question'. In J. Butler and A. A. Castagno, Jr. (eds.), *Transition in African Politics*, Boston University Papers on Africa, pp. 251–90. New York: Praeger

Horton, Robin. 1971. 'Stateless Societies in the History of West Africa'. In J. F. A. Ajayi and M. Crowder (eds.), *A History of West Africa* (2 vols.), vol. 1. London: Longmans

Jesman, Czeslaw. 1963. *The Ethiopian Paradox*. London: Oxford University Press

Kent, Raymond K. 1962. *From Madagascar to the Malagasy Republic*. New York: Praeger

Kuper, Leo. 1970. 'Continuities and Discontinuities in Race Relations: Evolutionary or Revolutionary Change'. *Cahiers d'études africaines* 10: 3 (39), 361–83

Lewis, I. M. 1958. 'Modern Political Movements in Somaliland'. *Africa*, 28: 3 (July), 244–61; 28: 4 (October), 344–63

Lofchie, Michael. 1963. 'Party Conflict in Zanzibar'. *Journal of Modern African Studies*, 1: 2, 185–207

Milcent, Ernest. 1967. 'Tribalisme et vie politique dans les Etats du Bénin'. *Revue française d'études politiques africaines*, 18 (June), 37–53

Moerman, Michael. 1967. 'Being Lue: Uses and Abuses of Ethnic Identification'. In June Helm (ed.), *Essays on the Problem of Tribe*, pp. 153–69. Proceedings of 1967 Annual Spring Meeting of the American Ethnological Society

Paques, Viviana. 1967. 'Alcuni problemi umani posti dallo sviluppo economico e sociale: Il case della Repubblica del Ciad'. *Il Nuovo Osservatore*, 8: 63 (June), 580–4

Rotberg, Robert I. 1967. 'Tribalism and Politics in Zambia'. *Africa Report*, 12: 9 (December), 29–35

Rothschild, Donald. 1969. 'Ethnic Inequalities in Kenya'. *Journal of Modern African Studies*, 7: 4, 689–711

Schwarz, Walter. 1968. *Nigeria*. London: Pall Mall Press

Shepherd, George W., Jr. 1966. 'National Integration and the Southern Sudan'. *Journal of Modern African Studies*, 4: 2, 193–212

Shils, Edward. 1957. 'Primordial, Personal, Sacred and Civil Ties'. *British Journal of Sociology*, 8: 2 (June), 130–45
Skinner, Elliott P. 1963. 'Strangers in West African Societies'. *Africa*, 33: 4 (October), 307–20
1967. 'Group Dynamics in the Politics of Changing Societies: The Problem of 'Tribal' Politics in Africa'. In June Helm (ed.), *Essays on the Problem of Tribe*, pp. 170–85. Proceedings of 1967 Annual Spring Meeting of the American Ethnological Society
Stavenhagen, Rodolfo. 1962. 'Estratificación social y estructura de clases (un ensayo de interpretación)'. *Ciencias políticas y sociales*, 8: 27 (January–March), 73–102
1963. 'Clases, colonialismo y aculturación: ensayo sobre un sistema de relaciones interétnicas en Mesoamérica'. *América Latina*, 6: 4 (October–December), 63–103
Suret-Canale, Jean. 1969. 'Tribus, classes, nations'. *La nouvelle revue internationale*, 130 (June), 110–24
Wallerstein, Immanuel. 1960. Ethnicity and National Integration in West Africa. *Cahiers d'études africaines*, 3 (October), 129–39
1967. *Africa: The Politics of Unity*. New York: Random House
1971. 'The Range of Choice: Constraints on the Policies of Governments of Contemporary African Independent States'. In Michael F. Lochie (ed.), *The State of the Nations*, pp. 19–33. Berkeley: University of California Press
Waston, J. H. A. 1963. 'Mauritania: Problems and Prospects'. *Africa Report*, 8: 2 (February), 3–6
Weber, Max. 1968. *Economy and Society* (3 vols). New York: Bedminster Press
Ziegler, Jean. 1967. 'Structures ethniques et partis politiques au Burundi'. *Revue française d'études politiques africaines*, 18 (June), 54–68

11 ❧ The two modes of ethnic consciousness: Soviet Central Asia in transition

By ethnic consciousness I mean the sentiment, shared by a group of people who define their boundaries in cultural terms (a common language, religion, color, history, style of life, and the like, or a combination of these), that they must seek to assert or extend their rights in the political arena in order to defend possibilities for their continued existence as a group and/or to maintain or improve their material conditions. Whether such a group prefers to call itself a nation, a nationality, an ethnic group, a tribe, a people, or any of the other sundry terms that are used is not very material to the substance of the fact that ethnic consciousness is an assertion in the *political* arena to defend *cultural* and *economic* interests.

Ethnic consciousness is eternally latent everywhere. But it is only realized when groups feel either threatened with a loss of previously acquired privilege or conversely feel that it is an opportune moment politically to overcome long-standing denial of privilege. For any particular group, this occurs periodically but not continuously.

Furthermore, the boundary lines of a group can only be perceived when it is ethnically conscious. It is the act of political assertion that defines the boundaries. Hence each periodic 'act' may in fact be that of a group with somewhat different boundaries, even though over a long period of time the successive acting groups use the same name and seem to have largely similar defining characteristics.

I have started with this somewhat tedious definitional process in order to insist on a fundamental premise of my argument: any 'ethnic' group exists only to the extent that it is asserted to exist at any given point in time by the group itself and by the larger social network of which it is a part. Such groups are constantly 'created' and recreated; they also constantly 'cease to exist'; they are thus constantly redefined and change their forms at amazingly fast rates. Yet through the physical maelstrom, some 'names' maintain a long historical continuity because at frequent historical intervals it has been in the interests of the conscious elements bearing this 'name' to reassert the heritage, revalorize the mythical links, and socialize members into the historical 'memory'.

Ethnic consciousness, being a political phenomenon, is a form of conflict. The conflict need not be violent, to be sure, though of course it often is. The nature of the conflict, however, may differ, and the form that ethnic consciousness may take may consequently differ as well. In the modern world-system there have been two quite distinct modes of ethnic consciousness occurring in two reasonably distinct arenas of the world-system.

The modern world-economy, within the framework of a single division of labor, contains core areas with a complex range of occupational activities, multiple social strata, a strong state machinery, and a relatively high overall standard of living (except for the bottom strata). It also contains peripheral areas, which have a narrower range of economic tasks, fewer social strata, a weaker state machinery, and a low standard of living for all but a thin upper stratum. It is evident that the forms of social conflict to be found in these two areas are quite different.

In peripheral areas, the main activity is agricultural labor. Groups of these laborers sharing language, customs, and usually religion as well find themselves compelled by the world market and the local political machinery to engage in hard work for relatively little pay. Their major economic complaint is too high taxation by the government, and their major contemporary demand has been for more educational facilities for their children, seeing the educational system quite correctly as the only likely route of social mobility.

Finding themselves the majority of the people in the area in which they live, these laborers also find that quite often their political rulers come from another ethnic group. This is of course true in all colonial situations in the modern world where the administration has been in the hands of people of radically different culture and geographical origin. This is also true in many regions of non-colonial states of the periphery where the national political leadership is largely or exclusively in the hands of one ethnic group, which, from the perspective of given geographic regions, is a stranger group.

To the extent that the local area in question has educated cadres, whose own chances of advancement are in fact blocked by the absence of political autonomy of the particular area, these cadres may begin to agitate for greater self-rule. They begin to react against the arrogant style of cultural assimilation practiced by the politically dominant forces and reassert traditional cultural values and boundary lines, or invent them.

When economic and political circumstances are such that the masses of the population respond positively to this agitation, we usually call this phenomenon 'nationalism'. Because nationalism has as its major slogan 'self-determination', and to have self-determination one must logically have a determinate unit, nationalism tends to be attached to territorial units, either already in existence or that can be seen as potential. However, because administrative units, especially those already in existence, almost never correlate perfectly with membership in linguistic, religious, or other cultural groupings – because, that is, they are almost always to some extent 'artificial' – ethnically conscious movements are normally faced with a choice, especially as the moment of political realization of aims draws near, between a territorial or a cultural definition of ethnicity. And usually, despite the presumed cultural base of the claims, they opt, out of *realpolitik*, for a territorial definition. This means that, on cultural grounds, the resulting entity has cultural minorities, which means that the problem remains, and the game can go on and on.

It also means that one man's ethnic consciousness is frequently another man's ethnic oppression. For territory is finite, and two 'groups' cannot both exercise sovereign control over the same area. Yet quite frequently two groups can lay claims of fairly equal plausibility to particular areas. At which point, more energy may be devoted to pursuing these rival claims than in any attempt to change the world-system that has maintained both 'groups' and the entire larger geographical area in peripheral status in the world-economy.

The ethnicity of core areas of the modern world is quite a

different affair. To be sure, there are certain surface similarities. The ethnic consciousness is defined in cultural terms and emphasized cultural renaissance. It has an objective greater equality in the political arena. And the underlying complaint is that of economic deprivation. But there the similarities stop.

Core areas of the modern world-economy have been for the past two centuries industrialized and urbanized areas. The role of agriculture has constantly declined until today only a small minority of the work force is involved in agricultural labor, and increasingly that labor is in fact highly skilled work.

The cities of the industrial areas tend to be ethnic hodgepodges in terms of the ancestry of the majority of the population. They are usually of multiple religions. Often they speak various languages, although the operation of the economy normally requires an official language as a *lingua franca*.

Any particular ethnic group tends to be only a minority of the population of the whole urban area, although they may be residentially segregated into 'ghettos'. If anything, the politically dominant ethnic group often constitutes the majority of the population, or the plurality, and comprises within it not only the political and economic elite but a large percentage of the professionals and of the most skilled workers. The multiple 'minorities' are divided into those of higher status whose members are recruited into higher-status jobs, and those of lower status whose members are recruited into subproletarian positions (unskilled labor and lumpenproletarian, marginal, or criminal employment).

The ethnic consciousness of the higher-status minorities tends to be entirely defensive, activated partially to break down remaining discriminatory barriers but increasingly to prevent incursions into their privilege by lower-status groups. One major mode of defense is their own assimilation into the dominant ethnic group, and it is frequently pursued. The political meeting ground of skilled workers of dominant ethnic group extraction and professionals and skilled workers of higher-status minority groups are institutions of the center-left (such as trade unions, 'liberal' or 'socialist' political parties, and the like).

Ethnic consciousness of the lower-status ethnic groups, however, is basically an urban phenomenon having strong roots in subproletarian elements. Since in the industrial urban areas education has usually been universal in recent years, these subproletarian elements are frequently joined by a stratum of so-called 'unemployed intellectuals', that is, persons who have been educated for positions that either do not yet structurally exist because of the insufficient degree of economic development or from which they are excluded because of their low ethnic origin. When these elements reject assimilation, it is most frequently the assimilation of the center-left institutions of which they are thinking.

The organization of such subproletarian elements tends to take on a tone of more radical ideology than in the case of rural workers in peripheral areas who are led by urban educated elements that see separation as a mode of obtaining substantial personal benefits. In the latter case, agitation often leads to constitutional reform that meets the demands of the leadership, who thereupon can become more 'conservative' in terminology.

In the subproletarian case, reform has a less promising outlook, largely because such elements confront in their demands not merely the upper privileged stratum of the society but a privileged middle stratum who already control the centre-left 'reform' institutions. Hence, there often occurs a process of 'radicalization'. If this ethnic movement has a firm territorial base, as in Quebec, it can lead to separatist demands, in which case, however, it involves sharing features of both forms of ethnic consciousness. If the territorial base is weak, as is the case with Blacks in the United States, the movement tends to have a less focused immediate goal, which means it is more difficult to organize but, once organized, more difficult to satisfy.

How does all this apply to Soviet Central Asia? As the various parts of Turkistan fell under Russian rule in the nineteenth century, these areas were drawn into the periphery of the capitalist world-economy. They were under colonial rule, which in Bukhara and Khiva was of the so-called indirect variety. Among the educated elements various forms of ethnic consciousness took root, for example the *jadid* (reformist) movement, and by the early twentieth century there flourished various overlapping and sometimes confused 'nationalist' sentiments: pan-Islamism, pan-Turanianism, Tatar nationalism, greater Bukhara, and so on.

Central Asia was in turn part of Russia, herself part of the semiperiphery of the world-economy. Faced in the late nineteenth century with the prospect of going backward rather than forward in industrialization – relative to developments in western Europe and North America – Russia underwent the October 1917 revolution. This upheaval was in part the expression of a demand for a national leadership, not tied to western European capitalist forces, that could bring about the industrial transformation of Russia, in part the expression of Russian peasant protest against the peripheral role of Russian agriculture (and their consequent exploitation), in part the expression of Russia's urban classes (especially the proletariat of skilled workers) for an expansion of their opportunities, political, economic, and cultural. It was, if you will, the expression of a class conflict in the world-economy that took on heavily ethnic clothing (heavier than its ideological leaders wished to admit at the time).

In ideological terms, Russia's colonies were an embarrassment for the communist leadership. In terms of their immediate collective objectives, maintaining these 'colonial' areas within the political hegemony of Russia was, however, vital to the political economy. The result was the uneasy compromise of the USSR. On the one hand, the USSR was a federation of sovereign republics with the right of secession, and the structure provided as well for a variety of lesser forms of political autonomy. This presumably ended the colonial status of the former outlying parts of the Russian Empire, insofar as they were guaranteed the various cultural appurtenances of self-government (especially language rights) and elected their own indigenous leadership. On the other hand, the USSR as such had a highly centralized state structure and was a very tight political system involving the primacy of the Communist Party of the Soviet Union. These two principles were not in perfect harmony. The evidence for this is clear in the frequent campaigns conducted over the years by the leadership of the CPSU against 'bourgeois nationalism' in the various republics and other autonomous units.

In practice, the Soviet leadership sought a pragmatic compromise that would achieve the objective of territorial integrity and economic coordination at the lowest possible political price. The papers in this collection tend to show how successful this policy was over the first fifty years of the USSR.

The leadership of the CPSU very early adopted, in the dispute of Stalin with Sultan Galiev, an operational principle that has guided them ever since. They indicated that they were open to any suggestions about possible ethnically defined administrative areas except those that would treat Central Asia (in any of its multiple versions) as a single entity. Evidently they felt that 'Central Asianism' would inevitably escalate into separatist pressures. Instead, they encouraged the crystallization of five 'nations' (in the official terminology) plus a few further 'nationalities'. Several of the studies in this collection argue that the CPSU leadership had to exert much energy to have these ethnic boundaries accepted. They also indicate that they had gained the support of large segments, but far from all, of the local cadres in this process of social definition.

Of course the central government demanded loyalty of the local leadership. They also demanded a certain sentiment of collective nationalism–Sovietism. And as an extra guarantee, they placed Russian personnel in number two positions of the various local Party organisms.

But in return, the central government pursued a policy of educational and agricultural development that was their boast and does them credit. Once again, the papers in this collection demonstrate the impressive degree to which educational and income gaps have been narrowed between Russia and Soviet Central Asia.

Soviet policy has consequently succeeded in two senses. The Central Asian areas of the USSR have manifested a remarkably low level of discontent, especially considering the fact that since 1917 all the rest of Asia has known so much nationalist turmoil and revolution. Secondly, nationalists in other parts of Asia (and elsewhere) have not for the most part considered Soviet Central Asia to be a 'colonial area' where a national liberation movement should be encouraged.

Is there then no problem? The problem comes, ironically, from the inner contradictions of a capitalist world-system. The USSR has reached the level of a core industrialized nation in the world-economy, still a capitalist world-economy. If she is to maintain this status and not regress she must further transform her industry into one with a major export component, and she must export not merely industrial products but machinery and electronic equipment as well. This requires the further industrialization and urbanization of European Russia. It also requires an expansion of population.

But European Russia is experiencing the kind of demographic slowdown that is precisely the consequence of the fact that an ever larger percentage of its population is going into the professions, or becoming highly skilled workers. There is in prospect a shortage of local people to fill the subproletarian positions in the economy. This is a situation that has faced every highly industrialized country in the world, especially since the Second World War. The only solution thus far found in western Europe and North America has been widespread importation of laborers. Not being citizens, or at least being only second-class citizens, these laborers have had little political influence not only with the government but with the trade union movement as well, and have worked at relatively low wage scales and in poor working conditions.

Although their problem is basically a class problem, the fact that class in this case is almost perfectly correlated with ethnicity, combined with the fact that the presumed class-defense organizations (traded unions and left-liberal political organizations) are in the hands of the middle-income stratum of workers (of largely upper ethnic origin), has meant that the subproletariat has sought to organize to defend its class interests in ethnic organizations.

Once organized, this subproletariat of the industrialized nations has tended to become 'radicalized' and to see parallels in its class-ethnic interests with those of the 'proletarian' nations of the 'Third World'. Indeed, it has begun to use the appellations 'Third World within', 'internal colonies', and the like. At which point a certain international political solidarity has begun to manifest itself.

Is it possible that the USSR will come soon to face the development of such subproletarian ethnic strata? Where will the workers come from who will soon be needed to fill subproletarian positions in the occupational structure of European Russia? From Turkey? From Bulgaria? Or from Soviet Central Asia?

It seems plausible to assume that the government of the USSR would find it least disruptive to encourage increased internal migration within the USSR and toward European Russia rather than away from it as heretofore – or rather toward it for unskilled workers, and away from it for the educated. And once large numbers of Central Asians find themselves located in the cities of European Russia, what will be the nature of their social relations with Russian workers? Will they organize themselves in ethnic associations? And what will be the *class* objectives of these ethnic associations, once formed? We can guess, by extrapolation from what has happened elsewhere, but we cannot be certain.

And should subproletarian ethnic strata in European Russia begin to make political demands, will they too consider themselves the 'Third World within'? Will the 'unemployed intellectuals' of the Soviet Central Asian republics join hands with the future educated segments of Central Asian extraction in European Russia who may sense 'institutional racism', and will they begin to 'radicalize', that is, attack the regime from the left? And if they do that, what will be the impact of such ideological currents on the undoubted remnants of more traditional 'bourgeois nationalism' in Soviet Central Asia? Finally, how will the radical elements of the rest of Asia (and Africa and Latin America as well) react to this phenomenon? Will they feel sentiments of political solidarity toward such groups? Again, these are all questions that it is too early to answer.

What is clear, it seems to me, is that Soviet Central Asia is today at a turning point, and that any analysis of the 'nationality question' must take into account the different ways in which ethnic consciousness and class consciousness intertwine, and hence the possible major shift in the political forms of expressing sentiments of 'Central Asianism'.

12 ❧ Class and class conflict in contemporary Africa

Class analysis of contemporary Africa has had a shaky history. Before the Second World War, most scholars who wrote about Africa scarcely took Africa seriously enough to use so contemporary and so 'European' a concept as class or class conflict to apply to the social structure of a colonial society (with the exception of writings about the rather special situation in South Africa). European analysts, particularly those linked with the French Communist Party, did undertake such analyses,[1] but they tended to be so mechanistic in their application of categories, especially in attributing to urban wage workers (the 'proletariat') an undue importance as a social and political force, that these analyses were discredited. Furthermore, when such movements as the *Rassemblement démocratique africain* and the trade unions broke their political links with the French Communist Party, they attached a rejection of class analysis to their general critique of communist political strategy.

An even more influential factor, however, was probably the emergence of a 'liberal-modernist' ideology among the younger western scholars. This group sought to take contemporary Africa very seriously. They found two groups of intellectual opponents. One was an 'old guard' of Africanist scholars and administrators who considered 'national' and nationalist phenomena in Africa as socially superficial and emphasized the continuing reality of 'traditional' tribal affiliations. A second was the main body of social scientists in Europe and North America who, having knowledge only of their own societies, wanted to apply their conceptual frameworks as mechanistically as did the ideologues of the French Communist Party.

1. The most elaborate of these appeared rather late. It is Raymond Barbé, *Les classes sociales en Afrique Noire* (Paris: Economie et politique, 1964).

To both these sets of opponents, the 'liberal-modernist' wing of scholars asserted that there was something new emerging in Africa, comparable perhaps to what was occurring in Asia and Latin America, but distinct from what was happening in the western world. This group further asserted that these phenomena had to be taken seriously on their own terms. The linguistic apparatus used to describe these 'new' African developments included terms like modernization, nation building, elites, integration. As for class, this group tended to take the position that this concept was only doubtfully relevant to the picture.[2]

As for the Africans themselves – both intellectuals and politicians – they found 'class' a nationally divisive concept (as indeed most found 'tribe'). They handled it by firmly denying its existence, or at least minimizing its significance.[3] That such a denial serves particular ideological functions for men in power seems so banal as to be scarcely worth noting.[4]

Thus by 1960, most analysts seemed to converge in an effort to bury class analysis in Africa.[5] However the 1960s were a traumatic decade for Africa in many ways. The aura of nationalist unity began to fade amidst the harsh daily realities of an independence which brought visibly widening income gaps for the African population, and military governments who made scarcely a pretense at intellectual appreciations of their own societies. Furthermore, the failure to 'develop' economically combined with the continuing resistance of the white redoubt of southern Africa to political change and majority rule tended to make very clear

2. Typical examples may be found in the special issue on 'African Elites' of the *International Social Science Bulletin*, 8: 3 (1956).

3. See the writings of any major African leader *circa* 1960, from Léopold Sédar-Senghor to Sékou Touré to Tom Mboya to Julius Nyerere. See the discussion in Robin Cohen, 'Class in Africa: Analytical Problems and Perspectives', *Socialist Register 1972* (London: Merlin Press, 1972), esp. pp. 231–4.

4. S. Ossowski made the best argument for this position in *Class Structure in the Social Consciousness* (London: Routledge and Kegan Paul, 1963). He argues that the positions of the political leadership of both the United States and the USSR reflect this phenomenon. See ch. 7.

5. Here and there some scholars spoke of these phenomena. See among others Martin Kilson, 'Nationalism and Social Classes in British West Africa', *Journal of Politics*, 20: 2 (May 1958), 368–87; Richard Sklar, *Nigerian Political Parties* (Princeton: Princeton University Press, 1963). I myself in 1962 discussed the class links of West African political parties. See 'Class, Tribe and Party in West African Politics', *Transactions of the Fifth World Congress of Sociology*, 3 (International Sociological Association, 1964), pp. 203–16, later published in expanded form in S. M. Lipset and S. Rokkan (eds.), *Party Systems and Voter Alignments* (New York: Free Press, 1967), pp. 497–518.

the world context within which African states operated. Some politicians began to talk of class conflict[6] and many African intellectuals began to theorize about Africa as a part of the 'peripheral capitalist' world.[7] Some began to criticize sharply the writings of what we have called the 'liberal-modernist' school, precisely because they ignored class analysis.[8]

This then is, if you will, the background in terms of intellectual history of the debate. It does not speak to the issues themselves. Can we speak of classes in contemporary Africa? Is class conflict a fundamental or even an important explanation of African political life? For those who argue 'no', the argument usually is based on the fact that some classes are largely 'missing' in Africa, or that 'ethnic' or other interpersonal links are far more determinative of political actions than class membership. Usually the negative position is couched, explicitly or implicitly, in a comparative frame: that while 'class' may be said to matter in Europe, it does not do so in Africa. This negative view, often expressed very cavalierly, seems to me to misread simultaneously the contemporary African scene, the real history of western Europe, and the arguments of classical Marxist class analysis.

Although the origin of the concept of class, and even of such key terms as proletarians, is derived from an analysis of Roman society,[9] the fond reference point of so many eighteenth-century and early-nineteenth-century thinkers, almost all of the concrete use of the terminology refers to capitalist systems. Indeed, it might be argued, although we shall not do it here, that the concept 'class' is historically specific to the capitalist mode of social organization. It might further be argued, and this I have done elsewhere,[10] that

6. For example, see Kwame Nkumah's last books, *Class Struggle in Africa* (New York: International Publishers, 1970).
7. Samir Amin is one of the most prominent of these. He is an Egyptian, but more importantly he is the Director of the African Institute of Economic Development and Planning, located in Dakar.
8. See for example Bernard Magubane, 'A Critical Look at Indices Used in the Study of Social Change in Colonial Africa', *Current Anthropology*, 12: 4–5 (October–December 1971), 419–30; cf. Archie Mafeje, 'The Ideology of Tribalism', *Journal of Modern African Studies*, 9: 2 (August 1971), 153–62.
9. Lorenz von Stein is probably the first to apply systematically the Roman concept 'proletarian' to the modern industrial world. See *The History of the Social Movement in France 1789–1850* (Totowa, New Jersey: Bedminster Press, 1964). Kaethe Mengelberg notes this in her introduction. See pp. 20–1.
10. See my *The Modern World-System: Capitalist Agriculture and the Origins of the European World-Economy in the Sixteenth Century* (New York and London: Seminar Press, 1974).

capitalism is to be located only in the form of world-system we have called a world-economy, and which has existed as a European system since about 1450, and as a global system since about 1815.

The peculiarity of the capitalist world-economy is that the boundaries of the economic and political structures are different. While the world-economy is defined as a system having a single division of labor, in a capitalist world-system the political units are states, which however vary in degree of strength *vis-à-vis* other states (the weakest form being the colony, which has no formal sovereignty at all). This results in the following situation. While a group's social activities are in some ultimate sense determined by their role in the world-economy, the object of their political activity (to secure or transform their position in the social system) is primarily directed at the state of which they are a member ('citizen').

This is very relevant to the confusion that surrounds the term 'class'. For class represents an antinomy, as a dialectical concept should. On the one hand, class is defined as relationship to the means of production, and hence position in the economic system which is a *world*-economy. On the other hand a class is a real actor only to the extent that it becomes class *conscious*, which means to the extent that it is organized as a *political* actor. But political actors are located primarily in particular national *states*. Class is not the one or the other. It is both, and class analysis is only meaningful to the extent that it is placed within a given historical context.

Nor is class consciousness the only form of consciousness. Empirically, it is obvious that within a capitalist world-economy ethno-national consciousness is a far more frequent phenomenon than class consciousness.[11] Furthermore, the interrelationship between class consciousness and ethno-national consciousness is not the same in states located in the periphery as against the core of the world-economy.[12]

11. Why this should be so I have discussed in 'Social Conflict in Post-Independence Black Africa: The Concepts of Race and Status Group Reconsidered', in Ernest F. Campbell (ed.), *Racial Tensions and National Identity* (Nashville: Vanderbilt University Press, 1972), pp. 207–26, and above, ch. 10.

12. There is even a further distinction to be made about the pattern to be found in the semiperiphery. For a discussion of this problem, see my 'Dependence in an Interdependent World: The Limited Possibilities of Transformation within the Capitalist World-Economy', *African Studies Review*, 17: 1 (April 1974), 1–26, and above, ch. 4.

We have suggested previously that there are two forms of ethnic consciousness.[13] Here we would like to argue that there are (at least) two forms of class consciousness, and that while the *form* of class consciousness and class conflict may be different in contemporary African states from that of, say, contemporary western Europe, they are both expressions of *class* interest. Not can *either* be understood without taking into account the position of each state within the world-economy. We can then evaluate for a given group the socio-economic consequences within this *world-economy* of particular class-oriented action undertaken at the *national* level.

As the European world-economy took form in the 'long' sixteenth century, various geographic regions moved into particular structural roles, and then provisionally could be said to have become locked into these roles. Thus, for example, Poland developed into a peripheral area, specializing in the production and export of wheat and wood. Over a period of 200 years (1450–1650), land was consolidated under the aegis of aristocratic owners, and peasants were bound to this land by legislation (the so-called 'second feudalism'). The indigenous commercial bourgeoisie was wiped out and replaced by merchants of foreign origin. Artisanry virtually disappeared. And the authority of the state steadily declined.

At the very same time, England developed in quite a different direction. Starting in 1450 as primarily an exporter of wool, with a state structure that had been bled by the Wars of the Roses, a commercial class still dominated by Italians and Hanseates, they were by 1650 part of the core of the European world-economy. Most of their agriculture and pasturage had been commercialized and divided between both large and small landowners. Agricultural workers were wage workers. Merchants were now only Englishmen. And England now forbade the export of wool but exported instead the 'new draperies'. The strength of the state machinery had steadily increased. Even the English Civil War was less a challenge of the strengthened

13. See my 'The Two Modes of Ethnic Consciousness: Soviet Central Asia in Transition?', in Edward Allworth (ed.), *The Nationality Question in Soviet Central Asia* (New York: Praeger, 1973), pp. 168–75, and above, ch. 11.

state than a quarrel over whose interests it should primarily serve.[14]

If we then look at the European world-economy, we notice that the division of labor had been made relatively (and of course transitorily) firm. As a result, such states as England and Poland (but of course not only them) varied not only in the strength of their state machineries but in the range of economic roles located within them, the 'nationality' of the tenants of these roles, and the degree of nation orientedness of various groups.

Thus, classes may be said to have emerged as objective realities within the world-economy. That is, an analyst can certainly discern distinctive economic roles, which relate to the capitalist mode of production. Owners of land, bullion, and ships were in an entirely different relationship to the market than workers who had nothing to sell but their labor (and who in the sixteenth century were for the most part constrained by law to sell their labor extremely cheap, as slaves, or 'serfs', or *encomendados*).

On the other hand, it is quite clear that conscious classes, that is groups seeking to legitimize their existence and secure political advantage, were only emerging in the core states (England, United Provinces, and to some extent France). Furthermore, the only group in the core areas that was becoming conscious of itself as a class was the bourgeoisie *of these areas*. Their consciousness was a mode of challenging the inherited privileges of strata who were no longer a relevant economic corporate group but whose social advantages were still encrusted and protected by law and custom, and who therefore remained a real social group but not a class (the 'aristocracy').

The developments of sixteenth-century Europe were essentially repeated in the nineteenth- and twentieth-century world with Africa developing along the lines that Poland had in the 'long' sixteenth century. That is, over 200 years (say 1750–1950), African areas were absorbed into the capitalist world-economy. Land was commercialized and concentrated (though for various reasons not on the scale of Poland). Various indigenous commer-

14. For some discussion of why Poland and England should have moved in opposite directions at this time, see my 'Three Paths of National Development in Sixteenth-Century Europe', *Studies in Comparative International Development*, 7: 2 (Summer 1972), 95–101, and above, ch. 2.

cial classes were squeezed out or reduced in role to the benefit of non-indigenous merchant elements. The role of the state structures were reduced to zero ('colonization').

In the core regions during this same period (now western Europe including Germany plus the United States), the internal diversity of economic role grew steadily greater and the state machineries ever more total in their control. Because this period of the history of the capitalist world-economy was marked by the displacement of capitalist agriculture by manufacturing as the primary source of profits, the industrial proletariat as such became a significantly large group in the *core* countries of the world-economy.

Because also in the nineteenth century, the core countries were virtually alone as manufacturing areas, this industrial proletariat was in a very weak bargaining position and hence suffered appalling conditions. Consequently, they developed a class consciousness of this proletariat to struggle politically against a now politically entrenched bourgeoisie.

In peripheral areas, such as Africa, developments were quite different. Class consciousness was not yet a relevant political tool. The indigenous capitalist landowners felt rather like their *confrères* of sixteenth-century Poland, that their interests lay in the smooth flow of international trade to which any kinds of struggle (either 'nationalist' or 'class') represented an interruption and a threat. The administrative bourgeoisie which emerged was at first too small to be politically significant.

With the further development of the world-economy, however, this latter group grew larger and in some areas (but largely not in Africa) a small indigenous manufacturing sector grew up. Thus in the twentieth century, we get the turmoil of revolt, but one primarily couched (certainly in Africa) in 'nationalist' terms, since what the administrative bourgeoisie was seeking was to replace (partially) external elements playing roles they felt they could perform. (And when 'nationalist' clothing would not work, 'tribalist' clothing could be substituted.)

The agricultural workers in Africa have not been class conscious within the nation since, as they have correctly seen, the action relevant to them is not there. A class conscious proletariat cannot emerge before in fact it represents a larger sector of the population.

Meanwhile, the same 'further development' of the world-economy in the twentieth century made possible the partial muting of the class conflict of the core countries by the absorption of skilled industrial workers into privileged sectors and by the increasing recruitment of subproletarian sectors from distinctive ethno-national groups.

This has been only the briefest of sketches of an extremely complex historical development. The object has been to suggest conceptual frameworks which would make possible a meaningful usage of class and class conflict in the analysis of contemporary Africa. The heart of our argument is based on the assumption that if one wishes to abstract some order out of the continuous flow of historical reality, it is important first of all to locate the 'primary contradiction' of a given political situation at a given time.

We are arguing that, in general, in a capitalist world-economy, the primary contradiction within *core* areas is to be located in the quarrel over the ambiguous and ambivalent role of the state structure, whose control is sought by different groups, both primarily located within its boundaries. This struggle, when it is sharp, is national in scope and 'class conscious' in terminology. This is what comes within the usual image of 'class analysis'.

In *peripheral* areas of the world-economy, however, the primary contradiction is not between two groups within a state each trying to gain control of that state structure, or to bend it. The primary contradiction is between the interests organized and located in the core countries and their local allies on the one hand, and the majority of the population on the other. In point of fact then, an 'anti-imperialist' nationalist struggle is in fact a mode of expression of class-interest. This is what Cabral means by using the term 'nation-class'.[15] That such an *expression* of the class struggle can also be a mode of muting it is of course the great danger, and this is the gist of the analysis of Fanon.[16]

The reality of class is not lessened by the very real resistance to class analysis, nor by its rarity as a political phenomenon. If class conflict were indeed the major preoccupation of most actors

15. Amilcar Cabral, 'The Weapon of Theory', in *Revolution in Guinea* (New York: Monthly Review Press, 1968), pp. 90–111.
16. Frantz Fanon, *The Wretched of the Earth* (New York: Grove Press, 1965), esp. pp. 121–63.

in the world-economy at any given time, the world-system would not long survive in its present form. The strength of ethno-national consciousness is in fact one of the most cohesive factors in the existing world-system. But strength and weakness are relative, not absolute. And above all, strength and weakness are measurements eternally in flux.

13 ❧ American slavery and the capitalist world-economy

The publication in 1974 of two major works on slavery in the United States has been an academic event. All the more so in that it has not escaped notice that the two interpretations – one steeped in the tradition of neoclassical economics, the other in Marxian historiography – are, at one and the same time, competing, overlapping, and complementary. The two books speak to, and are designed to speak to, the central socio-political tension of American national life: the systematic oppression of Blacks, its causes and consequences, economic, political, and social. It is therefore quite understandable that both books have been widely reviewed and have given rise to debate and controversy and many symposia. Indeed, an analysis of the reviews and commentaries would in itself give considerable insight into the contemporary American scene.

The authors of both books claim that, by reviewing historical reality, they are seeking to rescue the Black from unwarranted opprobrium. They do so, however, in strikingly different ways. Reduced to an extremely crude and oversimplified summary, Fogel and Engerman defend the Black against the charge of laziness and incompetence by arguing that the nineteenth-century slave in fact worked hard and efficiently, while Genovese defends him against the charge of having been weak or cowardly by arguing that the stance of 'accommodationism' and 'joy in life' was a subtle and efficacious form of resistance and probably the optimal political tactic for the period.

There are at least three different levels at which one could fruitfully criticize these works. One could discuss the social objectives of the authors and the ways in which their writing affects the contemporary political scene. Or one could discuss the concepts they have used to organize their material and how those are tied together theoretically. Or one could discuss the nature and quality of the evidence the authors put forward and the kinds of inferences they draw from it.

Both the first and the third kind of critical analysis have been widespread. With regard to their social objectives and consequences, both books have been heatedly attacked and passionately defended, especially *Time On the Cross*. Specifically, it has been argued (and denied) that the various 'rectifications' they attempt about the day to day reality of slave life end up as apologia, however unintended, for slave owners and slavery as a system. It is no accident, therefore, that many Black scholars have been quite angry about the books.

As for the process of evidence and inference, the two works illustrate quite different styles. Fogel and Engerman explicitly present their book as an example of the usefulness of cliometrics, 'a set of tools which are of considerable help in analyzing an important but limited set of problems' (p. 9).[1] Genovese says, on the other hand, that 'the subject of this book is the quality of life which largely defies measurement' (p. 676). The contrast between a 'scientific' and a 'humanistic' style (which is not at all a distinction, if there be one, between scientific and humane knowledge) is an old one, and despite the brouhaha of the publishers of *Time on the Cross*, no new twists are evident in the work of Fogel and Engerman. I leave quite to the side, furthermore, the criticisms of other cliometricians who argue that *Time on the Cross* is bad cliometrics, as I do the criticisms of Genovese by other Marxists who contend that *Roll, Jordan, Roll* is bad Marxism.

I leave them on the side. I do not necessarily agree or disagree. But I do not wish to be diverted from what I think would be useful: to discuss the theoretical adequacy of the interpretations. I do this out of a sense of intellectual priorities at this particular moment in history. I have a feeling that the methodological issues have been for the moment fully explored, at least as far as our governing theoretical frameworks permit. I believe too that the debate on the social functions of ideas, science as ideology, was clearly laid on the table in the 1960s, and that to pursue the matter

1. Unless otherwise indicated, all page references for *Time on the Cross* are to vol. 1.

further at this time is to escape into pastimes rather than to attack central issues. In my view, the key intellectual bottleneck at the moment is theoretical. We are facing the need to rethink and restate the conceptual frameworks we have inherited from the nineteenth century in order to understand and contribute meaningfully to the long world-systemic transition to socialism which has begun and in which we are living. Both books illustrate very well the nature of these intellectual difficulties.

First of all, neither book focuses on the problems of conceptualization. Fogel and Engerman are very aware of the social function of knowledge and indeed devote a good deal of space to the evolution of what they call 'the traditional interpretation of the slave economy' (passim, but esp. vol. 2, pp. 168–247). They attack the racist assumptions they assert underlay this so-called traditional interpretation, which they trace back to the 'racist myopia' of 'antebellum critics of slavery' (p. 215). The racism of the abolitionists in turn is explained by 'their greater physical separation from blacks', which made them more 'gullible [about] racial stereotypes' than slaveholders, and their upper-class 'conceptions regarding the behavior of all laboring folk', a failing 'they shared with slaveholders' (p. 136).

In addition, Fogel and Engerman constantly present their empirical evidence as surprising. Indeed their prologue offers us (pp. 4–6) ten 'principal corrections of the traditional characterization of the slave economy'. They promptly link these 'surprising' findings to the first concern by raising the question of 'how those who fashioned the traditional interpretation of the slave system could have been so wrong' (p. 6) and suggesting that the findings will 'not only expose many myths that have served to corrode and poison relations between the races, but also help to put into a new perspective some of the most urgent issues of our day' (pp. 8–9).

The one thing Fogel and Engerman do *not* do is to reconceptualize. It is not that they are unconcerned with theory. Rather, they assume that the theory with which they work is so adequate that all that is necessary is to do the cliometric research and then use the theory to interpret the findings. Thus volume 1 gives us the findings in narrative form and the interpretation and volume 2 the evidence and methods for the nitpickers. The epilogue to volume 1 discusses the 'implications for our times'. But so much is the theorizing based on unexamined assumptions that when the authors wish to outline their views on such an inherently controversial concept as 'exploitation', they refer us to *Webster's Third New International Dictionary*.

This problem is less severe with Genovese. He is not smug about the theory. Indeed, he recognizes that he is on difficult, indeed precarious, ground in his argument that the 'Old South, black and white, created a historically unique kind of paternalist society' (p. 4). In fact, much of his book can be taken as a plea for a reassessment of such central theoretical issues as the relationship of slaveholding to a capitalist world market, the constraints that religious and ethical world views place on the social relations of production, and the complex meanings of social interaction: 'Gratitude implies equality' (p. 146). Indeed, in an earlier article Genovese was so concerned about 'vulgar Marxism' which 'offers us the dead bones of a soulless mechanism' (Genovese 1968) that he spent the whole article denouncing a materialist analysis of slavery (that of Marvin Harris) and showing the usefulness, once properly reinterpreted, of two idealist accounts (those of Gilberto Freyre and Frank Tannenbaum).

So Genovese cannot be faulted for unawareness of theoretical issues. But he gets swept away in the majesty and wonderful complexity of his story. His subtitle is *The World the Slaves Made*, and he really offers us this, with rich texture and impressive scholarship. Indeed, the book is virtually an encyclopedic ethnography and, like all really good ones, offers immense pickings for future scholars. They will take, I am sure, many short descriptions and perceptive insights and expand them into a panoply of derived work.

Genovese offers us balance and perspective. But the reconceptualization he knows is needed peters out in a meandering apppendix on 'the fate of paternalism in modern bourgeois society: the case of Japan'. No doubt his way of presenting data as raising doubts about theory is far more fruitful than Fogel and Engerman's crisp assumption that they are validating theory, but it is not enough. Nor is it enough to engage in frequent and relevant comparisons to illuminate the data. For one has a feeling that the comparisons in both books are often between a concrete reality the authors know well and other situations about which myths or partial truths are perceived as empirical descriptions.

Since the bulk of each book is concerned with the actual findings, it is only fair to review them. And here we come up with a discovery that perhaps not everyone would expect (I did not): the pictures drawn in both books are very similar. The composite picture may be divided into four main parts: the issue of the efficiency of slave labor; the description of the extent of material and spiritual oppression of the slaves; the nature of family life; and the relationship of the most educated and privileged stratum of slaves to the others.

Efficiency is Fogel and Engerman's big thing. The typical slave field hand 'was harder-working and more efficient than his white counterpart' (p. 5). We even get statistical arguments that are quite precise. Slave farms are '28 percent more efficient' than southern free farms and '40 percent more efficient' than northern farms (p. 192).

As a result of this high efficiency, slavery was profitable. 'The discovery of a high and persistent rate of profit on slaves constitutes a serious, and probably irreparable, blow to the thesis that the price of slaves was largely attributable to conspicuous consumption' (p. 70). The discovery of the profitability of slavery 'throws into doubt' arguments that slaveholders were 'precapitalist' or 'uncommercial' or that they 'subordinated profits to consideration of power, life-style, and "patriarchal commitments"' (p. 71).

Furthermore, since slaves could be rented as well as bought and since 'hiring was not a minor or inconsequential feature of slavery' (p. 56), it followed that slavery was *not* 'incompatible with the shifting labor requirements of capitalist society' (p. 57).

And why was slavery so efficient? The answer is simple. The plantation was the original factory. The 'crux', the 'key' feature was the fact that slaves were organized into 'highly disciplined, interdependent teams capable of maintaining a steady and intense rhythm of work' (p. 204). The authors go further: 'ordinary slaves could be diligent workers, imbued like their masters with a Protestant ethic...' (p. 231). Thus it was that size of unit could be made to pay off. 'Economies of scale were achieved only with slave labor' (p. 194). Nor could such economies be achieved without the use of force. Fogel and Engerman find a superbly sterilized way of stating that point: 'The special advantage of slavery for agricultural production, then, is that it was a very cheap way of "compensating" slaves for the nonpecuniary disadvantages of gang labor' (p. 238).

We are told by Fogel and Engerman that Genovese disagrees, that Genovese thinks 'slavery was economically inefficient', although he is 'ambivalent on the issue of profitability' (p. 64). But to what extent does he disagree in fact? He does not disagree that slave owners responded to the market, reducing 'the size of their slave force for reasons of efficiency' (p. 401) and for the same reasons at other points engaging in hiring. He specifically criticizes Du Bois for overestimating the 'Puritan work ethic' (p. 311) of white European immigrants and agrees that slaves were willing 'to work extraordinarily hard', although he does add that they resisted 'the discipline of regularity' and 'responded to moral as well as economic incentives' (p. 313).

Nor does Genovese disagree that slave plantations could resemble 'factories in the field'. But he thinks that such a description, while correct for the great slave sugar plantations of the Caribbean, did not quite apply to the tobacco and cotton plantations of the US South. The system there was 'a halfway house between peasant and factory cultures' (p. 286). A difference to be sure, but not as sharp a contrast as Fogel and Engerman seem to think, and even Genovese to imply. Genovese does not think that slaves acted exclusively or totally as routinized workers, but does he in fact think that industrial factory workers do so? And do Fogel and Engerman? The actual pattern of work under modern capitalism does not fit Henry Ford's dream, despite all the efforts of Taylorism, as a plenitude of monographs have instructed us.

If there remain some differences between Fogel and Engerman and Genovese on efficiency, there are far fewer when it comes to discussing the quality of life. Life was difficult, both books argue, but it was no concentration camp (as Elkins and others had implied). As usual, Fogel and Engerman are more blunt: 'The material (and psychological) conditions of the lives of slaves compared favorably with those of free industrial workers' (p. 5). Less, they hasten to add, because conditions of slaves were so good than because those of free workers were so poor. And we do have to remember the previously cited 'nonpecuniary disadvantages of gang labor'. Conditions were not so good that anyone volunteered for the job. Genovese comes at the same theme from another entry point. He repeats on a number of occasions that in the nineteenth century, particularly between 1831 and 1861, the 'condition of the slaves...got better with respect to material conditions of life' (p. 51). Earlier the slaves *had* 'often suffered terribly', but in 'the nineteenth century the demands for improvement sounded on all sides' (p. 550).

Fogel and Engerman say that 'the average daily diet of slaves was quite substantial' (p. 113). Genovese seems to go along, as usual less fulsomely and more precisely: 'From the eighteenth century onward many slaves had a better diet than rural whites because they made an effort to raise vegetables' (p. 535). For Fogel and Engerman, 'the houses of slaves compared well with the housing of free workers in the antebellum era' (p. 116). Genovese makes the same comparison more negatively: 'The laboring poor of France, England, and even the urban Northeast of the United States, not to mention Sicily or Russia, lived in crowded hovels little better and often worse than the slave quarters' (p. 526).

Whippings were a part of the system, but scarcely as pervasive as generally thought, say Fogel and Engerman. 'Although some masters were brutal, even sadistic, most were not' (p. 146). Actually, as they see it, such whippings as occurred were a largely economic device. Free workers who shirked 'could be fired – left to starve beyond the eyesight or expense of the employer...Planters preferred whipping to incarceration because the lash did not generally lead to an extended loss of the slave's labor time' (p. 147). Once again, Genovese's emphasis is on improvement over time. Whipping in the nineteenth century replaced 'branding, ear cropping, and assorted mutilations' of earlier eras (p. 67). Overseers were held in check. 'No sensible shareholder wanted a man who could not maintain a certain level of morale among the slaves' (p. 15).

Fogel and Engerman congratulate themselves on rectifying the overstatements of the so-called traditional interpretation of slavery because 'it has diverted attention from the attack on the material conditions of black life that took place during the decades following the end of the Civil War. By exaggerating the severity of slavery, all that has come after it has been made to appear an improvement over previous conditions' (p. 260). No doubt a sound point. And Genovese goes one step further. In many ways, the situation was *worse* after the war. He says of family life for example: 'The postbellum record should not be projected backward' (p. 501).

The family is another arena of convergence. The destruction of the Black family under slavery is a 'myth' (p. 5), say Fogel and Engerman. Indeed, the family was 'of central importance' to the organization of the plantation, as the 'administrative unit for...distribution', as an 'important instrument for maintaining labor discipline', and as 'the main instrument for promoting the increase of the slave population' (p. 127). And the husband played 'the dominant role in slave society' (p. 141). Both planters and slaves agreed that it was important to 'encourage the development of stable nuclear families' (p. 142). Both Black promiscuity and widespread sexual exploitation of slave women are contentions for which there is 'virtually no evidence' (p. 135).

For Genovese, what did occur was a 'scandal', but the 'plantations hardly emerge from the statistics looking like the harems of abolitionist fantasy' (p. 145). As for marital infidelity, the evidence cannot sustain a charge that it was widespread. This charge 'may in fact largely reflect perceptions of postbellum conditions of social disorganization' (p. 467). As for family life itself, Genovese says that the data demand 'a reassessment of slave family life as having had much greater power than generally believed' (p. 451). The slaves created 'as much of a nuclear family norm as conditions permitted' (p. 452). The dignity of many men ('How many? No one will ever know') survived the indignities and 'came out of this test of fire whole, if necessarily scarred, to demonstrate that the slaves had powerful inner resources' (p. 491). As for the children, 'their early and formative years had offered a semblance of childhood, at least relative to the children of other laboring classes' (p. 505).

On the issue of the more privileged stratum of slaves, the approaches are quite different – for Fogel and Engerman, they represent the evidence of mobility, while for Genovese they pose the dilemmas of political opposition – but are the data so different? Fogel and Engerman say that slaves were 'fairly well-represented in most of the skilled crafts' (p. 38) and 'to a surprising extent...held the top managerial posts' (p. 39). Slave society 'produced a complex social hierarchy which was closely related to the occupational pyramid' (p. 40). Genovese says: 'The wealthier plantations resembled industrial villages, and substantial numbers of slaves acquired a high level of skill in a wide variety of trades' (p. 388). He does think, however, that this phenomenon was on the *decline* in the nineteenth century and attributes this to 'the South's growing dependence on northern manufactures and...increasingly exclusionist policies enforced by hostile white labor in the towns' (p. 389).

For Fogel and Engerman the politics of this middle stratum of southern society are simple. Despite higher pay and 'room for upward mobility...the scope of opportunity should not be exaggerated' (p. 152). Therefore it was 'on the talented, the upper crust of slave society, that deprivation of the peculiar institution hung most heavy' (p. 153). Thus they were the first to flee. They were seeking individual salvation. Genovese has a more complicated and generous vision. They were 'men between', striving 'to mediate between the Big House and the quarters, to lower the level of violence, to maintain order in the most human way available'. The driver, for example, mediated by 'instilling a more modern work discipline in his people' and at the same time offering 'some protection..against factorylike regimentation' (pp. 378–9). They both 'assumed the role of accommodationist and became the master's man' (p. 386) and 'provided the firmest social basis for a radical political leadership, as their repeated appearance in insurrectionary plots shows' (p. 394). Thus, for Genovese: 'The house servants did not so much stand between two cultures as they remained suspended between two politics' (p. 365).

Although the facts both books present seem to converge, time and again, the author's stances are strikingly different. Fogel and Engerman come to the data as calculating economic men. They try to figure out primarily why the firm acts as it does in terms of maximizing profit, and only secondarily how the worker operates within these parameters to extract advantage. Genovese is interested in the 'frog perspective', as Richard Wright called it. For him, the primary question is how the slave coped with an oppressive system, and only second how the slaveowner responded to the *political* action of the slaves.

This contrast explains why at least three major themes run through Genovese's book which are nowhere to be seen in that of Fogel and Engerman. One is the African legacy to Afro-American – 'a life-affirming faith that stressed shame and minimized guilt' (p. 247). The second is 'the development of the black nation within the American nation' (p. 449). The third, and by far the most important, is Black Christianity. I will not review here the panorama which provides indeed both the framework and the leitmotif of the book. I have no doubt that it represents Genovese's most substantial contribution and the one for which the book will be remembered.

In his view, in the 'dialectic of accommodation and resistance' (p. 658), the 'protonational consciousness' of the Blacks was 'expressed primarily through a religious sensibility' (p. 659). The book indeed closes on what I believe to be its true thesis: 'Black religion, understood as a critical world-view in the process of becoming – as something unfinished, often inconsistent, and in some respects even incoherent – emerged as the slaves' most formidable weapon for resisting slavery's moral and psychological aggression' (p. 659).

I have spent so much space outlining the presentations of data, because, as I have already said, they represent the thrust of both books, the residue left from reading them and studying them. Let me now turn to the theoretical issues that I believe are illuminated by both books but not dealt with in an ultimately satisfactory way.

The theoretical debate underlying these books concerns the nature of capitalism as a social system. Fogel and Engerman are adherents of the basic Smithian view that the search for profit via market exchange is a 'natural propensity' of humankind, operating as a kind of continuing psychological priority in all sane persons. The state sometimes interferes with this propensity, but the propensity is there nonetheless, unrestrained and unrestrainable – somewhat like the Freudian id which the ego contains but never subdues.

From this perspective, the 'traditional interpretation' of slavery was very disturbing. Of the five propositions Fogel and Engerman say define that interpretation (vol. 2, pp. 169ff.), the first four seem to indicate that slavery in the United States South represented economically irrational behavior: it was an unprofitable investment; it was economically moribund; slave labor was inefficient; slavery retarded growth.

Given their starting point, Fogel and Engerman were genuinely puzzled. Were these propositions true, why did slavery last so long, and why did it take a civil war to bring it to an end? The answer they come up with is at once simple and comforting. The propositions are not true. *Ergo*, there is no anomaly. This approach explains also why they do not pose other questions, such as how then to explain the outbreak of the Civil War, why slavery persisted longer in the southern states than in the Caribbean, why there was opposition to extending slave structures to the newly opening western areas of the United States. These questions are irrelevant to their purpose, which was to clear up an apparent anomaly in the data that would have called into question the basic theory.

The view of Fogel and Engerman is highly economistic. The state is a mere superstructure, and analysts should not dwell on its role excessively. Thus while the legal institutions of the antebellum South may have been 'pre-bourgeois', the economic structures were not. 'While the South developed a highly capitalistic form of agriculture, and while its economic behaviour was as strongly ruled by profit maximization as that of the North, the relationship between its ruling and its servile class was marked by patriarchal features which were strongly reminiscent of medieval life' (p. 129).

But this is only a minor variation on the theme of profit and property. People are a form of capital, *human* capital. 'Viewed in this light, the crucial difference between slave and free society rests not *on the existence* of property rights in man, in human capital, but on who may hold title to such property rights' (p. 233).

Genovese, starting from a Marxist perspective, faces entirely different dilemmas. For Marx, capitalism was a historically specific mode of production. It was not embedded in human nature, for human nature was an abstraction with no empirical reality.

Furthermore, it was a mode of production that came in a world-historical sequence. Over historical time, with the evolution of the material base of human societies (in terms of accumulated past labor embodied in machines and technology), new relations of production were established, which throughout all of known history involved the division of men into classes. Within each mode of production, groups tended to polarize into two basic classes, one of which (the smaller) exploited the other, thus generating a struggle between them, which eventually ended in the transformation of the system into another successive form.

Given this paradigm, the problem (as Engels made explicit in various famous leters) was not to explain the broad strokes of history – that could be easily and intelligently done, as demonstrated by the *Communist Manifesto* – but to explain the complicated detail: the long and murky 'transitions' from one mode of production to another, the workings of 'uneven development', the superstructural 'lags'. There have been three responses historically by Marxists to these complications: to ignore them, as do the 'vulgar Marxists', who turn out to be Smithians at heart; to be overwhelmed by them, as are the 'ex-Marxists', who usually become Weberians; to take them as both the key intellectual *and* the key political problem of Marxists. One type of current jargon calls this last response 'Gramscian', although to be sure Gramsci was by no means the only prominent Marxist thinker to make it. Both Lenin and Mao, to cite only the two most obvious, are clearly in this group. In any case, Genovese clearly states his indebtedness to Gramsci, in particular to his theories of hegemony and of political consciousness.

The problem for Genovese, given his strong evolutionary thrust, is the question of seeming 'regression'. 'At first glance, the legal history of Western Europe represents an anomaly. The law arose in early modern times on rational rather than traditional, patrimonial, or charismatic foundations, however many elements of these remained' (p. 44). It was *into* this system, in which private property was already ensconced, that slavery was introduced. Thus it is quite different from slavery in the ancient world, as Genovese makes clear. Genovese says that Fogel and Engerman concentrate on the economic costs of 'the reintroduction of precapitalist elements into the legal system' but that he, Genovese, is concerned rather with 'the effect of the imposed duality created by the reintroduction as well as the continuation of precapitalist ideas of power and property into an inherited system of bourgeois-shaped rational jurisprudence' (p. 46). Thus paternalism in a capitalist world was a reality, not an ideological fiction, although, adds Genovese, as with all human institutions its contradictions undid it. This happened because paternalism was a two-edged sword, and the slaves 'acted consciously and unconsciously to transform paternalism into a doctrine of protection of their own rights – a doctrine that represented the negation of the idea of slavery itself' (p. 49).

Thus we have an irony. Fogel and Engerman, avowed liberals, write what is to my mind one of the strongest politico-moral justifications for the theories of Karl Marx since Engels's *Condition of the Working Classes in England*. They argue with remarkable clarity that capitalists use the state machinery, both the carrot and the stick, to maximize their individual profits, and that the less individual freedom accorded the worker, the more profitable the system. On the other hand, Genovese, an avowed Marxist, might be said to make a case for conservative (idealist) theories about the ways in which political and cultural institutions tend to explain the largest part of historical reality. 'Only those who romanticize – and therefore do not respect – the laboring classes would fail to understand their deep commitment to "law and order"; life is difficult enough without added uncertainty and "confusion". Even an oppressive and unjust order is better than none' (p. 115). Ideologies, repeats Genovese over and over, are not merely 'self-serving and radically false'. They can also be an 'authentic world-view...developed in accordance with the reality of social relations', and hence embraced 'without hypocrisy' (p. 86). We cannot wish away paternalism with a sneer of contempt. It constituted in fact the 'rich experience' of the daily lives of slaves, who truly 'expressed admiration for the aristocratic features of southern life' (p. 115), while turning such admiration into 'a weapon of defense' (p. 116).

It is a striking feature of both works that they are so geogra-phically self-contained. Not that this is so unusual in modern social science. Nor do the authors fail to make 'comparisons'. Indeed both books abound in comparisons with other 'entities'. (I call them 'entities' because sometimes what are compared are firms, sometimes states, sometimes other groupings, and frequently a melange.) But at crucial points in the analysis, the fact that the American South was an arena in a *world*-economy is left out of consideration and hence the analysis is falsified.

Consider for example *Time on the Cross*. Chapter 1 is dutifully called 'The International Context of U.S. Slavery'. We are told of the origins of the Atlantic slave trade and the course of emancipation throughout the world. But it is only at the very end of the book that we learn, literally parenthetically, that 'most US cotton was consumed not in the United States but abroad' (pp. 245–6). There is no hint, even in passing, that British interests may have played a historic role in the perpetuation of slavery in the US South. Instead, we are told: 'Although it may be surprising to some readers, the main gainers from the gang system were not slaveholders but consumers of cotton' (p. 244). How carefully phrased. We are led to envisage the greedy customer buying a shirt cheap somewhere out there and thereby exploiting the Alabama fieldhand, when Fogel and Engerman know quite well that the bulk of the gain was creamed off by the primary 'consumers', the textile *manufacturers*.

Or take a theme which runs through both Fogel and Engerman and Genovese but which neither book explains very well: the relative material improvement of the conditions of the slaves in the decades immediately preceding the Civil War. This coincided, as Genovese notes (but Fogel and Engerman characteristically do not), with an increase in legal repression: more welfare, more 'rights', but also fewer manumissions. Genovese says of this apparent 'paradox' that the same men supported both trends and that their position 'made perfect sense' since it combined perpetual slavery with 'making it possible for [slaves] to accept their fate' (p. 51). But, if this is so, why was such a perfectly sensible solution only put into effect in 1831? Why not in 1731?

The answer gets us to the heart of the issue. In 1731 there was an international slave trade; in 1831 there was not, or at least there was none that permitted slaves to be brought from distant places to the United States. This change had come about because of both the industrial revolution of 1760–1830 and the definitive establishment of British world hegemony after 1815. Both the need for West Africa as a crop-producing area and the desire (and ability) to deny *European* competitors slave producers led to Britain's enforcement (selective, be it noted) of the abolition of the slave trade and encouragement in areas outside its own supply zones (such as the US South and Brazil) of emancipation.

These facts led quite directly to a number of phenomena mentioned in both books. It seems self-evident that if you cannot import new slaves from elsewhere (the United States from 1808 on) you have to reproduce them yourself and that this fact alone will require improvement of material conditions, including the encouragement of a stronger nuclear family. (It will also lead to tightening up on manumission.) Of course, there are contradictions, since this process makes slave labor more expensive, but then that is exactly what the incorporation of the West African external arena as a peripheral area of the capitalist world-economy did do, and why indeed slavery finally would disappear entirely. It disappeared *not* because it was incompatible with capitalism (here Fogel and Engerman are far nearer the truth than Genovese), but because it was incompatible with a capitalist world-economy that no longer had an external arena to bear the bulk of the cost of slave breeding.

Fogel and Engerman talk of a 'high break-even age' for US planters with regard to slaves – hence medical care for slave children and encouragement of fertility of slave women 'while slaveowners in other parts of the hemisphere appear to have discouraged it' (p. 155). Precisely. 'Of all the slave societies in the New World, that of the Old South alone maintained a slave force that reproduced itself' (Genovese, p. 5). And why? Because in Brazil, for example, at that time they were still importing slaves from Mozambique, and it *cost less* to buy an adult slave than to rear your own (because of loss of mother's work time, costs of child rearing, etc.).

But notice how bizarrely these facts come out in Fogel and Engerman. They tell us that in Jamaica (unlike the United States), life expectation fell below the 'break-even age'. Let us ignore the fact that for Jamaica they are talking of the eighteenth century and for the Old South of the nineteenth. Let us merely see what comes next: 'Consequently, during most of the eighteenth century, masters in colonies such as Jamaica discouraged family formation and high fertility rates, preferring to buy adult slaves in Africa rather than to rear them' (pp. 155–6). Consequently? It was just the opposite. As long as plantation owners could buy slaves in Africa, who cared about the break-even age which was calculated on the basis of owning slaves throughout their life cycle? The 'consequently' illustrates in the clearest possible way the fundamentally unhistorical nature of the analysis of Fogel and Engerman. But, of course, if capitalism is a natural propensity, why bother with mere history – inaccurate, confusing, anecdotal?

Or consider the rejection by Fogel and Engerman of the contention of Hinton Rowan Helper, made in 1857, that the South was a 'colonial dependency'. Not so, say Fogel and Engerman, for were it so, 'how are we to characterize the states that occupy the territory running from the western border of Pennsylvania to the western border of Nebraska?' And, presumably even more telling: 'The South's large purchases of manufactured goods from the North made it no more of a colonial dependency than did the North's heavy purchases of rails from England.' The South (were it a separate nation) would have stood fourth in the world in wealth, exceeded only by Australia (top of the list – did you not know that in 1860 Australia had the highest per capita income in the world?), the North, and Great Britain. 'Indeed, a country *as advanced as Italy* [italics mine] did not achieve the southern level of per capita income until the eve of World War II.' And finally: 'The true colonial dependencies, countries such as India and Mexico, had less than one tenth the per capita income of the South in 1860' (p. 249).

With so much obfuscation, where do we begin? In the uncomplex world that Fogel and Engerman construct there are a few 'real colonies', presumably badly off, maybe (dare I suggest it?) even exploited, and *all the rest* of the world is composed of countries that are presumably equal trading partners in a system wherein comparative advantage reigns supreme and per capita income measures how hard you work ('efficiency'). Absent from this world is unequal exchange: peripheralization leading to a *variety* of economic roles for the peripheral areas of the world-economy, which have different modes of labor control (raw material cash-crops based on slave labor for the US South contrasted with food cash-crops based on small freeholds in the US

'West'); the concept of a semiperipheral area (such as the US North), at once exploiting and exploited and seeking to break loose and become a core nation by snapping the economic umbilical cord of the South to Great Britain. 'As advanced as Italy?' An Italy just achieving the political framework with which to compete in the world-economy, an Italy whose South became a major labor reserve for the United States, Brazil, and the Italian North precisely at the moment when slavery was finally disappearing (was it so coincidental? See Ianni 1965).

Genovese, by contrast, never oversimplifies. But occasionally his stress on complexity prevents clarity. His book is an exercise from beginning to end in the subtle intertwinings of a 'paternalist' structure. But what of the elementary question: is paternalism *in contradiction with* capitalist social relations? I have the sense that for Genovese the answer is an impatient of course – in 'contradiction with', though of course not 'incompatible with'. Let me suggest another possible approach. The particular form of paternalism which Genovese describes is, as I am sure Genovese would agree, quite different from classical feudal social relations, and is on many continua somewhere between the latter and purely market-oriented contractual relations. Units based on this form of paternalism can be seen as units in transition, ones resisting capitalization, ones whose power to survive needs to be explained. This is essentially Genovese's approach, it seems to me, and one firmly in the Maurice Dobb version of Marxist analysis in which Genovese specifically places himself (p. 688, n. 71).

But suppose the forms Genovese is describing are not transitional or remnants or pockets of resistance but the heart and essence of capitalism as a mode of production, which could be seen as a system that contains within its economic arena *some* firms largely based on contractual wage labor and *some* (even most) firms based on one variant or another of coerced or semicoerced semiwage labor. If we make this simple switch of perspective, which must of course be argued, we see the whole picture in a very different light. The slave owners were then indeed capitalists, as Fogel and Engerman argue, not, however, because all rational men are, but because they were operating in a capitalist world-economy. And a slave owner who did not allow market considerations to loom large in his firm's operation would sooner or later go bankrupt and be replaced by one who did. That southern planters developed a different ideology from that of New England mill owners (and were they as different as Genovese implies?) is simply the reflection of differing interests within a single capitalist world-system. That they tried to use the state (whether within the Union or by creating the Confederacy) to defend their interests, that is the name of the game.

From the slave owner's point of view, the slave received a wage. He received annually the sum of the cost of purchasing him (or raising him if he was born to a slave), maintaining him during his work years and old age, and policing him (the *extra* costs of supervision entailed by the slave status), divided by the years of effective work. By measuring output in comparison with annual wage we can easily compute a productivity ratio. It is complicated but eminently feasible to compare the cost of a slave's output with the cost of the contractual wage laborer who receives regular payments plus perquisites only during his effective work time (at least until the twentieth-century welfare state measures entered into the wage picture) and must spread this money over the life cycle of the nuclear family. Employers were no doubt aware of rough equivalencies, or thought they were. Coercion (as opposed to contract) reduces the total wage, as Fogel and Engerman clearly demonstrate, but the optimal wage (that is, the one yielding the greatest income to the slave owner per dollar spent on slave maintenance) was one that combined 'force and pecuniary income'. They add '*more* pecuniary income per capita than they would have earned if they had been free small farmers' (p. 239), but of course they omit the non-money income ('subsistence') of the free small farmers. Thus coerced or semicoerced semiwage labor is, and has been from the beginning of capitalism as a world-system, a phenomenon of peripheral areas of the capitalist world-economy, while contractual labor is concentrated (largely, but not exclusively) in core areas.

The slave owners responded to a market. This does not mean they were not responsive to 'other' considerations: the social status of slaveholding, the guarantees of an available work force. But do these not involve also economic benefits? Certainly these 'other' considerations evolved into an immense superstructure which was not a hypocrisy, but if the social relations were truly in contradiction with long-term economic rationality, could they have survived in a capitalist world?

The key methodological issue is the unit of analysis. Given their neoclassical orientation, the logical unit for Fogel and Engerman is the firm, and they tend to use it. They do so inconsistently, as do most neoclassical economic historians, because so many questions cannot be treated at the level of the firm. But they handle the difficulty – one is tempted to say, neoclassically – by blurring it. Else they would have to reopen their premises. But for Genovese, the analysis revolves presumably around a mode of production. Yet he never quite uses the term. Why not? Why does he speak of slave *society*, paternalist *society*, slavery as a *system*? In the end these are all euphemisms for 'state' or the quasi-state which was the Old South – as though *states* have modes of production. A state no more has a mode of production than does a firm. The concept 'mode of production' describes an *economy*, the boundaries of which are precisely a preliminary empirical question of the utmost relevance to an understanding of 'class rule'. The South, certainly in the years 1831–61, the years with which both books are centrally concerned, was part and parcel of a *world*-economy whose mode of production was *capitalist*, and within which owners of large-scale cash-crop plantations utilized, to the extent they could, such state structures as they could control (or largely control) to make it possible for them to extract the largest share of the surplus value being produced by productive workers.

Slavery was thus very useful to them, particularly the variety of it ('paternalism') which evolved, for all the reasons (most of which seem to me plausible) that Genovese (and even Fogel and Engerman) adumbrate. But it did not fit the interests of competing groups, who evolved ideologies to help them eliminate it.

Slavery of course did not serve the interests of the slaves, in however paternalist a form. We must never forget that no one volunteered to be a slave. Slaves organized as best they could to defend themselves and improve their lot. Here Genovese has done us an immense service in showing what a legally repressed group of proletarian workers can do, operating within the laws and the ideological constraints imposed by their oppressors. He makes a very telling comparison of the class actions of slaves and contractual wage workers. '[Small group desertions, which were frequently designed only as a temporary action,] parallelled strikes by free workers, for they aimed at winning concessions within the system rather than at challenging the system itself. But, like strikes by free workers, they contained a germ of class consciousness and demonstrated the power of collective action. In both respects they combatted the sense of impotence that the slaveholders worked so hard to instill in their slaves' (p. 656).

This comparison, in my view valid, has great implications which are not developed, ones that go counter to the theme of a unique paternalist slave society. Genovese tells us over and over that concessions to slaves were made, in some part because of benevolence or prudence of the whites (whether slaveholders or abolitionist allies), but in large part because the slaves in some way seized their 'rights'. It was not easy. Genovese reminds us of Fanon's dictum: 'It is always easier to proclaim rejection than to reject' (p. 701, n. 9). But it was done. It does not help, however, for us to fail to be clear that what the slaves accomplished in the antebellum South was the accomplishment of proletarian workers in a peripheral arena of the capitalist world-economy.

References

Fogel, Robert William and Stanley L. Engerman. 1974. *Time on the Cross* (2 vols.). Boston: Little, Brown & Co.

Genovese, Eugene D. 1968. 'Materialism and Idealism in the History of Negro Slavery in the Americas'. *Journal of Social History*, 1: 371–94

1974. *Roll, Jordan, Roll: The World the Slaves Made*. New York: Pantheon Books

Ianni, Constantino. 1965. *Il sangue degli emigranti*. Milan: Ed. di Comunità

14 ꝫ Class formation in the capitalist world-economy

Social class as a concept was invented within the framework of the capitalist world-economy and it is probably most useful if we use it as historically specific to this kind of world-system. Class analysis loses its power of explanation whenever it moves towards formal models and away from dialectical dynamics.

Thus, we wish to analyze here classes as evolving and changing structures, wearing ever-changing ideological clothing, in order to see to whose advantage it is at specific points of time to define class memberships in particular conceptual terms. What we shall attempt to show is that alternative *perceptions* of social reality have very concrete consequences for the ability of contending classes to further their interests. In particular, there are two arguments about the fundamental paradigm of analysis: is class a polarized concept or a multimodal one? Are affiliations to class groupings more or less fundamental or significant than affiliations to 'status groups' or ethno-nations? We shall argue that the debate about the paradigm turns out in the end to be the crucial debate and to play a central role in class organization.

Before however we can proceed to analyze the nature and workings of social classes, and the process of class formation, we must specify the mode of functioning of this world-system in which they are located. There are three basic elements to a capitalist world-economy. First, it consists (metaphorically) of a single market within which calculations of maximum profitability are made and which therefore determine over some long run the amount of productive activity, the degree of specialization, the modes of payment for labor, goods, and services, and the utility of technological invention.

The second basic element is the existence of a series of state structures, of varying degrees of strength (both within their boundaries, and *vis-à-vis* other entities in the world-system). The state structures serve primarily to distort the 'free' workings of the capitalist market so as to increase the prospects of one or several groups for profit within it. The state acts on the market in the short run by the use of its legal prerogatives to constrain economic activities within or across its borders. But it also acts on the market over the long run by seeking to create institutional proclivities (from the conveniences of established currency and trade channels, to taste preferences, to limitations of knowledge of economic alternatives), such that some persons or groups 'spontaneously' misjudge the economic activity that would in fact optimize their profits, a misjudgment which favors some other group or groups that a particular state wishes to favor.

The third essential element of a capitalist world-economy is that the appropriation of surplus labor takes place in such a way that there are not two, but three, tiers to the exploitative process. That is to say, there is a middle tier, which shares in the exploitation of the lower tier, but also shares in being exploited by the upper tier. Such a three-tiered format is essentially stabilizing in effect, whereas a two-tiered format is essentially disintegrating. We are not saying that three tiers exist at all moments. We are saying that those on top always seek to ensure the existence of three tiers in order the better to preserve their privilege, whereas those on the bottom conversely seek to reduce the three to two, the better to destroy this same privilege. This fight over the existence of a middle tier goes on continually, both in political terms and in terms of basic ideological constructs (those that are pluralist versus those that are manicheist). This is the core issue around which the class struggle is centered.[1]

These three tiers can be located repetitively throughout all the institutions of the capitalist world-economy: in the trimodal economic role of regions in the world-economy: core, semiperi-

---

1. Marx himself underlines the political importance of the third tier, the middle stratum: 'What [Ricardo] forgets to mention is the continual increase in numbers of the middle classes,...situated midway between the workers on one side and the capitalists and landowners, on the other. These middle classes rest with all their weight upon the working class and at the same time increase the social security and power of the upper class.' *Theorien über den Mehrwert* (Kautsky edition, 1905–10) book II, vol. 2, p. 368, translated in T. B. Bottomore and Maximilien Rubel, *Karl Marx: Selected Writings in Sociology and Social Philosophy* (London: Watts and Co., 1956), pp. 190–1.

phery, and periphery;[2] in the basic organizational structure of the productive process (the existence of a foreman role); in the trimodal patterns of income and status distribution in core capitalist countries; in the trimodal pattern of political alliances (left, center, and right), both at the world and national levels.

Once again, let me underline my position: I am not arguing that three tiers *really* exist, any more than I am arguing that two poles *really* exist. I am indifferent to such Platonic essences. Rather, I am asserting that the class struggle centers politically around the *attempt* of the dominant classes to create and sustain a third tier, against the *attempt* of the oppressed classes to polarize both the reality and the perception of the reality.

That is to say, classes do not have some permanent reality. Rather, they are formed, they consolidate themselves, they disintegrate or disaggregate, and they are re-formed. It is a process of constant movement, and the greatest barrier to understanding their action is reification.[3] To be sure, there are patterns we can describe and which aid us to identify concrete realities and explain historical events. But the patterns themselves evolve over time, even within the historically bound phenomenon of the modern capitalist world-economy.

The division of the populace into tiers of relative privilege often takes the form of ethno-national groupings. Max Weber challenged the Marxian perception of social reality by asserting that what he called 'status groups' (*Stände*) were a parallel phenomenon to social classes, and that the two realities cross cut. I do not accept this position. I believe 'class' and what I prefer to call 'ethno-nation' are two sets of clothing for the same basic reality.[4] However, it is important to realize that there are in fact

2. On the way in which the semiperiphery is to be distinguished from the core and the periphery, see my 'Dependence in an Interdependent World: The Limited Possibilities of Transformation Within the Capitalist World-Economy', *African Studies Review*, 17: (April 1974), 1–26, and above, ch. 4.

3. Lucien Goldmann defines reification as 'the replacement of the qualitative by the quantitative, of the concrete by the abstract', a process he argues is 'closely tied to production for the market, notably to capitalist production...'. 'La Réification', in *Recherches dialectiques* (Paris: Ed. Gallimard, 1959), p. 92.

4. I have spelled out in some detail my views on the Marx–Weber controversy, and the ways in which I think Weber errs by becoming paradoxically a 'vulgar Marxist', in 'Social Conflict in Post-Independence Black Africa: The Concepts of Race and Status Group Reconsidered', in Ernest Q. Campbell (ed.), *Racial Tensions and National Identity* (Nashville: Vanderbilt University Press, 1972), pp. 207–26, and above, ch. 10.

two sets of clothing, so that we may appreciate how, when and why one set is worn rather than the other. Ethno-nations, just like social classes, are formed, consolidate themselves, disintegrate or disaggregate, and are constantly re-formed.

It becomes thus part of any concrete analysis to identify the stage at which specific classes or ethno-nations are found: whether a given stratum is an emerging, established, or a declining social class. I would further like to argue that the classic Marxian terminology about social classes refers in fact to these three aspects of the evolution of classes. Emerging classes are classes *an sich*. Established classes are classes *für sich*. And false consciousness is the defense of the interests of a declining social class.[5]

If we argue that classes and ethno-nations reflect the same social reality, we must furnish some rationale for the existence of two forms. We shall seek to do this by assessing what are the purposes (or advantages) of a social group taking on one or the other identity.

Let us start with social classes. There is a short-run logic in the formation of a class. It is that the gradual perception of common interests (that is, similar relationships to the ownership and control of the means of production, and similar sources of revenue) and the construction of some organizational structure(s) to advance these interests is an indispensable aspect of bargaining (which is the form that all short-run struggle takes). The traditional distinction between objective class status and subjective class membership (common to the majority of both Marxists and functionalists) seems to me totally artificial. An objective class status is only a reality insofar as it becomes a subjective reality for some group or groups, and if it 'objectively' exists, it inevitably will be felt 'subjectively'. The question is not there, but in the degree

5. False consciousness presumably refers to the inability of a group to perceive (and *a fortiori* to admit) that they are members of a given social class. The most obvious explanation of such behavior is that the group sees some advantage in this 'misperception'. If a group of office assistants fails to acknowledge the growing 'proletarianization' of the work force of large bureaucratic structures, or a 'lesser nobility' refuses to admit that they are operating as agricultural capitalists quite like non-noble 'gentry', but insist they are of a different 'stratum' than others performing basically similar economic tasks, they are exhibiting 'false consciousness'. The benefit they hope to draw from this is to retain privileges associated with an earlier status which they fear will lose by acknowledging that the class to which they once belonged (or to which their predecessors belonged) has 'declined' because of the evolving structure of the capitalist world-economy.

to which the 'objective' reality takes the 'subjective' form of class consciousness rather than the form of ethno-national consciousness.

It would seem logical to deduce that short-run organizing is engaged in primarily when the overall political alignment of forces is such that those who organize can reasonably expect significant short-run bargaining advantages. Needless to say, the very success of the process vitiates its polarizing impact on the political system. This is the phenomenon that Lenin called 'economism' and the New Left more recently called 'co-optation',

But class consciousness also has long-run significance. It is the clearest route to the acquisition of power within a given state structure by any group numerically larger than one that is politically dominant in that state structure. Whether this acquisition of power is sought theoretically by parliamentary or insurrectionary means, the basic thrust is 'democratizing'. This is, it seems to me, what we mean when we call the French Revolution a 'bourgeois democratic revolution'. In the eighteenth century, the bourgeoisie did not have a primary role in the governance of the French state, and in the nineteenth century it did. This basic shift came about as a result of 'bourgeois class consciousness'.

The self-negating aspects of such 'class' assumptions of power are a basic theme of the unhappy critics on the sidelines of modern history, especially in the last half-century. See Claudel's trilogy on the impact of the Napoleonic era (*L'otage, Le pain dur, Le père humilié*) or di Lampedusa's novel on the social consequences of the *Risorgimento* (*The Leopard*) or Djilas' analysis of the Yugoslav revolution in *The New Class*.

While I do not condone the basic pessimism that pervades such works, they point (without truly understanding it) to a phenomenon that is real enough. As long as we have a capitalist world-economy, the state machinery is inevitably 'prebendal' in spirit, in that control of the state machinery leads to differential access to resources in a system in which production is for profit rather than for use. Hence such power is, if you will, 'corrupting', even of those who assume it in order presumably to transform the social structure. We have all been so bedazzled by the phenomenon of bureaucratization in the modern world that we have missed the more important fact that bureaucratization can *never* occur at the level of political decision making of a state structure within a capitalist world-economy.

And yet both Weber and Marx pointed to this fact. Weber, whose works are the fount of contemporary theorizing about bureaucratization, said nonetheless: 'Exactly the pure type of bureaucracy, a hierarchy of *appointed* officials, requires an authority (*Instanz*) which has not been appointed in the same fashion as the other officials.'[6] And Marx offered as one of the prospects of socialism precisely the end of this anomaly. What else did Engels mean by the 'withering away of the state' except the end of precisely this kind of private use of collective machinery? The Karl Marx who denounced the 'idiocy of rural life' surely did not envisage a bucolic, unstructured Utopia. Rather Engels caught his sense accurately when he wrote: 'State interference in social relations becomes, in one domain after another, superfluous; and then dies out of itself; the government of persons is replaced by the administration of things, and by the conduct of processes of production. The state is not "abolished". *It dies out*.'[7]

How this absence of prebendal opportunities will operate in a socialist world is not to the point here. What is to the point is to notice the limitations of the seizure of state power (limitations, not irrelevance) to the achievement of class objectives within the capitalist world-economy.

Thus, classes are formed – to bargain in the short run, and to seize state power in the long run – and then disintegrate by virtue of their success. But they are then re-formed. This is what Mao Tse-Tung meant when he said of the People's Republic of China, 'the class struggle is by no means over.'[8]

This continuous re-eruption of the class struggle after each political resolution is in my view not a cyclical process, however, but precisely a dialectical one. For the 'establishment' of a class,

6. Max Weber, *Economy and Society* (3 vols., New York: Bedminster Press, 1968), vol. 3, p. 1123.
7. Frederich Engels, *Socialism: Utopian and Scientific* (New York: International Publications, 1935), p. 42. In other versions, the italicized phrase 'it dies out' has been translated as 'it withers away'. Weber, unlike Marx and Engels, was not looking foward to a 'withering away' of the state. Quite the contrary. He saw the politician as the guarantor of 'responsibility', and the danger to be avoided was the one who acted as though he were a bureaucrat and therefore became a *Kleber*, one who sticks to his post. See Weber, *Economy and Society*, vol. 3, pp. 1403–5.
8. See my 'Class Struggle in China?', *Monthly Review*, 25: 4 (September 1974), 55–9.

however transient the phenomenon, transforms – to a greater or lesser extent – the world-system and thus contributes directly to the historical evolution of this world-system.

Let us now turn to the alternative organizational form: that of ethno-nations. Here too, we can distinguish between short-run and long-run uses. In the short run, the formation of an 'ethno-nation' serves to alter the distribution of goods according to some arbitrarily defined status – kinship, language, race, religion, citizenship. Ethno-nations defend or seek to acquire privilege through partial or total monopolies, distinguishing the group and creating organizational cohesion by the manipulation of cultural symbols.[9]

Ethno-national consciousness is the constant resort of all those for whom class organization offers the risk of a loss of relative advantage through the normal workings of the market and class dominated political bargaining. It is obvious that this is frequently the case for upper strata, who thereby justify differential reward on one or another version of racist ideology. Furthermore, insofar as dominant groups can encourage a generalized acceptance of ethno-nationalism as a base for political action, they precisely achieve the three-tiered structure of exploitation which helps maintain the stability of the system.[10]

9. In an unpublished paper, Michael Hechter argues that industrialization, far from diminishing ethnicity, leads to 'the proliferation of the cultural division of labor'. He concludes that 'so long as substantial regional and international economic inequalities persist, it is reasonable to expect the cultural division of labor to be perpetuated'. 'Ethnicity and Industrialization: On the Proliferation of the Cultural Division of Labor' (mimeographed), p. 10.

10. While this is readily apparent to many analysts in terms of the function of ethnic groups within nation-states, it is less frequently observed that the creation and reinforcement of state structures as such performs exactly the same stabilizing function for the world-system. One author who sees this clearly is Francisco Weffort. In a criticism of authors who see a 'contradiction' between class struggle in the market and a trans-class perspective of struggle on the basis of oppressed nationhood, Weffort argues:

For example, did there exist, in the almost complete Argentine integration into the international market of the nineteenth century, a *real* contradiction between State and market? Was not the Argentine State itself, making use of the attributes of sovereignty, one of the factors of this incorporation?

To understand this example a bit, it is clear that the oligarchy controlled the State, but who gave to the Argentina of that era its sense of being a Nation, other than this very oligarchy? My view is that the existence of the Nation-State, or call it autonomy and political sovereignty, is not sufficient reason for us to think that there has come about a contradiction between Nation and market in the country that is integrated into the international economic system. On the contrary, under certain internal social and political conditions (which can only be specified by means of class analysis), the groups who have hegemonic power, or who are those who give content

But ethno-nations that have to rely on overt legislated monopolies are on weak grounds. They are highly visible in their open
challenge to the universalistic ideology of the primacy of the
capitalist market, which is reflected in the political ideology of
'liberalism'. It is possible to maintain legislative discriminations
for long periods of time, as we all know. Nonetheless, the more
enduring form in which privilege is maintained is the creation
of *de facto* but informal privileged access to non-state institutions
(education, occupation, housing, health), optimally through the
operation of a totally 'individual' attribution of advantage. By
refusing to 'discriminate' in particular situations which 'test' one
individual against another, the institution abstracts the totality of
social factors which accounts for differential performance, and
hence widens rather than narrows existing inequalities.[11]

This subtle mechanism of defending upper class interests has
become more important in recent years precisely because of the
increased difficulties of using cruder mechanisms as a result of
the ever more effective organization of oppressed classes. It is

to the idea of the Nation, may use political autonomy to advance economic
integration.
'Notas sobre la "teoría de la dependencia"; ¿Teoría de clase o ideología nacional?'
Revista Latinoamericana de Ciencia Política, 1: 3 (December 1970), 394.
See also Amicar Cabral's useful concept of the 'nation-class'.
We are not unaware that in the course of the history of our people, there have
emerged class phenomena, varying in definition and state of development...[But]
when the fight against colonial domination begins, it is not the product of one class
even though the idea may have sprung up from the class which has become aware
more rapidly or earlier of colonial domination and of the necessity of combatting
it. But this revolt is not the product of a class as such. Rather it is the whole society
that carries it out. This nation-class, which may be more or less clearly structured,
is dominated not by people from the colonized country but rather by the ruling
class of the colonizing country. This is our view, and hence our struggle is essentially
based not on a class struggle but rather on the struggle led by our nation-class
against the Portuguese ruling class.
Interview published in *Anticolonialismo*, 2 (February 1972).
11. It is precisely this danger to which Marx pointed in the *Critique of the Gotha Programme*.
One of the clauses of the Programme called for 'equitable distribution of the proceeds
of labour'. Marx commented:
What we have to deal with here is a communist society, not as it has *developed* on
its own foundations, but, on the contrary, as it *emerges* from capitalist society;...
    This *equal* right is an unequal right for unequal labour. It recognizes no class
differences, because everyone is only a worker like everyone else; but it tacitly
recognizes unequal individual endowment and thus productive capacity as natural
privileges. *It is therefore a right of inequality in its content, like every right*...To avoid
all these defects, right instead of being equal would have to be unequal.
V. Adoratsky (ed.), *Karl Marx: Selected Works* (New York: International Publications,
n.d.) vol. 2, pp. 563–5.

precisely thus to counter this newly prominent phenomenon of 'institutional racism' that the world has seen in the twentieth century an increasing expression of class consciousness in ethno-national forms.

It is no accident that the great social revolutions of the twentieth century (the Russian, Chinese, Vietnamese, Cuban) have been at one and the same time 'social' and 'national'. To be 'social', they had to be 'national', whereas those 'revolutions' which claimed to be 'national' without being 'social' (for example, that of the Kuomintang) could not in fact defend 'national' interests. It is similarly not at all accidental that oppressed lower strata in core capitalist countries (Blacks in the United States, Québécois in Canada, Occitans in France, etc.) have come to express their class consciousness in ethno-national terms. To be sure, this breeds confusion. But there is *less* confusion in the advantages drawn by the upper class hangers-on of an oppressed ethno-nation than in the failure of the working-class movements in the core capitalist countries to represent the interests of the weakest strata of the proletariat (of 'minority' ethnic status) and thereby prevent a growing gap – both objective and subjective – between the interests of workers of upper ethnic status and those of lower ethnic status.

Yet the confusion, if less serious, is nonetheless there. And promotion of ethno-national minorities most frequently results simply in a shift in location of the privileged stratum, and a restructuring of ethno-national dividing lines.

So are we then back where we started? Not at all. We must maintain our eye on the central ball. The capitalist world-economy as a totality – its structure, its historical evolution, its contradictions – is the arena of social action. The fundamental political reality of that world-economy is a class struggle which however takes constantly changing forms: overt class consciousness versus ethno-national consciousness, classes within nations versus classes across nations. If we think of these forms as kaleidoscopic reflections of a fundamental reality which has a structure seldom visible to the naked eye of the observer (like the world of the atom for the physicist), but one that can in fact be perceived as an evolving pattern, then we may come closer to understanding the social reality of the capitalist world-system of which we are a part, the better and the faster to transform it.

Part III

Political strategies

---

15 ᴥ Old problems and new syntheses: the relation of revolutionary ideas and practices

It is appropriate in a lecture series that honors Pitirim A. Sorokin to start with an insight from his work. In 1941, during the Second World War, Sorokin published a *cri de coeur* called The Crisis of Our Age. It was a sort of application to the problems of our time of his major work, *Social and Cultural Dynamics*.

Sorokin based his analysis on a kind of grand dialectic of ideas. He saw three kinds of mental constructs, which he called ideational, idealistic and sensate systems. These systems are reflected in all spheres of mental activity – in the fine arts, in epistemologies, in ethics, in law, in social organization. If we take the sphere that interests the university most of all, the one he calls systems of truth, we see very clearly Sorokin's framework of analysis. Ideational truth, he tells us, is 'the truth revealed by the grace of God', and may be called 'the truth of faith'. Sensate truth is 'the truth of the senses, obtained through our organs of sense perception'. Both are partial truths and dangerous when they arrogate to themselves the whole field of truth. There is however a third truth, which we are led to infer is less partial:

Idealistic truth is a synthesis of both, made by our reason. In regard to sensory phenomena, it recognizes the role of the sense organs as the source and criterion of the validity or invalidity of a proposition. In regard to supersensory phenomena, it claims that any knowledge of these is impossible through sensory experience and is obtained only through the direct revalation of God. Finally our reason, through logic and dialectic, can derive many valid propositions

231

[through the logic of human reason]...Human reason likewise combines into one organic whole the truth of the senses, the truth of faith, and the truth of reason.[1]

For Sorokin, these systems of truths are located in different orders. Although the historical sequencing is not always crystal clear, it seems that Sorokin believes that human history (or at least Graeco-Roman-western history) has seen up to now a pattern of oscillation between ideational and sensate cultures, but that the world (or rather the western world) was going through a crisis in the twentieth century which could conceivably be resolved by the adoption of the synthesis that he called 'idealistic' culture.

One does not have to agree with Sorokin's formulation of the problem (and I do not) to see that he was addressing himself to a real historical issue – the widespread sense that the world order which had bloomed in the nineteenth century was not permanent and infinitely perfectible, but faulty and transitional. Sorokin called that world order a sensate system of culture. I call it a capitalist world-economy. But it is clear we are talking about the same thing.

For Sorokin, the period since 1914 has been a period of the 'disintegration of sensate culture'. This manifests itself as a deterioration of the 'systems of meanings and values'. For example:

In social science, the deterioration of sensate culture means a progressive replacement of the generations of Ibn-Khaldun, Vico, Locke, Montesquieu, Adam Smith, Herbert Spencer, A. Comte and Karl Marx by a host of scholars united in big research corporations led by 'social science managers and social science committees'. Industriously they will cultivate in their scholarly treatises either a misleading preciseness, or a painful elaboration of the obvious, or a scholarly emptiness, with all the Alexandrian erudition and all the thoroughness of 'trained incapacity'.   (p. 30)

In the larger society, we see the emergence of the 'partisans of the Absolute ethical norms', many of them becoming 'stoics, ascetics, and saints'.

The soul of the society in transition will be split into the *Carpe diem* on the one hand, and on the other into ideational indifference and negative attitude toward all the sensory pleasures. Society itself will be increasingly divided into open, perfectly cynical sinners with their 'Eat, Drink, and Love for tomorrow is

1. Pitirim A. Sorokin, *The Crisis of Our Age: The Social and Cultural Outlook* (New York: E. D. Dutton and Co., 1942), pp. 81–2. Unless otherwise specified, other quotations in this paper are from this book and will be identified only by page numbers.

uncertain', and into the ascetics and saints who will flee the sensory world into a kind of refuge, new monasteries, and new deserts. (p. 301–2)

And finally, 'the disintegration of the sensate phase means a multiplication of the conflicts within its systems of meanings and between its human agents and groups' (p. 303).

The use of a dialectical mode, the denunciation of the moral emptiness of sensate culture and the intellectual vacuity of empiricist reasoning makes Sorokin into a critic of the social order and one whose criticism parallels Marx and the Marxists. But he rejected the parallel. A member of the Kerensky government overthrown by the October Revolution, Sorokin went into exile in the United States, into the heartland of the sensate culture he was denouncing. For Sorokin regarded Marxism not as the antithesis of the values of sensate culture but as a further elaboration of its values, and in particular the value of materialism. Marx thus was defined in effect as the intellectual culmination of Descartes, Locke, and the Enlightenment rather than as Marx perceived himself, the heralder of a contrasting perspective reflecting the values and needs of a different social class, the proletariat.

Who was right? When fifty years after the Russian Revolution, the leaders of the Chinese Communist Party said of the leaders of the Communist Party of the Soviet Union that they were 'revisionists' returning to the 'capitalist road', were they not saying with Sorokin that the system established in the USSR represented no real shift away from 'sensate culture', from a capitalist mode of production? To be sure; but the Chinese were also saying that this was not inevitable, that one *could* break with the old system, provided one recognized that merely changing some economic and political institutions, though necessary, was not sufficient. To complete the process of transition, to continue to pursue the class struggle, the Chinese engaged in a *cultural* revolution. Thus the Chinese posed for themselves and for us the question of the proper and possible relation of revolutionary ideas and practices.

Sorokin was perfectly right in perceiving the 'disintegration' of the world of nineteenth-century Europe. Of course, this has been a common insight of many twentieth-century thinkers. The First World War marked the end of an era in at least three senses. First, the ruling classes of the world realized that their previous beliefs, in the permanence of British (white) hegemony in the world, in the unending beneficence of scientific progress, and in the virtues of bourgeois liberalism as the summit of human wisdom and morality, were not merely elements of an ideology they had used to deceive others. They had largely deceived themselves as well. This realization had its roots in the long economic downturn of 1873–96 and its intellectual expression in the malaise of the so-called *fin de siècle* intellectuals. But the 1914–18 war transformed mere intellectual forebodings into generalized fears of the whole of the western bourgeoisie – hence, the wide reception given to a book like that of Spengler on *The Decline of the West*.

There was a second sense in which the First World War marked the end of an era. Throughout the nineteenth century, the working classes had organized politically for revolution in Europe. But aside from the short-lived Paris Commune of 1870, there had been no real insurrection. However in 1917, there was – in Russia. And it succeeded. Even if parallel attempts at revolutions failed elsewhere – in Hungary, in Germany – a revolutionary party of the proletariat had come to power in a state and stayed in power. And it was a large and potentially very powerful state. Whatever else may be said about it, the October Revolution changed the face of world politics and undermined, just by having occured, a major pillar of the political stability of the world capitalist system.

There was a third sense in which the First World War was a turning point. The capitalist world-system was attacked not merely by the workers of Europe, but by the peoples of the colonial and semicolonial world. Rumblings, insurrections, mass movements, even changes in governments occurred in China, India, Turkey, Mexico. It is easy now to see that this marked the opening skirmishes of a world-wide struggle of movements of national liberation against Europe's world political hegemony, which had been based on the latter's temporary technological advantages and deep-rooted racism. The objectived long-term economic crisis plus objective evidence of the ability of the oppressed to organize successfully made those who held power and privilege lose the bloom of arrogant and smug self-confidence, and face their future with anxiety and hatred.

The dominant groups (or at least their intellectual and political elites) gave up the hope and belief that the existing system could last forever, and replaced this dangerous illusion with a pragmatic strategy to put off the awful day as long as possible. Yes, capitalism would someday end; yes, in the long run, socialism would come. But, John Maynard Keynes reminded them, politics and economics were really concerned with the present and the immediate future; after all, 'in the long run, we are all dead'. So too in 1942, Joseph Schumpeter published *Capitalism, Socialism and Democracy*, in which he demonstrated with cold and ruthless logic why capitalism (the system he unreservedly and unashamedly adored) would inevitably be superseded by socialism (which he saw as some kind of return to a primitive darkness). But, as a last comfort to the living, he reminded the reader that capitalism was at that moment still vigorous and kicking: 'From the standpoint of immediate practice as well as for the purpose of short-run forecasting – and in these things, a century is a 'short-run' – all this surface may be more important than the tendency toward another civilization that slowly works deep down below.'[2]

When a ruling class no longer believes it will survive indefinitely, when it senses that time is on the side of the oppressed and that all it can do is postpone fundamental change, it changes its strategy of rule. It replaces disdain with cunning. And cunning requires a judicious mix of ferocity and concession.

It seems to me quite easy then to understand the politics of the half-century since the First World War. The world has known unthinkable displays of ferocity (from gas ovens in Auschwitz to napalm in Vietnam) and remarkable displays of concession (from welfare state reforms in industrialized countries to decolonization in Asia and Africa).

The net result of this gigantic world-wide effort is more difficult to ascertain. No doubt it has helped the capitalist world-economy to survive. For, although we are today in the beginning of another world economic downswing comparable to that of 1873–96, the system still has a lot of staying power. And yet, it is also clear that, despite both the ferocity and the concessions, the forces that stand for the destruction of the capitalist world-economy are more deep rooted, well organized, and efficacious than ever.

This then is the theme I wish to evoke: what is the relationship

2. Joseph Schumpeter, *Capitalism, Socialism and Democracy* (New York: Harper and Brothers, 1942), p. 163.

during this long and difficult world struggle of the ideas and the practices of revolutionary movements? Is the world likely to emerge at the end of this struggle with a world order that fulfils the promise of the revolutionaries or one that contains the hobgoblins brandished by the tenants of present advantage? And what is our role – as individuals, and as members of social strata having interests in the distribution of world rewards – in this battle of transformation, in this world class struggle?

Let us start by looking at what has happened to the forces of revolution since 1917. The Russian Revolution sealed a world-wide break among what might be loosely termed oppositional elements, a break that had been in the making since at least 1848. There were those who believed that the progressive evolution of a capitalist economy moved towards its perfecting, towards the elimination of its disparities (as inefficiencies), towards the slow equalization of the distribution of reward. This group argued that the only proper role of 'progressive' forces was to hasten the arrival of the Kingdom of God by proclaiming the faith and converting the sinful, who would give evidence of their repentance by agreeing to appropriate reforms. Today, such people are called social democrats or liberals, according to local custom. And then there were those who thought quite the contrary. This second group saw the push of history, or the dialectical process of social life, as one in which imperfect systems over time exaggerate their imperfections, make acute their contradictions, polarize still further the distribution of reward, and that the only proper role of 'progressive' forces was to organize rationally to win the struggle. The latter group, for a long time called communists (but today the use of this term no longer has the clear connotations it once had), have often been accused of being prophets and hence secular fanatics. But it could be argued that their image of ongoing struggle was less visionary and more realistic than the image held by the liberals of the slow perfectibility of mankind via ratiocination.

In any case, this split took very concrete organizational form between the First and Second World Wars. One group organized primarily in the Second International; the other in the Third. The social democrats sought to achieve their objectives by a loyal participation in national parliamentary processes. In a few countries, they succeeded in becoming the government (alone or in coalition) for varying lengths of time. They also organized in trade unions. When in power, they supported the kind of social legislation which created the framework of the welfare state. Reflecting the interests primarily of 'middle strata' of well-paid skilled workers (including the so-called professionals), they showed political strength (under one label or another) only in western Europe, North America and Australasia.

Parallel 'middle strata' (middle in terms of privilege in the world-economy) were also to be found in Asia, Africa, and Latin America, although more of them were concentrated in bureaucratic roles and fewer in industrial ones than in Europe and North America. Because in these latter cases the upper strata were in part or in whole 'foreigners' from a national perspective (unlike in Europe and North America), the national organizations of these middle strata put the emphasis on *national* rather than *social* reallocations of resources. Instead of calling themselves social democrats, they called themselves populists or nationalists and, with some exceptions, came to participate in governments only after the Second World War.

Essentially, social democrats in core countries of the capitalist world-economy and populist-nationalists in the peripheral countries represented the same interest groups, espoused the same underlying *Weltanschauung*, and promoted the same genre of reforms, *mutatis mutandis*. What should be observed very clearly about the political history of these groups is that, although they came increasingly to participate in governments, they never anywhere held such power that they could destroy or even seriously cripple the economic viability of the network of world private economic and financial enterprises which they claimed to regard as their antagonist. And the concessions they were able to wrest from the upper strata were in large part due to the fear by the latter of the forces represented by the Third International.

No doubt, in the light of the expanded world production of the twentieth century, these 'middle strata' received real material rewards. But one has to live in the fantasyland of the lunatic right to believe that either social democracy or Third World nationalism has fundamentally altered the mode of functioning of the capitalist world-economy, and in particular that it has meant any substantial

increase in either material benefit of non-material psychic satisfaction for the bottom strata of the world's population.

One does not have to take my word for it, or that of any other
analyst. One merely has to look at the contemporary ability of
the social democratic and Third World nationalist movements
to mobilize effective political support from these bottom strata to
see how the latter have rejected them. In countries where several
parties compete in elections, these lower strata habitually abstain
for the most part, and engage in the multifarious forms of chronic
guerilla sniping. In much of Asia, Africa and Latin America, the
army is used to contain their revolts.

Let me be clear about what I have been saying. I do not say
that social democratic and nationalist movements have *never* been
able to mobilize mass support. Nor do I say that they have *never*
enacted important social reforms. I am saying that these important
social reforms have turned out to benefit primarily the 'middle
strata' materially (and hence the 'upper strata' politically), and
that the lower strata have quite markedly shown their awareness
of this and repugnance of it. Of course, this repugnance has not
always been able to manifest itself in a politically efficacious form,
but that is in large part because of repression and not false
consciousness. What often passes as 'false consciousness' of the
oppressed is frequently only their prudent pretence in a dangerous
situation. Thus, in terms of its own ostensible objectives, social
democracy has turned out to be a monumental failure whose
short-term glories have failed to bear the test of time and whose
achievements are sung not by poets but by fat-cat *apparatchiks*,
whose rhetoric has lost all semblance of youthful idealism. (The
character of the union representative in *On The Job*, a play by
Montreal's new young proletarian playwright, David Fennario,
makes vivid how far the worm has turned.)

If the Second International (and the analogous Third World
nationalist movements) have been such a failure, what of the
Third? It is right that we assess it with the same severe criteria
we have just used for the Second. We must start with its central
organizational dilemma between the First and Second World War.
The Third International was composed of one party in power, the
Communist Party of the Soviet Union (CPSU) and a very large
number of parties out of power, only a few of whom could claim

large organized strength. This led consciously, and probably inevitably, to the central role of the CPSU in the Comintern. But since the CPSU was the state of the USSR and the state was the CPSU, in effect the Comintern was an international structure of one state and allied parties elsewhere, each party separately and even all together organizationally subordinate to the Soviet leadership.

Furthermore, this state took a specific internal form. Surrounded by enemies who literally wished to destroy it, the Soviet regime gave priority to physical survival. It is only the period immediately following the Russian Revolution that we call 'War Communism', but in a sense this would be a good title to give to the whole period of Stalin's rule. The ideological consequence of besiegement was 'socialism in one country'. The international organizational consequence was to make the defence of the Soviet state a priority for all parties in the Comintern. The internal organizational consequence was not merely the one-party regime (by no means foreordained in 1917) but the very extensive purges and the systematic use of terror. Thus, an evaluation of the politics of the Third International reduces itself to (or must at least be centered around) an evaluation of the Soviet experience.

One of the few things in which there has been remarkable world-wide consensus since say 1956 has been the misdeeds of Stalin. He has had virtually no defenders – in the western world, in the USSR or eastern Europe, in Asia, Africa, or Latin America. Even in China, which nominally defends him, it is well to remember that Stalin's misdeeds *vis-à-vis* China are very central to the consciousness of Chinese leaders. The Chinese defend Stalin primarily in order to attack his Soviet critics, Khrushchev in particular.

Such quasi-unanimity arouses the suspicion that the consensus is based on some ideological motives. In any case, let us try to draw a sober balance sheet. On the negative side, there are a long series of charges. There is the charge of monumental unnecessary cruelty, not a charge which revolutionaries can afford to take lightly. (It is after all the hallmark of the defenders of the status quo to excuse cruelty by arguments of historical inevitability while simultaneously minimizing its extent.) The second charge is that by utilizing the Comintern as an agency of the Soviet state, the CPSU seriously undermined the 'national-rootedness' of revolutionary forces in the core states of the world-economy. The history of the French Communist Party is a notable case in point. This charge is really double. By forcing the French Communist Party to cut itself from its own national realities, it weakened its abilities to obtain support. But worse, when this pressure was relaxed in the post-Stalin era, no path remained for the French Communist Party to 'prove' its national-rootedness except to become a social democratic party.

A third charge is that the focus on the primary needs of the Soviet state also hurt revolutionary movements in the peripheral countries of the world-economy. Right after the Russian Revolution, starting with the Baku Congress of 1920, there was an attempt to create a world alliance of revolutionary socialist movements in Europe and what today are called national liberation movements, particularly from Asia. An epigram was coined: 'The road to Paris lies through Peking and Calcutta.' But the flexibility required for such a strategy ran against the grain of Comintern priorities. And consequently, it may be argued that far from being a spur to revolutionary forces in Asia, the Comintern served as a constraint, that the Chinese and Vietnamese made their revolutions *despite* the Comintern, thanks more to the global folly of Japanese aggression than to the comradely support of the CPSU.

The fourth charge is that by conceiving of the problem as that of building 'socialism in one country', the CPSU achieved precisely the opposite. The CPSU forgot the dialectical relationship between transformation within the Soviet Union and evolution of the capitalist world-economy (of which it remained structurally a part). It thus created a variant of state capitalism to the benefit of a bureaucratic bourgeoisie rather than a political rampart of world socialist forces, whose internal transformation would have served as an imperfect model of the future world while being an actual element in the transition. This too is a double charge. On the one hand, this error led to collusive *détente* with the forces that dominate the capitalist world-economy, and hence (at least in the view of some) to the literal restoration of capitalist classes in power. But there is another negative consequence. Because the Soviet state was incorrectly held up as a model of 'socialism', many of those outside the USSR who were disillusioned with the Soviet state applied their criticism to socialism itself. There is no question but that from Khrushchev's 1956 speech at the 20th Party Congress to today, one of the political burdens of revolutionary forces anywhere is the need to aplogize for the 'model' that went astray. Perhaps time will erase this need, but the moment is not yet.

This then is a formidable condemnation of the Soviet experience. And yet, and yet – there is another side to the coin. There is first the purely national side. In 1914, Russia was well on its way to a form of incorporation into the world-economy that would probably at best have led to her subordination to west European interests, in a style and manner comparable to that of Canada *vis-à-vis* the United States: semi-industrialized, semi-well off, and not at all autonomous, even culturally. The Mensheviks, like the CCF, might have controlled a province or two but not the central government. This fate Russia has been spared. It is a self-centered powerful state, indeed a 'superpower'. And the explanation is to be found in the Russian Revolution of 1917 and the fact that the CPSU under Stalin was able to survive the Second World War and emerge by the 1950s as a major industrial nation.

You may well feel that this accomplishment is no greater than that of social democratic reforms, that all this means is that Russian middle strata were allowed some of the same limited share in the world pie achieved by middle strata in Europe and North America. And this may be fair if one takes a stance of Olympian aristocratic disdain. But obviously if you are a Russian, you may feel differently.

But if this were all the achievement, it would be meager from the standpoint of the rest of us. The achievement of the Soviet state, including as an indissociable part of it the Stalinist era, was greater than that. It demonstrated first of all the enormous vulnerability of the world capitalist system to organized revolutionary opposition. This is the 'spectre' that Marx brandished but Lenin materialized. This is what made Spengler tremble and Sorokin optimistic (yes, optimistic) about the 'disintegration of sensate culture'. We have talked just before of the negative impact the Soviet experience has had on world revolutionary psychology, on the realization of political consciousness. The negative impact is real, but it must be weighed against the positive impact. Mao's 'paper tiger' was Lenin's doing.

Nor is this all. It was more than a question of world class

consciousness, however vital that is. It was a question of *rapports de force*. The Soviet Union created the space that made it possible for others to operate. We have already suggested that the political achievements of social democracy (the welfare state) could never have been so considerable without the pressure of the Comintern. And when today at the United Nations the delegate of the USSR says that the Great October Socialist Revolution was a critical variable in the acceptance by the colonial powers of the logic of decolonization, he is stating a truth of which every bourgeois nationalist in Asia or Africa is very aware and for which, in a corner of his heart, he is even grateful.

Nor did the creation of world social space for opposition forces merely benefit the social democrats and the nationalists. For the national liberation movements, too, have been direct beneficiaries. It is true that Soviet assistance to the Chinese Communist Party from the 1920s to the 1940s was fitful, unintelligent, and ultimately ungenerous. It is true that the road to Yenan, and from Yenan, was taken against Soviet counsel, indeed against Soviet subversion of the Chinese party. But nonetheless, the fact that the USSR held first Nazi Germany and later the USA at bay, the fact that its existence legitimated revolutionary struggle, was of enormous benefit to the Chinese Communist Party, to the Vietnamese, and to others. One must distinguish between deliberate Soviet policy (quite often wrong headed, sometimes even counter-revolutionary), and the objective impact of the Soviet role in the capitalist world-economy.

Thus, if we are to assess the half-century since the First World War, I think it is unquestionable that the Third International achieved more of its ostensible objectives than the Second, and that, if we were to analyze both of them in terms of the objectives of socialist movements in the nineteenth century, the Third International showed itself more faithful to these objectives than the Second, and was therefore in those terms far more 'progressive'.

Today the Third International is no more. And the Second International is a shell. Today, the split in the 'socialist camp' between the USSR and China seems very profound and unlikely to heal in the foreseeable future. Today, we are faced with the decline of the hegemony of the United States, which had picked up the pieces after the *pax britannica* crumbled of its economic contradictions, and which had provided the cement that held together the world-system since the First World War. Today, the peripheral nations have at last learned the effectiveness of trade union solidarity, the first fruits of which are the remarkable financial transfers to oil-producing nations achieved by OPEC. Today we are all required therefore to rethink the means by which we can shorten the transition from the lingering system of world capitalism to its successor, world socialism. And we must do it in the light of what has occurred in the past half-century in the struggle between those who would shore up the system a little longer (and who are neither incompetent nor thus far all that unsuccessful) and those who would use, in Sorokin's language, the 'logic of reason', rather than either the 'logic of faith' or the 'logic of the senses' to establish a more rational world structure.

Let me start by making a guess about the geopolitical alignments that will emerge in the next twenty years or so. This guess may be far off, but if we are calculating probabilities and therefore strategies we must at least discuss it. I would start by seeing the likelihood of a link-up between the European Economic Community and the Comecon countries. Such a link-up makes a lot of sense on various dimensions. For western Europe, it would guarantee an immense market and resource base with which to emerge as the leading economic force at the end of the present world economic contraction. For the USSR, it would guarantee the kind of advanced technology it needs to overcome its stagnant economic level. Politically, it could only be based on an updated version of social democracy. But this would of course delight the middle strata not only of western but also of eastern Europe, especially if we bear in mind that social democracy need not mean political literalism. If such an alliance were able to include parts of the Arab world as well, it would have a fair chance to achieve world hegemony.

In counterpoint to this old dream of the 'heartland' finally achieved, there might be two poles of resistance. One would be China which could conceivably work out a political arrangement with Japan. The other would be the United States, wounded but scarcely moribund. Obviously, the two oppositional poles might be attracted towards some kind of tactical alliance. Given European economic strength and a putative US–Chinese alliance, some of the multinationals and the big banks now centered in the United States might begin to shift their focus of decision-making and capital accumulation to Europe.

If such a picture is even remotely plausible, I would see three major centers of political struggle and class conflict. One would be in China, the second in the United States, and the third in the semiperipheral states of the world-economy.

Let us start with China. The point of the Great Proletarian Cultural Revolution was the strong sense by Mao Tse-Tung and his associates that China was starting on the same path the USSR travelled ('the capitalist road'), and would have soon been on this path unless a conscious and continuing organizational effort were made to combat this tendency. The reasoning went something like this. Since the state governed by a communist party remains inevitably part of the capitalist world-economy, even if it nationalizes its internal means of production and even if it preaches socialist ideology, there are constant pressures on the state to utilize what might be called 'profitability' criteria in decision making. To the extent that these pressures are yielded to, the state bureaucracy and economic managers acquire vested class interests in maintaining and extending such criteria, until the socialist political thrust is lost.

How do Mao Tse-Tung and his allies hope to stem this social erosion of the revolutionary movement? Fundamentally, their answer is by politicization, the 'mass line', whereby the political intelligence of the mass of the population in China, the true proletarians, hold the incipient class formations of the middle strata in check. This politicization takes the form of study and self-criticism, of open questioning of bureaucratic decisions, of requiring regular periods of work as one of the masses for cadres, etc.

There are two problems with this. One is that it requires regular 'recharging' of the batteries. And who will do this? Thus far, Mao Tse-Tung himself has played an important role. But obviously he will soon be out of the picture. If one institutionalizes such mass watching over the cadres, will not the institutional structures be merely new bureaucracies? The second problem is that whenever one emphasizes the primacy of politics over considerations of technical efficiency, the risk is that the damage to the level of overall production will be real, and hence there is a pressure to swing back. If in addition China is allied in any way with such states as Japan or the United States, will these pressures not be even greater?

To each of these problems, the Chinese seem to say that they represent difficulties but ones that are not impossible to overcome, that mass political involvement of the proletariat has never been tried as they are trying it and that it has untapped potential to solve the classic dilemmas of the virtues of spontaneity opposed to the virtues of organization. Let us hope they are right. But this is why I say China is one critical arena of political conflict. Because if the Chinese can in fact main an ideological equilibrium despite the pressures, they will have not merely solved the problem the CPSU could not solve, but they will make it more possible for the rest of us to utilize collective self-transformation as a mode of transforming the world-system.

The second critical arena I see is the United States. We have become used to thinking of the United States as the command post of world capitalism. But suppose the exigencies of economic processes make this so no longer. Suppose the 'decline' goes faster than it did for Great Britain. Don't forget that Great Britain sold its soul early to the United States in return for having its economy shored up artificially. But will anyone play this role for the United States? There does not seem to be a likely candidate on the horizon. If over the next ten years or so, the United States suffers massive unemployment, while Europe does not, and if some important multinationals begin to abandon ship, the internal politics of the United States will take on quite another cast.

As long as the United States was the world hegemonic power, the structures of 'consensus liberalism' worked reasonably well. It is only in such an atmosphere of relative well-being that the tactic of 'repressive tolerance' described by Marcuse can in fact play a role. This explains the relative internal political calm of the period 1945–65. (After 1865, world hegemony was beginning to come into doubt, and internal class contradictions found open organizational expression anew, particularly in the Black Power movement.) This relative internal calm may now be 'transferred' to Europe. It will no longer be possible in the United States.

When concensus liberalism is no longer possible, when the class battles become more acute, then it is likely that new political formations arise and contest each other in the political arena. Fantastic as it may seem, it is by no means implausible that in the next twenty years in the United States (and I speak now only of the United States) we see two mass movements come into being: one a variant of a fascist movement, and one a variant of a revolutionary socialist movement. Old themes yes, but also new syntheses.

The program of a fascist movement would be xenophobic, militaristic, racist, repressive, and anti-intellectual. The social basis of such a movement would be all those, of whatever class level, who would see their relative privilege crumbling. It would be a reaction of fear rather than of hope, oriented to today rather than to today and tomorrow. But then this has always been true of fascist-type movements. How much support it would get from the Establishment, and at what point it would get such support, is as yet uncertain.

What then would a revolutionary socialist movement look like? If it were to make any headway, it would have to be fundamentally antiracist and internationalist (in the sense of understanding US internal struggles as an inherent part of the world-wide struggle going on throughout the capitalist world-economy). The social basis of such a movement would have to be the true American proletariat, which more than that of any other 'white' country is a non 'white' population – principally Blacks and Spanish-speakers. Thus speaking to the old theme of the 'national question' in a new way would be crucial. For only if an American movement could simultaneously harness the political firestorm of the oppressed ethnics and also mobilize a significant segment of white workers could it in fact have a chance of success.

Obviously, the geopolitical role the US government will play will be a function of which of these two prospective movements will in fact turn out to be stronger. The triumph of a fascist movement will almost surely mean war, probably with the USSR.

Let me now turn to the third arena in which the resolution of internal conflict will determine, in an immediate sense, the evolution of the world-system. This is in what I call the semi-periphery, that is all those states who play an intermediate role in the world-economy: large along at least one crucial dimension (population, skilled manpower, total industrial output, per capita income), tending to produce manufactured goods for an internal market and weaker neighbors but still an exporter of primary products, playing the role of peripheral partner to core countries and core partner to some peripheral countries.

There are a large number of such countries in the world today: Brazil, Venezuela, and Mexico; Algeria, Egypt, and Saudi Arabia; Iran, India and Indonesia; Nigeria, Zaïre, and South Africa; and yes, Canada. We must start by noting that these countries as a group will benefit from the altered pattern of the world-economy in periods of economic contraction. Basically, semiperipheral countries have improved bargaining power *vis-à-vis* core countries in downswings (as opposede to upswings) of the world-economy. In upswings, the crucial shortage is that of capital (world industrial production expanding rapidly) and therefore capital investors (located in core countries) can choose in which semiperipheral country to invest and can therefore exact advantageous terms. In downswings, the crucial shortage is markets to realize profits (world industrial production contracting relatively), and therefore purchasers of goods, particularly of capital goods (located in part in semiperipheral countries) can choose from which core country to purchase, and can therefore exact advantageous terms.

The world has now entered into such a downswing. The semiperipheral countries have begun to play on their new advantage. But this time we have a new additional factor. A downswing also involves a relative shortage of primary commodity production. This is one of the reasons for relative contraction of industrial production. Eventually, of course, commodity production will expand to meet the needs but in the meantime there are suddenly favorable terms of trade for primary producers.

The last time such a period occurred was in 1900–13 with a resultant quantum jump in the world production of cash crops. But politically this period had been preceded by intensive colonization in Africa, southeast Asia, and Oceania by European states. This meant that the profits from the improved terms of trade went precisely to the same core countries from which it was gotten. What the left hand lost the right hand got.

Now, precisely because of 1917 and its consequences, the world has been largely 'decolonized'. Thus when OPEC achieves a reallocation of world finance flows, the core capitalist countries alternately yelp, menace, and see if they can't 'recycle' the petrodollars. OPEC however is a model that is being emulated. The crisis of 'recycling', that is of retransferring the financial flows, is a world crisis, but it is also an internal crisis of the semiperipheral countries.

Here too, as in China and the United States, there are two paths to follow, each of which has significant internal strength (or will have), and in which, therefore, the political battle is critical. On the one side are the middle strata in these countries who see their own protection in shoring up the world capitalist system (even if in their countries they are not private entrepreneurs but state bureaucrats). Basically this group would gravitate towards a negotiated alliance with the emergent Euro-Soviet new core of the capitalist world-economy. The counter group would perhaps be less cohesive, and would vary according to the disparate structures of these various states. But it would center around a radical nationalist coalition, seeking more self-centered and autonomous economic transformation. Whether any of these coalitions would include formations one might call revolutionary socialist movements is an open question. The world geopolitical options of such coalitions, where they came to power, would in part be a function of who won or was winning in the Chinese and US internal struggles. If the latter resulted, either together or separately, in offering genuine revolutionary poles of opposition, this would attract the radical nationalists of the semiperipheral countries. But if not, not.

We have sought to review the fifty years since the First World War and the twenty-five years to come as the beginning phase of the world-wide transition from a capitalist world-system to a socialist world-system. This transition will not be completed in a mere twenty-five years. But if we are to make rapid progress, it is important to reflect critically upon initial experiences and to conduct the struggle at critical nodes.

Shall we be optimistic? Sorokin seemed not to be. At the end of his book, he said: 'But from the lessons of history concerning life and death, the blossoming and sickness of society, man hardly learns anything' (p. 325). But this pessimism derives largely from his ambivalent views about cyclical theories of change. Sometimes he seems to say they are a never-ceasing pendulum. Sometimes he seems to find a way out.

He does say that if there is a way out, there must be a 'fundamental reorientation of values, [a] thoroughgoing change of mentality and conduct...' (p. 326). Is Mao Tse-Tung not saying the same thing, precisely in the light of the Soviet experience? But the possibility of change seems to cheer Sorokin up. He ends his book with a statement I should like to make my own:

Hence [because of the need for a fundamental reorientation of values] the crisis itself, and hence the inevitability of a fiery ordeal as the only available means of teaching the otherwise unteachable. *Volentem fata ducunt, nolentem trahunt.* The more unteachable we are, and the less freely and willingly we choose the sole course of salvation open to us, the more inexorable will be the coercion, the more pitiless the ordeal, the more terrible the *dies irae* of the transition. Let us hope that the grace of understanding may be vouchsafed us and that we may choose, before it is too late, the right road – the road that leads not to death but to the further realization of man's unique creative mission on this planet! *Benedictus qui venit in nomine Domini.* (p. 326)

16 ✢ Fanon and the revolutionary class

Preface to an article

This article is the continuation of a conversation. I knew Frantz Fanon at two moments of his life, and had long conversations with him. The first time was in the summer of 1960, when he was full of life and passion. It was in Accra and he was serving as the representative of the Provisional Government of the Algerian Republic, responsible for links to the government of Ghana and secondarily to other governments and movements in Black Africa. The second time was in the fall of 1961 when he was dying of leukemia in a hospital in Washington, DC, dying but still full of life and passion. He had just written *Les damnés de la terre*, a book composed with speed during the remission he had between his first and second (fatal) bout of illness, written speedily out of fear he might not complete it.

In this second period, Fanon had developed an intense curiosity about the United States, where he found himself. He wanted to know what made America tick and what were the prospects for revolution, particularly among the Blacks. At one moment of our conversation, referring to I no longer remember what, he suddenly said angrily: 'Vous américains, vous n'êtes pas prêts à vous dialoguer. Vous vous monologuez toujours.' I have always remembered this admonition, though it was not directed at me personally.

In the 1970s, the USA is happily no longer the all-powerful hegemonic power she was in 1961, a reality that had twisted the consciousness of all Americans. Perhaps the moment has come when the United States, and most particularly the American left, can enter into a dialogue with their comrades in the struggle elsewhere. Fanon believed that the function of critical intelligence

250

is to illuminate and make rational the work of militants. It is in this spirit that I should like to consider his views on class consciousness and revolutionary movements.

*

The failure of voluntarist revolution and ideas [in the 1960s] has discredited the writers associated with them. But it should not obscure the genuine defects of the Marxist analysis which prevailed in the 1950s and to which Fanon drew attention.   E. J. HOBSBAWM (1973, p. 6)

If Marx was not a Marxist, then Fanon surely was not a Fanonist. Fanonism, if I seize the essence of the now countless pejorative (and even some favorable) references to it, is said to be a belief that peasants are more revolutionary than urban workers, that the lumpenproletariat is more revolutionary than the proletariat, that the national bourgeoisie of the Third World is always hopeless, that violence is always purgative, and not only intellectuals but even cadres cannot be relied upon to make the revolution, without spontaneous explosions from the base. While each of these contentions can be backed up by numerous quotations from Fanon, and each reflects a partial truth which he stated, their combination as 'Fanonism' seems to me to miss the whole point of what Fanon was arguing.

A discussion of 'Fanonism' uncovers all the issues of revolutionary strategy and political tactics. The passion of the intellectual debate is an expression of political divisions *on the left*. I shall therefore ignore the occasional dyspeptic and usually ill-informed critic on the right and limit this discussion to those supporters and critics who share with Fanon a basic rejection of contemporary inequalities and oppression and a willingness to engage in militant action to change the world.

If one reads the set of such articles and books, one finds oneself amidst what the French call a 'dialogue of the deaf'. The same words recur throughout – bourgeoisie, proletariat, peasantry, lumpenproletariat – but the nature of these concepts and the empirical realities they are supposed to reflect, seem to be drawn from different universes, only occasionally intertwined. I should like to untangle this skein, in order to get at the nub of the issue. In order to to this, I shall review both the nature of the criticisms of 'Fanonism' in the light of what I believe Fanon's views were, and also whom I believe Fanon was attacking and why some of these people are counterattacking. It is only with this underbrush cleared away that I think we can begin seriously a dialogue on the left appropriate for the 1970s.

The degree of the confusion can be seen by noticing the disparity in the answers to the question most authors seem to ask: was Fanon a Marxist? The affirmative camp includes a variety of critics. Enrica Collotti-Pischel argued: 'The Marxist element in Fanon is quite large' (1962, p. 838). She felt that 'Fanon and Mao Tse-Tung are really on the same line, along with Ho Chi Minh, Castro and other leaders of the anticolonial revolution' (1962, p. 837). Fredj Stambouli agreed: 'Fanon's approach...remains in the tradition of Marxist–Leninist interpretation' (1967, p. 523). So did Tony Martin: 'but he was Marxist in the sense that Lenin or Castro or Mao are Marxist' (1970, p. 385). E. J. Hobsbawm put it more cautiously: 'Fanon is incomprehensible outside the context of Marxism and the international communist movement' (1973, p. 6). And Adolfo Gilly should probably be counted in the same group: 'He was not a Marxist. But he was approaching Marxism through the same essential door [used in Marx's analyses of historical events, a concern with what the masses do and say and think]' (1965, p. 2).

But, on the other side, Nguyen Nghe saw him as an 'individualist intellectual' (1962, p. 27) and implied he was a 'Trotskyist' (1963, p. 28). Similarly, Imre Marton accused Fanon of a 'subjectivist interpretation' (1965, 8/9, p. 56), reflecting 'the illusion of the petty bourgeoisie' (1965, 8/9, p. 59). For Jack Woddis, like Regis Debray and Herbert Mareuse, Fanon used 'the slogans of anarchism' an ideology that is 'an expression of the viewpoint of the petty bourgeoisie' (1972, p. 402). Renate Zahar seemed to be answering Enrica Collotti-Pischel when she said: 'Nonetheless, the analogy between the ideas of Fanon and the Chinese and Cuban theories of the anticolonialist revolution is quite superficial...' (1970, p. 100). The most recent and most negative evaluation was that of Azinna Nwafor who called upon readers to 'vigorously combat the erroneous formulation of Fanon on the role of social classes in the African revolution', contrasting these misconceptions with 'a concrete and correct analysis, adoption of appropriate practical measures of which Cabral already serves as a rich source and unerring guide' (1975, p. 27). Peter Worsley by contrast saw considerable overlap in the views of Fanon and Cabral (1972).

The last twist is that of Dennis Forsythe who said that Worsley's characterization of Fanon as a Marxist is 'misleading', though Fanon is also not an 'anti-Marxist'. For Forsythe, 'the divergent tendencies in Fanon's theorizing from Marxian analysis', divergencies that could also 'be detected in the works of Mao T'se-Tung, Che Guevara and Regis Debray...constitute an advance on Marxian analysis as far as the Third World is concerned' (1970, p. 4). Forsythe concluded that the 'Third World finds itself and speaks to itself through the voice of Fanon, just as Marx spoke up for the impoverished urban masses in the European context' (1970, p. 10).

What is it that those authors who consider Fanon 'un-Marxist' complain of? It is surely not his emphasis on the legitimate place of violence in the revolutionary process. Indeed, his 'Marxist' critics seem to go out of their way to make it clear they appreciate this part of Fanon's arguments, even if they demur on some nuances. (See Nguyen Nghe 1962, pp. 23–6; Marton 1965, 7, pp. 39–46; Woddis 1972, pp. 25–30, although Woddis insists that 'armed struggle' should only be seen as one type of a wider category, 'political struggle'.)

What they object to is rather his view of the politics of the various classes in the 'colonial world'. This is a crucial issue, for it has implications about 'class alliances' within and across frontiers. Let us review each of the four key class terms used by Fanon: proletariat, lumpenproletariat, peasantry, and bourgeoisie.

The phrase of Fanon that shocked the most, and was meant to shock the most, was this:

It has been pointed out repeatedly that, in colonial territories, the proletariat is the core of the colonized people most pampered by the colonial regime. The embryonic proletariat of the towns is relatively privileged. In capitalist countries, the proletariat has nothing to lose; it has everything to win in the long run. In colonized countries the proletariat has everything to lose.   (1961, p. 84)

From around the world, they snapped back. The Vietnamese communist, Nguyen Nghe, retorted:

The working class in the colonies does not constitute a privileged class in the sense that Fanon means, that is, one pampered by the settlers; it is privileged in the revolutionary sense of the word, by the fact that it is in the best position to observe first-hand the mechanisms of exploitation, to conceive the road to the future for the whole of society.   (1962, p. 31)

For the Hungarian communist, Imre Marton, '...even in sim-
plifying social realities in the extreme, we may still conclude that
it is impossible to place on the same plane the proletariat and the
national bourgeoisie...[The proletariat] is a class subjected to
exploitation by foreign capital, but also by national capital (1965,
8/9, p. 52). And the British Marxist, Jack Woddis, faults Fanon
on the simple accuracy of his 'incredible claim' that African
workers under colonialism were pampered:

All the available facts and statistics, which Fanon either ignored or of which
he was not even aware (and if it was the latter, it was totally irresponsible for
him to make such sweeping statements without even bothering to find out what
were the real facts) completely refute Fanon's claim. Nearly all official and
semi-official reports are compelled to admit that under colonial rule the African
worker, far from being 'pampered', had to put up with deplorable conditions.
Low paid, ill-clad, ill-housed, ill-fed, undernourished, diseased – this was too
often the condition of the typical African worker.   (1972, p. 108)

One wonders can Fanon and these authors be talking about the
same people? A closer look reveals they are not quite. Who is then
included in this proletariat which Fanon says has everything to
lose?

It is made up in fact of that fraction of the colonized people which is necessary
and indispensable for the proper functioning of the colonial machine: street-car
conductors, taxi-drivers, miners, dockers, interpreters, male-nurses, etc. These
are the elements who constitute the most faithful clientele of the nationalist
parties and who by the privileged place they occupy in the colonial system
constitute the 'bourgeois' fraction of the colonized people.   (1961, p. 84)

One additional quote will more clearly identify this 'pampered'
proletariat of Fanon who are but a 'bourgeois' fraction:

The great error, the congenital vice of the majority of political parties in the
underdeveloped regions has been to follow the classic schema of appealing first
of all to the most conscious elements: the proletariat of the towns, the artisans
and the civil servants, that is, to an infinitestimal part of the population *who
scarcely come to more than one per cent.*   (1961, p. 84; italics added)

Is this proletariat, who *along with the civil servants and the artisans*
are less than one per cent, the 'typical African worker' of whom
Woddis was talking? Clearly not, for Woddis says that Fanon's
argument 'fails to take account of the peculiar class structure of
Africa where, during the colonial period in which Fanon pretends
the workers enjoyed a special luxury, the overwhelming majority
of workers were *casual, unskilled migrant labourers or seasonal
workers in agriculture*' (1972, p. 102; italics added). Did Fanon then

fail to notice this group of whom Woddis talks? Not at all, but as we shall see, he called them lumpenproletarians and peasants. We will come to the question later of which terminology is more useful. Here I limit myself to pointing out that, by a semantic confusion, Woddis is attacking a straw man.

Nguyen Nghe's critique is more discriminating:

[The Fanonian conception involves] to begin with the error of placing in the same class the dockers and the miners with the interpreters and the male-nurses. The former constitute the true proletariat, the industrial working class (in the colonies, we must also locate here the workers on large plantations); the latter form part of the petty-bourgeoisie, also a revolutionary class, but with less resolution and follow-through.   (1962, p. 30)

Since Nguyen Nghe just previously cited Truong Chinh, 'theoretician of the Vietnamese revolution', as saying that the four classes that 'make up the people' and 'constitute the forces of revolution' are 'the working class, the class of peasant workers, the petty-bourgeoisie, and the national bourgeoisie', we must note that Nguyen Nghe is speaking of still a different group from both Fanon and Woddis, for his 'industrial working class' includes workers on large plantations ('peasants' in Fanon's usage) but excludes 'interpreters and male-nurses'. The latter become petty bourgeois, 'also revolutionary but with less resolution and follow-through'. But once again, is there not an element of word juggling here? Nguyen Nghe's less resolute 'petty-bourgeois' and Fanon's unreliable 'proletarians' seem to be, at the very least, overlapping categories.

If we move to a discussion of the lumpenproletariat, the debate becomes perhaps clearer. Neither Nguyen Nghe nor Marton really discussed the lumpenproletariat. But in Woddis' attack on Fanon, they played a central role. Woddis, relying on Marx, made the quite correct point that for Marx the lumpenproletariat served mainly as 'the bribed tool of reactionary intrigue' although, on occasion, it could play a positive role. 'But as a class, or rather sub-class, it would only be *swept* into movement by the proletariat at a time of revolution; it could certainly not initiate or lead a revolution' (1972, p. 80). What Woddis did *not* do is tell us who exactly are the lumpenproletarians and what their relationship is with the 'casual, unskilled migrant labourers' he included in the proletariat. It seems that for Woddis the actual lumpenproletariat is limited to 'the real *déclassés* (1972, p. 82) or, on the very same page, 'the declassed and criminal elements'. If declassed is supposed to refer to those who have shifted *downward* in life style as a result of changed class location of the adult, and not merely to uprooted migrants from country to city, one wonders if there are *any* declassed elements in Africa today, or even in the Third World generally. One certainly wonders if there are many.

This is not the group in any case Peter Worsley thought of when he read Fanon:

> It is a great mistake to think of them statically, as constituting a separate category – lumpenproletarians – sharply marked off from the peasants as if they were really a fixed and consolidated social class, firstly, because they are ex-peasants, anyhow, and secondly, because they are essentially *people in process.* They are *becoming* townsmen – eventually, they hope, a part of the settled, employed urban working-class population. But they are a long way from being absorbed and accepted into urban society. They are outcasts, marginal men, travelers between two social worlds, occupants of a limbo to which most of us would think hell preferable, but which for them represents a great improvement in many respects upon the village life they have abandoned.   (1969, pp. 42–3)

A more sophisticated skepticism about the lumpenproletariat has been expressed by Robin Cohen and David Michael whose attack was directed less against Fanon than what they called 'an identifiable "Fanonist tradition" [that] has been established by Peter Worsley, Oscar Lewis, Peter Gutkind, and others' (1973, p. 32). The complaint of Cohen and Michael about the 'Fanonists', but one that might equally be made about Woddis, was that they assumed the marginality of the lumpenproletariat, whereas:

> The lumpenproletariat is much less alienated from the neo-colonial economy than the Fanonists imply. Many of them, indeed, have an important stake in the system and live, like parasites, off the productive labour of others – whether it be through dependence on the income of employed kin, through theft or through the provision of services like prostitution.   (1973, p. 36)

Furthermore, Cohen and Michael believed that the very category may be a dubious researcher's taxonomy which groups together as 'street people' such varied types as 'beggars, religious ascetics and prophets, the physically disabled and insane' plus another whole segment of the population among whom '. . . distinctions need to be drawn between those who are de-employed, those who are intermittently employed, those who have given up all hope of securing employment, those who still seek jobs and those who have accommodated themselves to a socially disapproved livelihood as thieves, pimps or prostitutes' (1973, pp. 37–8). These are helpful precisions for a discussion of political tactics. For the moment, we simply note that this makes clear that Fanon was indeed talking of a far larger social category than Woddis suggested.

It is about the peasantry that we find Fanon's second shock-quote:

> It is quite clear that, in colonial countries, the peasantry alone is revolutionary. It has nothing to lose and everything to gain. The peasant, the declassed person, the starving person is the exploited person who discovers soonest that violence alone pays. For him, there is no compromise, no possibility of coming to terms.
>
> (1961, p. 46)

Nguyen Nghe was struck by the vigor of the affirmation. He called on us 'simultaneously to capture the profound truth of Fanon's affirmation, to appreciate the inestimable support of the peasant masses for the revolution', – and to see where Fanon went wrong. 'The peasant, *by himself*, can never attain revolutionary conscious-ness; it is the militant coming *from the towns* who will discern patiently the most capable elements among the poor peasants, educate them, organize them, and it is thus only after a long period of political work that one can mobilize the peasantry' (1962, p. 29; italics added). The peasantry *alone* is revolutionary! The peasant, by himself, can *never* attain revolutionary consciousness! We are amidst a confrontation of the Algerian and Vietnamese experiences, of the failure to create a revolutionary party and the success. Nguyen Nghe continued:

> The poor peasant may be a patriot and die heroically gun in hand, but *if he remains a peasant*, he will not be able to lead the revolutionary movement...The Vietnamese People's Army is made up 90% of peasants but the revolutionary leadership *has not defined itself* as a peasant leadership, and the leaders seek to inculcate in the militants an ideology that is not peasant, but proletarian.
>
> (1962, p. 31; italics added)

Nguyen Nghe went further. He suggested that the success *and the limits* of the *Chinese* experience depended precisely on the role the peasantry played in it:

> Even far-off Yenan received messages and men continuously from Shanghai located several thousand kilometers away; without this osmosis Yenan would have become the refuge of a mere sect, cut off from historical experience, destined sooner or later to disappear...
>
> It is probable that certain negative aspects of the Chinese revolution are due to too strong a peasant imprint, to too long a stay in the countryside of many leaders and militants.
>
> (1962, pp. 32–3)

Once again, who are the peasants? Nguyen Nghe sometimes talked of peasants, sometimes of *poor* peasants. Woddis said that 'one should not ignore that the peasantry is, in general, based on the petty ownership of the means of production'. But he then proceeded to tell us:

The peasantry is really not one homogeneous class. If one can imagine, for example, a tube of toothpaste open at both ends and being squeezed in the middle, one has to an extent a picture of what happens to the peasantry. From an army of smallholders *a mass of poor and often landless peasants* is squeezed out at the bottom, while a small stratum of rich peasants employing wage labour emerges at the top. In other words, the peasantry is in a stage of break-up into three distinct strata with largely different interests. *In fact, the poor landless peasant often ends up as the wage labourer* exploited by the rich peasant.

(1972, pp. 59–60; italics added)

It should be clear that Fanon's starving peasant is scarcely Woddis' rich peasant. He is quite probably Woddis' 'poor and often landless' peasant who, as Woddis notes, often ends up as the 'wage labourer', in short, as a proletarian. Remember Nguyen Nghe also specifically cited wage workers on plantations as proletarians. So Fanon's peasants turn out to be Nguyen Nghe's and Woddis' proletarians, or almost.

Let us look finally at the fourth major class-category, the bourgeoisie. The plot thickens. For in many ways we are coming to the key question for which the debate about the working classes serves as camouflage. What does Fanon say of the bourgeoisie?

The national bourgeoisie which comes to power at the end of the colonial regime is an underdeveloped bourgeoisie. Its economic strength is almost nonexistent and in any case incommensurate with that of the metropolitan bourgeoisie it hopes to replace... The university graduates and merchants who make up the most enlightened fraction of the new state are noteworthy by their paucity, their concentration in the capital city, and the kind of activities in which they engage: trafficking (*négoce*), farming, the liberal professions. Among this national bourgeoisie one finds neither industrialists nor financiers. The national bourgeoisie of underdeveloped countries is not involved in production, invention, construction, labor. It is completely routed towards intermediary-type activities... In the colonial system, a bourgeoisie that accumulates capital is an impossibility.

(1962, p. 114)

Thus, incapable of fulfilling the historic role of a bourgeoisie, it must be combatted because the national bourgeoisie 'is good for nothing' (1961, p. 132).

The condemnation is global. And it is this unwillingness to find *any* virtue in the national bourgeoisie that seems to exasperate most of his critics. Imre Marton chastised Fanon for concentrating exclusively on the relations of the national bourgeoisie with 'imperialist forces'. He forgot, says Marton, the existence of a socialist bloc which has the consequence, for *some* countries, of inducing the national bourgeoisie '...under the pressure of the popular masses...to conduct in international affairs a meaningfully anti-imperialist policy and at home a policy which, to various degrees, takes into consideration certain political and economic aspirations of the popular masses' (1965, 8/9, p. 51) Woddis repeated the same theme: 'But it is equally true that the very existence of a socialist system provides new possibilities for the national bourgeoisie to secure help in building its independent economy and in lessening its dependence on imperialism, and in this very process to come into conflict with the imperialist powers' (1972, p. 95).

Amady Ali Dieng, agreeing with Marton, added that Fanon had neglected the 'generally accepted' distinction in Marxist writings between the national bourgeoisie 'which exploit an internal market whose interests are opposed to those of imperialism', and a 'bureaucratic and comprador bourgeoisie...whose interests are closely linked to those of imperialism'. Apparently fearing this distinction might however serve to classify in the camp of the people some of Africa's most reactionary politicians, Dieng quickly added a footnote. 'This conception [of a national bourgeoisie] excludes the Ivory Coast rural bourgeoisie from the ranks of the national bourgeoisie for they are based on the cultivation of coffee and cocoa and thus have their interests tied to imperialism by virtue of the fact that their market lies outside the Ivory Coast' (1967, p. 26). But, since there is scarcely a 'bourgeois' anywhere in Africa who is not involved in cash-crops or other enterprises linked directly to a *world* market, once we exclude the Ivory Coast rural bourgeoisie, we should have to exclude many others and we would end up with a nearly empty category. At which point, would not Dieng's 'bureaucratic and comprador bourgeoisie' in fact heavily overlap with Fanon's national bourgeoisie?

As we have moved through the class categories we have noted semantic confusion after semantic confusion. How strange! Is Fanon so difficult to read? It is true his style was 'literary' and far from 'precise'. It is true that he reveled in rhetorical flourish.

But the texts are neither abstract nor abstruse. They are filled with concrete referents and earthy descriptions. It should not have been so difficult to seize the essence – unless one didn't want to.

Whom was Fanon attacking? We must put him in his context. He wrote his major work in 1961 in the seventh year of the Algerian war of national liberation. Independence was in sight. The previous year, in 1960, fifteen African states had become independent, in large part, as Fanon well knew, in the wake of the Algerian struggle. In the summer of 1960, the Congo 'collapsed', and the counterrevolution in Africa showed its teeth. Fanon was in the Congo as a representative of the Algerian provisional government at the height of the first crisis and futilely sought to rally the independent African states behind Lumumba. Lumumba's murder must have been announced just as he began to write *The Wretched of the Earth*.

Furthermore, the Algerians had fought a long war, with only belated and begrudging support from the French Communist Party and the USSR. They had little reason to be grateful to Imre Marton's 'socialist camp'.

Finally, it is indeed historically true for Algeria that the urban proletariat had made more revolutionary noise than it engaged in action, and that the revolution did begin in the rural areas, 'spontaneously' (that is, outside the established organizational structures, and against them).

Fanon found the Algerian revolution an island of health in a sea of neocolonial governments in Africa whose reality he saw clearly far earlier than most observors. While much of the world left was celebrating the advent of the single-party states in Africa, Fanon cried out: 'The single party is the modern form of the dictatorship of the bourgeoisie, without mask, without make-up, unscrupulous, cynical' (1961, p. 124).

Burned by Europe, and twice shy. There too is another issue full of emotion. It is no accident that Fanon, the Martinican, educated in France, struggling for Algeria, should have become the hero of the Black Panther Party in the United States and other Black militants. Eldridge Cleaver wrote that *The Wretched of the Earth* became 'known among the militants of the black liberation movement in America as "the Bible"' (1967, p. 18). Huey Newton said they read Fanon, Mao, and Che (1973, p. 111). Stambouli

defended Fanon's 'haste...to abandon European models' by
pointing to 'the inadequacy of these models for the reality of
ex-colonial countries' (1967, p. 528). Collotti-Pischel defended
Fanon's attack on the inadequacy of the *action* of the European
left:

> It is difficult today for a European Marxist to contest, in good faith, the truth
> of Fanon's thesis that, in the struggle of colonial peoples for independence and
> development, the European masses have in every way sinned by absenteeism
> and impotence...when they 'did not directly align themselves in colonial
> questions with our common oppressors (*padroni*).'   (1962, pp. 857–8)

For Imre Marton on the contrary, the models of Europe, like the
action of the European left, were quite adequate: 'Fanon detaches
the internal conditions of the countries of the Third World from
the general laws governing our epoch...What is merely a specific
form becomes for Fanon a specific content, in opposition to
socialism as it has been realized in the socialist countries' (1965,
8/9, p. 60). Surprisingly, Nguyen Nghe went further in this regard.
He charged Fanon with a 'refusal of modern values' which
condemned the Third World countries to 'stay in their rut':

> We cannot begin history over, as Fanon claims. We fit ourselves into the currents
> of history, or rather we must figure out how to do so. However much we hate
> imperialism, the primary duty, for an Asian or an African, is to recognize that
> for the last three centuries, it is Europe that has been in the avant-garde of
> history. Europe has placed in the arena of history at least two values which had
> been lacking for many Asian and African countries; two values which go
> together, even if at certain moments or in certain places they were not
> necessarily linked: the renewal of productive forces, and democracy.
>   (1963, p. 34)

Nguyen Nghe's charge that Fanon wished to begin history over
is quite off the mark. It is simply that Fanon had a more acerbic
view of Europe's accomplishments. 'This Europe which never
ceased talking about Man, never ceased proclaiming that she was
concerned only about Man, we know today with what sufferings
humanity has paid for each of the victories of its spirit' (1961,
p. 239). But in any case what concerned Fanon was less the past
than the future. 'Remember, comrades, the European game is
finished forever; we must find something else' (1961, p. 239). If
Africa wants to imitate Europe,

> ...then let us confide the destinies of our countries to Europeans. They will
> know how to do better than the most gifted among us.

But we wish that humanity advance one small bit,...we must invent, we must discover...

For Europe, for ourselves and for humanity, comrades, we must grow a new skin, develop new concepts, try to create a new man.   (1961, p. 242; italics added)

It is precisely on the questions of class structure in the world-system, and the class alliances that are essential for a revolution, that Fanon looked for 'a new skin', and 'new concepts'. Far from rejecting European thought, in which he was deeply embedded himself, he took the title of his book from the *Internationale*, and he took his starting point from the *Communist Manifesto*: 'Workers of the world unite! You have nothing to lose but your chains.' He simply said, let us look again to see who has how many chains, and which are the groups who, having the fewest privileges, may be the most ready to become a 'revolutionary class'. The old labels are old skins, which do not correspond *fully* with contemporary reality.

Fanon did not offer us the finished analysis. He issued the clarion call for this analysis. Marie Perinbam, it seems to me, caught this point exactly: 'Fanon was not analysing a revolution; he was trying to sustain one, and to create others...Fanon's hypothesis about the spontaneously revolutionary peasantry, far from being an appraisal of a particular situation, was a rallying idea, a myth, a symbol of committed action' (1973, pp. 441, 444). This is why Stambouli could say about Fanon's conception of the role of the peasantry that it aroused the most criticism and that it was the part of his argument that was 'perhaps the least understood' (1967, p. 526).

The key tactical issue is how the sides line up in the world struggle, and Fanon was in this matter skeptical of certain received truths. In 1961, his arguments seemed more heretical than they do in the 1970s after so many ideological landmarks have been called into question by the profound split in the world communist movement.

Enrica Collotti-Pischel isolated clearly on the key theoretical issue of what may be called the Leninist heritage about which Fanon was raising questions:

In substance the origin of the colonial problematic within the Comintern was two-fold. On the one hand there were the political and even more generally human consequences of the Leninist thesis of the world struggle against imperialism, the indispensable unity of the proletarian and colonial revolutionary struggle, the denunciation of the acceptance of colonial oppression on the part of the majority of European social-democrats. On the other hand, there were the whole set of arguments that resulted from the extension to the colonies of concepts elaborated by Marxists primarily in order to take a position on the problem of the *national* question and which were characterized, at least initially, by factors typically growing out of the particular situation of the problems of national minorities in Europe, that is, out of the heritage of the disintegration of European multinational states. (1962, pp. 840-1)

The solution to this problematic was the 'theory of revolution in two stages', a bourgeois-democratic stage followed by a socialist stage, each stage implying a different class alliance.

In effect, various of his critics are attacking Fanon for assuming that the first stage must necessarily go astray, that it can and must be 'skipped'. Whereas, say they, it cannot be skipped and will only go astray if adventurist neglect of the primacy of the proletariat undermines the ability of the working classes to check the bourgeoisie *while collaborating with it,* and thereby, in Woddis' phrase, 'complete the aim of national liberation' (1972, p. 113), or as Nguyen Nghe argued:

Endowing armed struggle with absolute metaphysical value leads Fanon to neglect another aspect of the revolutionary struggle, which was not even discussed in his book, the problem of the union of social classes, of different social strata for national independence and, once peace has been restored, for the building of a new society. (1963, p. 28)

Perhaps the most credible criticism along this line has been made by Basil Davidson who argued that in the one place other than Algeria where Fanon applied his own theories, his judgment was shown to be mistaken. This was in Angola where Fanon was an early strong supporter of the UPA of Holden Roberto against the MPLA of Agostinho Neto.

The proof of Fanon's error, or of the error of the conclusion which others drew from what he preached or was thought to preach, may be seen most easily of all in the experience of Angola. The almost completely unprepared rising of the Kongo people in March 1961 was very 'Fanonist' in conception, but it led to disaster, whereas the progress of the Angolan national movement under MPLA leadership, very 'non-Fanonist' in this context, has led to continual expansion and success. (Davidson 1972, p. 10)

This is no doubt a strong argument, to which can best be replied what the most generous of Fanon's sharp critics, Nguyen Nghe, had to say: 'If Frantz Fanon were still alive, how many things might he have still learned, in the light of the Algerian experience?'

(1963, p. 26). And, one might add, in the light of everything that has happened since Nguyen Nghe wrote?

What is it that we can learn, in the light of Fanon's critique of the inadequacies of revolutionary theory of the 1950s, plus the concrete experience of the 1960s? One thing, I think, is that the trinity of terms which we have to describe the 'working classes' or the 'poor' – proletariat, peasantry, and lumpenproletariat – are in many ways misleading because of connotations that may be said to describe the realities of nineteenth-century Europe (and even that?), but do not really correspond with the twentieth-century world.

Peasantry is a term that groups together proletarians and bourgeois, and assumes a kind of socio-geographic separateness of country and city which precisely has been breaking down. Lumpenproletarian is simply a Marxian euphemism for what the bourgeoisie once called the 'dangerous classes' and breeds confusion.

I would think the most useful distinctions to make is first of all between proletarians and semiproletarians, that is between those who derive their *life*-income from wage labor and those who, in their life-income, receive one part from wage labor and one part from other sources such as access to usufruct of primary production; doles from family, the state, or the public; and theft. Such a distinction will make it clear why Tony Martin is correct in saying that, for Fanon, 'the lumpenproletariat is but an urban extension of the peasantry' (1970, p. 389). It is because the semiproletarians, in most cases and especially in the peripheral countries of the world-economy, are indeed obliged to move back and forth over their lifetime from urban to rural areas in order to eke out the non-wage segment of their *life*-income.

Once one makes the distinction one between the proletariat and the semiproletariat, it is easy to see how Fanon's ideas can be applied to the 'advanced capitalist countries' as well as to the Third World, as Worsley did: 'the notion of the "Third World" refers to a set of *relationships*, not to a set of *countries*. It also points to the special misery of peasantry, *lumpenproletariat*, and to the broad division between the White "Lords of Human Kind" and the "Natives" of the earth whether these be in Harlem or in Hong Kong' (1972, p. 220). It is in this context that we can understand the formulation of Eldridge Cleaver: 'In both the Mother Country and the Black Colony, the working class is the right wing of the proletariat and the lumpenproletariat is the left wing... We definitely have a major contradiction between the working class and the lumpenproletariat.' (Cited in Worsley 1972, p. 222.)

The historic process of capitalism is that of proletarian*ization*. It is far from being completed, if it ever will be. In this process, those who are only semi-employed during their working *life* must scrounge to survive. They are at once more desperate and more mobile than the permanently employed, however much the latter are exploited. It seems difficult not to agree that the semiproletarians are indeed the 'wretched of the earth', and that they are the most likely group to engage spontaneously in violence.

It is curious that Fanon ever should have been attacked for a supposed belief in the unremitting virtues of spontaneity. The chapter on spontaneity after all is entitled 'The grandeur *and the weaknesses* of spontaneity'. It is in this chapter that he says 'The leaders of the insurrection come to see that even very large-scale *jacqueries* need to be brought under control and oriented. These leaders are led to renounce the movement as a mere *jacquerie* and therefore transform it into a revolutionary war' (1961, p. 102). Fanon is neither denying the need for revolutionary *organization* (quite the contrary) nor denying the importance of ideological commitment. He is assessing which groups are most likely to be willing to take the first and hardest steps in a revolution, the serious beginnings. Those who wait for the 'right moment' risk waiting for Godot.

Fanon did not therefore endorse any and all forms of violence. His language is quite clear in this matter: 'The impetuous wolf who wanted to devour everything, the sudden gust of wind which was going to bring about an authentic revolution risks, if the struggle takes long, and it does take long, becoming unrecognizable. The colonized continually run the risk of allowing themselves to be disarmed by some minor concession' (1961, p. 105). This is why political organization and ideological clarity are imperative. But nonetheless, said Fanon, it is from the mass of semiproletarians that the militants are likely to be drawn.

There is another distinction to be drawn in our map of class relationships, one within the proletariat proper. It is that between those proletarians who live at or near the level of minimum subsistence adequate for this maintenance and reproduction and little else and those wage workers who receive a substantial income permitting a 'bourgeois' style of life but which they spend more or less as they earn it. This group is frequently called 'petty bourgeois', a term Fanon tends to avoid. The key fact to note is the absence of a secure property base for this style of life and therefore the risk for an individual of losing the high income, the reward for skill *and conformity.*

This 'labor aristocracy' (if one can stretch one's image of Lenin's term to cover not merely skilled workers but cadres, technicians, and professionals) are in a 'social contract with the true bourgeoisie, in which their collective individual remunerations are the political counterpart of their essential conservatism. This 'social contract' works both ways. When any particular segment is threatened with exclusion from advantages or not admitted to it, it will become 'militant' in its demands. In the colonial countries, these are the 'bourgeois fraction' of whom Fanon wrote and whose intentions and actions as 'leaders of nationalist movements' he denounced.

Was Fanon then against a 'revolution in two stages'? It all depends on the interpretation. Collotti-Pischel noted that Mao Tse-Tung accepted this formula, but she added:

The fundamental difference between the position of Mao and that of Stalin was precisely in this different sense of the function of dialectic in the historical process:...the national-bourgeois phase in Mao is significantly more transitory and provisional than in Stalin. What mattered was not the development of the phase, but its overcoming.   (1962, p. 847)

As for Fanon, his answer was no less clear: 'The theoretical question posed about underdeveloped countries over the last fifty years, to wit, can the bourgeois phase be skipped or not, must be resolved at the level of revolutionary action and not by thinking about it' (1961, p. 131). Is this so wrong?

Rereading Fanon in the light of the history of revolutionary movements in the twentieth century should lead us *away from* polemics and into a closer analysis of the realities of class structures. The fetish of terminology often blinds us to the evolution of the phenomena they are supposed to capture. Fanon suspected strongly that the more benefits strata drew from an existing unequal system, the more prudent they would be in their political activity. He pushed us to look for who would take what risks and then asked us to build a movement out of such a revolutionary class. Have the history of the years since he wrote disproved this instinct? I fail to see how and where.

References

Cleaver, Eldridge. 1967. *Post-prison Writings and Speeches.* New York: Vintage Ramparts

Cohen, Robin and David Michael. 1973. 'The Revolutionary Potential of the African Lumpenproletariat: A Skeptical View'. *Bulletin of the Institute of Development Studies*, 5 (October), 31–42

Collotti-Pischel, Enrica. 1962. '"Fanonismo" e "questione coloniale"'. *Problemi del socialismo*, 5, 834–64

Davidson, Basil. 1972. Review of Y. T. Museveni *et al.*, *Essays in the Liberation of Southern Africa*, and K. W. Grundy, *Guerilla Struggle in Africa*. *Anti-Apartheid News* (September), 10

Dieng, Amady Ali. 1967. 'Les damnés de la terre et les problèmes d'Afrique noire'. *Présence africaine*, 62 (2), 15–30

Fanon, Frantz. 1961. *Les damnés de la terre*, Cahiers libres 27–8. Paris: Ed. Maspéro. (The English translation is frequently careless and misleading, particularly when dealing with the nuances of precisely the controversial concepts discussed in this paper. I have therefore made all my own translations.)

Forsythe, Dennis. 1970. 'Frantz Fanon: Black Theoretician'. *The Black Scholar*, 1 (March), 2–10

Gilly, Adolfo. 1965. 'Introduction'. In Frantz Fanon, *Studies in a Dying Colonialism*, pp. 1–21. New York: Monthly Review Press

Hobsbawm, E. J. 1973. 'Passionate Witness'. Review of Irene L. Gendzier, *Frantz Fanon: A Critical Study. The New York Review of Books*, 22 February, pp. 6–10

Martin, Tony. 1970. 'Rescuing Fanon from the Critics'. *African Studies Review*, 13 (December), 381–99

Marton, Imre. 1965. 'A propos des thèses de Fanon'. *Action* (revue théorique et politique du Parti Communiste Martiniquais), 7 (2), 39–55; 8/9 (3/4), 45–66

Newton, Huey P. *Revolutionary Suicide*. New York: Harcourt, Brace, Jovanovich

Nghe, Nguyen. 1963. 'Frantz Fanon et les problèmes de l'indépendance'. *La Pensée*, 107 (February), 23–30

Nwafor, Azinna. 1975. 'Imperialism and Revolution in Africa'. *Monthly Review*, 26 (April), 18–32

Perinbam, B. Marie. 1973. 'Fanon and the Revolutionary Peasantry – The Algerian Case'. *The Journal of Modern African Studies*, 11 (September), 427–45

Stambouli, Fredj. 1967. 'Frantz Fanon face aux problèmes de la décolonisation et de la construction nationale'. *Revue de l'Institut de Sociologie*, 2/3, 519–34

Woddis, Jack. 1972. *New Theories of Revolution.* New York: International Publishers

Worsley, Peter. 1969. 'Frantz Fanon: Evolution of a Revolutionary – Revolutionary Theories'. *Monthly Review*, 21 (May), 30–49

1972. 'Frantz Fanon and the "Lumpenproletariat"'. *Socialist Register*, pp. 193–230

Zahar, Renate. 1970. *L'oeuvre de Frantz Fanon*, Petite collection Maspéro 57. Paris: Maspéro

17 ~ An historical perspective on the emergence of the new international order: economic, political, cultural aspects

The 'new international order' is, at one and the same time, a program and an analysis. It is a program of social transformation; it is an analysis of why such social transformation is possible or even probable.

As a program it is couched in the Aesopian language of the United Nations. Caught amidst the linguistic differences of east and west, north and south, the United Nations has invented a suitably flat expression which is unexceptionable, since the only thing on which everyone can agree is that the 'new' may be desirable.

It is often said that what distinguishes so-called 'traditional', premodern systems from the modern world is that the premodern systems were unchanging whereas the modern world-system makes (technological) change its central focus. This is in fact false. Premodern societies were constantly changing, and the modern world has been, when all is said and done, a remarkably slow-changing world. Nonetheless there is an important difference between the two in their ideologies of change: in premodern systems, whenever there was real change it was justified by arguing that no change had occurred. In the modern world, whenever real change does not occur, it is justified by asserting that change has in fact taken place.

Bearing in mind then the meaninglessness of the invocation of newness, we will approach this subject skeptically. What is in fact new in the international order? And in what temporality is it new? For time is not singular. Indeed there is even more than one *dimension* of temporalities.

There is first of all Braudel's 'plurality of social time...indispensable to a common methodology of the social

269

sciences'.[1] This is his now fam̲o̲u̲s̲ ̲d̲i̲s̲t̲i̲n̲c̲t̲i̲o̲n between the *longue durée* which is 'slow-moving, sometimes practically static',[2] the 'conjunctural' which is the turn in a cyclical movement and is medium-term, and the episodic or short-term (*événementielle*) which is 'the tempo of individuals, of our illusions and rapid judgment –...the chronicler's and journalist's time'.[3] Braudel asserts that we must explicitly recognize the multiple social times because otherwise our models have no meaning: '...models are of varying duration: they have the same time-value as the reality they record. And for the social observer, this time aspect is of prime importance – for even more important than the profound structures of life are their breaking points and their sharp or gradual deterioration under opposing pressures.'[4] For make no mistake about it. Even the 'slow-moving, sometimes practically static' *longue durée* changes. The long term is not the same, for Braudel, as 'the *very long-term*, sheltered from accidents, conjunctures and breakdowns',[5] the time of qualitative mathematics and of Claude Lévi-Strauss, about whose very reality Braudel, the historian, casts a doubtful eye: 'if it exists, [the very long-term] can only be the time-period of the sages...'[6]

Thus, Braudel gives us two dimensions along which time may be divided. There is first of all the variety of social times. And then there is the division between all finite social time, however slow-moving, and the eternal time of the sages (and the qualitative mathematicians, another name for universalizing social scientists).

There is however a third dimension of time, one bequeathed to us by the Protestant theologian, Paul Tillich. It is the distinction between *chronos*, 'formal time' and *kairos*, 'the right time'. This distinction, found within the Greek language, was used by Tillich to assert the difference between quantitative and qualitative time:

Time is an empty form only for abstract, objective reflection, a form that can receive any kind of content; but to him who is conscious of an ongoing creative life it is laden with tensions, with possibilities and impossibilities, it is qualitative

1. Fernand Braudel, 'History and the Social Sciences', in Peter Burke (ed.), *Economy and Society in Early Modern Europe* (New York: Harper Torchbooks, 1972), p. 13.
2. *Ibid.*, p. 20.
3. *Ibid.*, p. 14.   4. *Ibid.*, p. 32.
5. *Ibid.*, p. 33.   6. *Ibid.*, p. 35.

and full of significance. Not everything is possible at every time, not everything is true at every time, nor is everything demanded at every moment.[7]

We do not have to share Tillich's theology to recognize the importance of this other dimension of time, and to ask ourselves if perhaps Tillich was right in being 'convinced that today a kairos, an epochal moment of history, is visible'.[8]

I should thus like to discuss three temporalities: the *longue durée* of the modern world-system; the secular trends and cyclical rhythms of that system; and the *kairos*, the moment of transition in which we are living today.

How long is a *longue durée*? That too depends on which structures we are analyzing. The structures of social geography, of the ecological underpinnings of our social relations, are finite but nonetheless millenial. The structures of civilizations, of the cultural forms in which we clothe our social action and even more of the cultural barriers we erect, are multisecular, if not millenial. The structures of the social economy, of the modes of production which determine the constraints within which social action occur, are perhaps shorter still, albeit still 'long', still multisecular.

The modern world-system is a capitalist world-economy, whose origins reach back to the sixteenth century in Europe. Its emergence is the result of a singular historic transformation, that from feudalism to capitalism.[9] This capitalist world-economy continues in existence today and now includes geographically the entire world, including those states ideologically committed to socialism.

In order to appreciate what is new and not new in the international economic order, we must first have a clear view of what this economic order is and how it differs from other economic orders. We must elucidate what is capitalism, in what ways it represents a change from prior systems and presumptive or possible successor ones. We could of course say that 'capitalism' has always existed and may always exist. And if we define capitalism as merely the use of stored dead labor, then this is

7. Paul Tillich, 'Kairos', in *The Protestant Era* (Chicago: University of Chicago Press, 1948), p. 33.
8. *Ibid.*, p. 48.
9. The argument that this transition was singular and not repeated on many successive occasions in different 'societies' or 'social formations' is spelled out in my 'From Feudalism to Capitalism: Transition or Transitions?' *Social Forces*, 55: 2 (December 1976), 273–83, and above, ch. 8.

surely true, or at least has been true for tens of thousands of years. And it is unlikely to cease to be true. But this is to ignore the fundamentally different ways in which human groups treat their capital. The usefulness of capitalism as a term is to designate that system in which the structures give primacy to the accumulation of capital *per se*, rewarding those who do it well and penalizing all others, as distinct from those systems in which the accumulation of capital is subordinated to some other objective, however defined.

If we mean by capitalism a system oriented to capital accumulation *per se*, capitalism has only existed in one time and place, the modern world since the sixteenth century. Earlier there had been capitalists. There had even been embryonic or proto-capitalist systems. But there had not yet been the *kairos*, 'the moment of the fulness of time',[10] which permitted the emergence of a capitalist *system*. These previous social structures were such as to circumscribe the individual capitalists found within them, quash those forces that sought to change the social economy in a capitalist direction, and in general destroy the fruit of 'enterprise'.

What distinguishes capitalism as a mode of production is that its multiple structures relate one to the other in such a way that, in consequence, the push to endless accumulation of capital becomes and remains dominant. Production tends always to be for profit rather than for use. In a capitalist system, the realization of profit is made possible by the existence of an economy-wide market, which is the measure of value even for those economic activities that do not pass through it directly. Many may seek to escape the market mechanism in a capitalist world-economy. But the claim that one has succeeded is an idelogical stance, which any particular more disinterested observer can take for what it's worth.

What provides the continuity of a capitalist world-economy through its *longue durée* is the continuous functioning of its three central antinomies: economy/polity; supply/demand; capital/labor. The coexistence of these three antinomies is defining of capitalism, and the way their contradictions fit into each other is the clue to the dynamics of the system as a whole.

10. Tillich, 'Kairos', p. 33.

What is the nature of these three antinomies?

Economy/polity: 'Economy is primarily a "world" structure but political activity takes place primarily within and through state structures whose boundaries are narrower than those of the economy.'

Supply/demand: 'World supply is primarily a function of market-oriented "individual" production decisions. World demand is primarily a function of "socially" determined allocations of income.'

Capital/labor: 'Capital is accumulated by appropriating surplus produced by labor, but the more capital is accumulated, the less the role of labor in production.'[11]

The *continuity* of the capitalist world-economy from the sixteenth century to today is found in the interacting pressures generated by these three antinomies which have determined the largest part of social behavior throughout the history of the system. Perhaps the exact percentage of social behavior this matrix explains has varied somewhat over time, rising from the sixteenth to the late nineteenth and early twentieth centuries, and declining slightly since, but the concept of capitalism can be used to denote a single system whose boundaries of time and space are those in which this matrix has predominated. There was a before (and an outside); there will be an after. What lies between and within is capitalism.

The antinomy between the 'world'-wide economy and the multiple polities accounts for the continuing pressure towards state 'formation' and centralization, the creation of a world-wide state *system*, and the particular form of imperialism which thrives better on 'informal empire' than on direct political colonization.

Unequal exchange is the principal outcome of this antinomy. Unequal exchange has to do not with the initial appropriation of surplus value, but its redistribution, once created, from peripheral to core regions. The absence of a world-empire, a single state encompassing the whole world-economy, makes it structurally impossible for any ruling group to yield to pressures in favor of production for use-value, even were it so inclined. State

11. These definitions are cited from 'Patterns of Development of the Modern World-System', research proposal of the Fernand Braudel Center for the Study of Economies, Historical Systems, and Civilizations, published in *Review*, 1: 2 (Fall 1977), 111–45.

structures that attempt to do so penalize their cadres and citizens in material ways, thus creating internal (as well as external) pressures against the maintenance of such a policy.

States therefore have tended to fall back into another role, as agents maximizing the division of the world surplus in favor of specific groups (sometimes located within their borders, sometimes located outside). Of course, not all states are equally successful in this attempt – a function of the ways in which the capital/labor and supply/demand antinomies determine their ever-changing capacities to affect the world market, as well as their ever-changing tactical postures.

States in which core activities are located have achieved the most efficacious state structures relative to other states. That is both the consequence of the nature of their economic activity and of the socio-economic groups located within its limits, and the cause of their ability to specialize in core-like activities. States in which peripheral activities are concentrated are conversely weak, and are weakened by the very process of economic peripheralization. The semiperipheral *state* is precisely the arena where, because of a mix of economic activities, conscious state activity may do most to affect the future patterning of economic activity. In the twentieth century, this takes the form of bringing socialist parties to power.

State machineries have interfered with the workings of the world market from the inception of capitalism. Moreover, the states have formed, developed, and militarized themselves each in relation to the others, seeking thus to channel the division of surplus value. In consequence, *all* state structures have grown progressively stronger over time absolutely, although the *relative* differences bewtween core and peripheral areas have probably remained the same or even increased. This steady expansion of state machineries, sometimes called bureaucratization, sometimes called the rise of state capitalism, has not yet changed the nature of the contradiction between an economy whose structural forces transcend the frontiers of any state, however powerful, and thus render the world-economy still resistant to a fundamental political reordering of social priorities of production. In short, capitalism still survives.

The antinomy of supply/demand at the level of the world-economy is the necessary consequence of the economy/polity antinomy. The absence of an overarching political structure has made it virtually impossible for anyone (or any state) effectively to 'limit' world supply. Supply is a function of the perceived profitability of production, whether the producer is a household, a private firm, or a state enterprise, and whether the profit is consumed by the producers or reinvested. Hence, world-wide, production is 'individual', anarchic, and competitive. Production proceeds as long as it seems more profitable to produce than not to produce. Rising real prices will of course stimulate production. But even declining real prices will do the same at first, as individual producers run after absolute profit by expanding quantity to make up for low profit ratios per item. Only a true 'crash' slows the process down, thereby eliminating the weak producers and increasing the world concentration of capital.

That these 'crashes' are systematic is the other side of the economy/polity antinomy. The states 'lock in' demand by stabilizing (within a certain range) historic expectations of allocation of income. The state-wide class struggles between capital and labor result in political compromises that generally last at least decades, if not more, and which determine approximate ranges of wage levels. While each struggle is state-wide, the role of the state in the world-economy is a major constraint on the kind of compromise reached.

At any given time, therefore, world-wide demand is 'fixed' – the vector of the multiple state-side outcomes of their internal class struggles. World supply meanwhile is steadily expanding, following the star of capital accumulation *per se*. The absence of effective interstate coordination – even today – has led historically to these 'crashes'. When a 'crash' occurs, world supply momentarily declines. But more importantly, it enables the state-wide political compromises to be reopened, leading over time (at least in some states) to a reallocation of income such that world demand once more exceeds world supply and the upward spiral of capital accumulation can safely resume its heady pace.

It is the combination of the workings of the economy/polity antinomy and that of supply/demand that gives the capital/labor antinomy its particular forms. For if it were simply a matter that a bourgeois obtains surplus value from the proletarian he employs, and that this were the only (or at least the 'ideal') form of surplus value extraction, we could not account for the fact that the pure bourgeois/proletarian social relation is a minority social relation throughout the whole history of the capitalist world-economy – even today, even in so-called 'advanced capitalist states'.

If it were true that surplus value is only created when a propertyless proletarian receives 'wages', why would it not have been the case that the capitalist system engendered nothing but this social relation? The classical answer is that there has been 'resistance' coming from 'feudal' (semifeudal, quasi-feudal) groups, a resistance that has been both un-'progressive' and irrational from the perspective of the social economy as a whole. But when an 'irrationality' lasts centuries, and seems to be sustained precisely by those groups who are said to be dominant politically (the bourgeoisie, or the capitalist classes), then we should at least investigate the possibility that our analysis is askew.

I contend that when a product is produced for exchange, and value is created greater than the socially necessary amount needed to reproduce the labor that created the product, there is surplus value, whatever the nature of the social relation at the work place. And whenever the actual producer has expropriated from him – via the market, the state, or direct coercion – a part of this surplus value, we have evidence of exploitation. It will be said that something like this happens in pre-capitalist systems. And it does, with one crucial difference: the exploitation is *not* maximized over time and space, because capital accumulation *per se* takes second place in these other systems to other socio-political considerations. The mark of a capitalist system is that it rewards accumulation *per se*, and tends to eliminate individuals or groups who resist its logic.

Having said this, we must now look to see what social relationship optimizes the expropriation of surplus value. It is often said that proletarian wage labor does this, because it creates a market (often specified as the 'home market') for the realization of profit. It does do this, but the direct producer as consumer of finished goods is only one part of the picture. The other part is the direct producer as participant in the division of the surplus value. This double role of the direct producer is the heart of the contradictions of the capitalist system. The bourgeois increases his potential profit as the part of the surplus value the direct producer receives approaches zero, except that the bourgeois risks not realizing his profit at all, unless world-wide demand remains high enough, a function in large part of widening the distribution of the surplus value.

Hence, the bourgeoisie as a 'world' class is pushed in two opposite directions simultaneously: towards dispensing the 'biologically' minimum wage,[12] and towards partial income reallocation (that is, higher wages). The collective response of the world bourgeoisie takes the form of a functional split. Most direct producers receive the 'biologically' minimum wage. Some receive more.

Here however we come to another contradiction. The world bourgeoisie is not a unity but an alliance of competing groups whose *individual* interests go against those of the collective. *Individually*, capitalist firms tend to maximise profits by increasing production. Hence over time, in order for the expanding production to find appropriate markets, an increasing number of direct producers must receive more than the 'biologically' minimum wage. But if this tendency goes too fast the bourgeoisie risks losing the rate of profit that is their *raison d'etre*.

Since we are still talking of the *continuities* of capitalism, we must look at how capitalists have handled these contradictions over time. The optimal way to arrange that a direct producer receive only the 'biological' minimum is to have him and his household produce it for their own account, while producing the 'surplus' without 'remuneration' (or with very little) for the legal account of a bourgeois, provided however that the bourgeois can adjust the quantity of production of surplus value to his immediate needs in terms of the world market. The ideal arrangement for this is one of the many varieties of so-called 'quasi-feudal' relations in which the cash-crop sector or industry is controlled by an enterprise.

A full-time, life-long proletarian wage laborer will always (at least over time) receive a larger part of the division of surplus value than a part-time, part-life-long proletarian (our so-called

12. I am aware that what seems to be 'biologically' minimum is itself a function of social definition. Yet behind this variation, there does lie a true bottom line.

quasi 'serf' or semiproletarian). Not only can full-time proletarians organize and defend class interests more effectively, but the supervision costs are high if the bourgeois wishes to obtain a work efficiency as high as that from the semiproletarian at the latter's rate of real income. Hence, proletarian wage labor is a *pis aller* from the individual capitalist's viewpoint. Nonetheless, collectively the bourgeoisie needs it, both for 'efficiency' of expanded production, and to provide an expanding market.

In short, the capitalist system requires proletarian wage labor to exist but as little as it can get away with. Its dilemma is that the supply/demand antimony regularly forces it to expand the size of the world-wide wage labor proletariat.

We have outlined the *continuities* of capitalism, in the *longue durée*. Our description of these continuities points up their contradictions and resulting cyclical rhythms. The ways in which these contradictions are regularly resolved may be summarized as the secular trends of capitalism. These trends are the opposite of continuities; they are the conjunctures of ongoing development and transformation of the system as a whole.

I will be briefer on the secular tendencies, and outline only four of them, each of which involves movements towards asymptotes, and hence temporally bounded, since one cannot expand the curves indefinitely.

(1) There is the process of *expansion* of the world-economy – the pushing of outer boundaries of the world-economy to the limits of the earth, the conquest of the 'subsistence redoubts' within. The dynamic of this expansion is located in the crises caused by the supply/demand antinomy. Each wave of expansion has revitalized demand. But the physical limits of such expansion are being approached today.

(2) There is the process of *proletarianization*, the conversion of 'quasi-feudal' semiproletarians into proletarian wage labor, determined by the joint workings of the supply/demand and capital/labor antinomies. The process of proletarianization saves short-run profits (expanded demand) at the expense of long-run profits (increased share of surplus-value to the direct producer). As long as expansion continues, proletarianization does not reduce the share of surplus value to the world bourgeoisie as the expanded amount of primary accumulation

is greater than the reallocated surplus value. But as the rate of expansion slows down, further proletarianization will cut into the global share of surplus value retained by the bourgeoisie.

(3) There is the *politicization* which accompanies the process of proletarianization and which takes the multiple forms of parties, workers' movements, national (and 'ethnic') liberation movements, etc. The picture is complex but the global impact is double. On the one hand, it creates a vast current of anti-systemic groups, including now organizations of the semi-proletariat, which are becoming too numerous simply to repress or coopt. There is a threshold of collective size that is being approached. On the other hand, to counter this growing trend, the upper strata must reinforce (and purchase the services of) their cadres - military, political, cultural.

(4) Thus, we come to the fourth trend, which I shall call the *janissarization* of the ruling classes. As the working classes grow more political, it enables the cadres of the bourgeoisie (the technicians, the professionals, the managers) themselves to impose their demands on the legal owners of economic firms. This means *de facto* a partial redivision of surplus value *within* the bourgeoisie, from the top strata to their cadres. Furthermore, since these cadres are disproportionately located in core states, this affects the politics of these states which become welfare-state oriented or social democratic. On the one hand, this redistribution is at the immediate expense of the top strata and not of the direct producers. On the other hand, this redistribution *presupposes* the continued expropriation of surplus value from the direct producers, and has not thus far diminished it in any significant way. This is the phenomenon of the expanding tertiary sector of the industrial states, breeding conspicuous content and political complacency based on indifference to the 'barbarians' of the periphery. The obverse of this however is a dispersion of political will on the part of the bourgeoisie, no longer able to act with deft and firm swiftness of purpose. As janissarization increases, the ability to resist or coopt the politicized world working classes diminishes.

Thus we come to our third temporality – that of the *kairos*, the 'right time', the moment of choice and transition. The fact is that we are already there – inside this third kind of time, which is not the time of a moment, but of an epoch.

The twentieth century has seen the steady growth of anti-systemic forces throughout the world. For every step backward (via regression or cooptation) there have been two steps forward. Any plausible measurement of the strength of anti-systemic forces will yield a linear upward curve. Beginning with the Russian Revolution in 1917, and greatly accelerating after 1945, one state after another has begun to claim it is on the road to socialism (or, indeed, already there). Since the collapse of the unity of the world communist movement, it is no longer easy to find a commonly accepted definition of what constitutes a socialist state, since many self-designated socialist regimes do not recognize the legitimacy of other self-designated ones.

These so-called socialist states are in fact socialist movements in power in states that are still part of a single capitalist world-economy – our familiar economy/policy antinomy. These 'socialist' states find themselves pressed by the structural exigencies of the world-economy to limit their internal social transformations. They are not therefore in fact socialist economies, though we may be willing to call them socialist polities. They are caught in the dilemmas not only of the supply/demand antinomy but of the capital/labor one as well.

Nonetheless, these regimes represent an important part of the anti-systemic forces, and their existence has altered the world alignment of power. It is said that in nineteenth-century France, there were two parties: the party of order and the party of movement. These were not organizations but broad structural thrusts. This language is even more appropriate as a description of the contemporary world-economy.

The secular trends of capitalism have accelerated the contradictions of the system. The result is that the world finds itself at the *kairos*.

The first contradiction is in the movements of popular sentiment. Nationalism and internationalism have served both as anti-systemic forces, and also as modes of participation in the system. The socialist party or national liberation movement in a semiperipheral or peripheral state may in riding the crest of nationalism serve as an expression of the party of movement; the same party or movement may aid other parties or movements in other countries in the name of international solidarity. But nationalism has also been a primary means of denying the class struggle, and internationalism has often been a figleaf for imperialism.

All this has become increasingly clear. The examples are by now numerous. And this very clarity itself creates a pressure on the anti-systemic regimes that works against the temptation of their cadres to join the party of order. The forces that push for movement are becoming more difficult to tame, perhaps too difficult to tame, even for revolutionaries with credentials. Thus, the party of movement is now more than the expression of the will of its leaders; it is the reflection of a structural thrust, itself the outcome of the successive conjunctures of the capitalist world-economy.

And, on the other side of the political battle, a second contradiction has become acute. The party of order is rent by an internal split which, far from healing, is steadily becoming wider. There are two organizational forces that have simultaneously grown stronger and more complex: the multinational corporations on the one hand, and the state machineries of the core states on the other. The relationship of these two forces has become an ambivalent one. On the one hand, they support each other constantly. On the other hand, their interests frequently diverge. The corporations exist to make profit, and hence are ready to make alliances with whatever groups they need to deal with in order to maximize these profits over the medium and long run. The state machineries must however necessarily respond primarily to the needs of its own citizens, especially in the core states. Insofar as the cadres everywhere are demanding a larger share of the pie, their collective interests stand opposed to that of the multinationals, whose major recourse has been, will continue to be, to play one set of national cadres off against another.

As long as the world-economy is expanding over all, this contradiction can be contained. But as we approach limits, the constraints imposed upon all economic actors may lead to increasingly acute conflict between regimes in (at least some) core states and the multinationals. As with the party of movement, so the party of order may now be more than the expression of the will of its leaders. But in this case, the structural pressures are towards fission, and therefore the weakening of the ability to stand up against the party of movement.

We may now return to our opening discussion on the new international order. The very discussion is part of the *kairos*. The language is Aesopian to cover over the struggle between the party of order and the party of movement. But the Aesopian language cannot last. It is an attempt to keep us all operating within the temporality of conjuncture, when an understanding of the temporality of the *longue durée* will make it clear that we are participating in the *kairos*. This attempt will not succeed.

Tillich ended his essay on the *kairos* with a question and an answer:

One question may still be raised, and we offer a brief answer to it: 'Is it possible that the message of the kairos is an error?'

The answer is not difficult to give. The message is always an error; for it sees something immediately imminent which, considered in its ideal aspect, will never become a reality and which, considered in its real aspect, will be fulfilled only in long periods of time. And yet the message of the kairos is never an error; for where the kairos is proclaimed as a prophetic message, it is already present; it is impossible for it to be proclaimed in power without its having grasped those who proclaim it.[13]

13. Tillich, 'Kairos', p. 51.

Concluding Essay

18 ✦ Class conflict in the capitalist world-economy

Social class was not a concept invented by Karl Marx. The Greeks knew it and it re-emerged in eighteenth-century European social thought, and in the writings that followed the French Revolution. Marx's contribution was three-fold. First, he argued that *all* history is the history of the class struggle. Secondly, he pointed to the fact that a class *an sich* was not necessarily a class *für sich*. Thirdly, he argued that the fundamental conflict of the capitalist mode of production was that between bourgeois and proletarian, between the owners and the non-owners of the means of production. (This is in contrast to the suggestion that the key antagonism is between a productive and non-productive sector, in which active owners were grouped with workers as productive persons as opposed to non-productive rentiers.)

As class analysis came to be used for revolutionary ends, non-revolutionary thinkers by and large put it aside, many if not most fervidly rejecting its legitimacy. Each of Marx's three major contentions on class has been subject to violent controversy ever since.

To the argument that class conflict was the fundamental form of group conflict, Weber responded by arguing that class was only one of three dimensions along which groups were formed, the other two being status and ideology, and that these three dimensions were more or less equal in relevance. Many of Weber's disciples went further and insisted that it was status group conflict that was primary or 'primordial'.

To the argument that classes existed *an sich* whether or not, at given points of time, they were *für sich*, various social psychologists insisted that the only meaningful construct was a so-called

283

'subjective' one. Individuals were members of only such classes as they considered themselves to be.

To the argument that the bourgeoisie and the proletariat were the two essential, polarized groups in the capitalist mode of production, many analysts responded by arguing that more than two 'classes' existed (citing Marx himself), and that 'polarization' was diminishing over time rather than increasing.

Each of these counterarguments to the Marxian premises had the effect, to the extent that they were accepted, of vitiating the political strategy derived from the original Marxist analysis. One riposte therefore has been to point to the ideological bases of these counterarguments, which of course was done many times. But since ideological distortions involve theoretical incorrectness, it is in fact in the long run more effective, both intellectually and politically, to concentrate on discussing the theoretical usefulness of the competing concepts.

In addition, the running assault on the Marxian premises about class and class conflict have combined with the realities of the world to create internal intellectual uncertainty in the Marxist camp, which has taken three forms over time: debate on the significance of the so-called 'national question'; debate on the role of specified social strata (particularly the 'peasantry' and the 'petty bour-geoisie' and/or the 'new working class'); debate on the utility of concepts of global spatial hierarchization ('core' and 'periphery') and the allied concept of 'unequal exchange'.

The 'national question' first began to plague Marxist (and socialist) movements in the nineteenth century, especially within the Austro-Hungarian and Russian empires. The 'peasant ques-tion' came to the fore between the two world wars with the Chinese Revolution. The dependent role of the 'periphery' became a central issue after the Second World War, in the wake of Bandung, decolonization, and 'Third Worldism'. These three 'questions' are in fact variants of a single theme: how to interpret the Marxian premises; what in fact are the bases of class formation and class consciousness in the capitalist world-economy as it has historically evolved; and how does one reconcile descriptions of the world in terms of these premises with the ongoing political definitions of the world by the participating groups.

I propose, in view of these historical debates, to discuss what the nature of the capitalist mode of production tells us about who in fact are bourgeois and proletarians, and what are the *political* consequences of the various ways both bourgeois and proletarians have fit into the capitalist division of labor.

What is capitalism as a mode of production? This is not an easy question, and for that reason is not in fact a widely discussed one. It seems to me that there are several elements that combine to constitute the 'model'. Capitalism is the *only* mode of production in which the *maximization* of surplus creation is rewarded *per se*. In every historical system, there has been *some* production for *use*, and *some* production for *exchange*, but only in capitalism are all producers rewarded primarily in terms of the exchange value they produce and penalized to the extent they neglect it. The 'rewards' and 'penalties' are mediated through a structure called the 'market'. It is a structure but not an institution. It is a structure molded by *many* institutions (political, economic, social, even cultural), and it is the principal arena of economic struggle.

Not only is surplus maximized for its own sake, but those who use the surplus to accumulate more capital to produce still more surplus are further rewarded. Thus the pressure is for constant expansion, although the individualistic premise of the system simultaneously renders *constant* expansion impossible.

How does the search for profit operate? It operates by creating legal protections for individual firms (which can range in size from individuals to quite large organizations, including parastatal agencies) to appropriate the surplus value created by the labor of the primary producers. Were all or most of this surplus value however consumed by the few who owned or controlled the 'firms', we would not have capitalism. This is in fact approximately what had happened in various pre-capitalist systems.

Capitalism involves in addition structures and institutions which reward primarily that subsegment of the owners and controllers who use the surplus value only *in part* for their own consumption, and in another (usually larger) part for further investment. The structure of the market ensures that those who do not accumulate capital (but merely consume surplus value) lose out economically over time to those who do accumulate capital.

We may thereupon designate as the bourgeoisie those who receive a part of the surplus value they do not themselves create and use some of it to accumulate capital. What defines the bourgeois is not a particular profession and not even the legal status of proprietor (although this was historically important) but the fact that the bourgeois obtains, either as an individual or a member of some collectivity, a part of the surplus that he did not create and is in the position to invest (again either individually or as part of a collectivity) some of this surplus in capital goods.

There is a very large gamut of organizational arrangements which can permit this, of which the classic model of the 'free entrepreneur' is only one. Which organizational arrangements prevail at particular moments of time in particular states (for these arrangements are dependent on the legal framework) is a function of the state of development of the world-economy as a whole (and the role of a particular state in that world-economy) on the one hand, and the consequent forms of class struggle in the world-economy (and within the particular state) on the other. Hence, like all other social constructs, the 'bourgeoisie' is not a static phenomenon. It is the designation of a class in the process of perpetual re-creation and hence of constant change of form and composition.

At one level, this is so obvious (at least given certain epistemological premises) that it is a truism. And yet the literature is cram packed with evaluations of whether or not some local group was or was not 'bourgeois' (or 'proletarian') in terms of a model organizational arrangement derived from some other place and time in the historical development of the capitalist world-economy. *There is no ideal type.* (Curiously enough, though the 'ideal type' is a Weberian methodological concept, many Weberians in practice realize this, and *per contra* many Marxists in fact constantly utilize 'ideal types'.

If we accept that there is no ideal type, then we cannot define (that is, abstract) in terms of attributes, but only in terms of processes. How does an individual become a bourgeois, remain a bourgeois, cease being a bourgeois? The basic way one becomes a bourgeois is achievement in the market. How one gets in a position to achieve initially is a subordinate question. The routes are various. There is the Horatio Alger model: differentiation out of the working classes by dint of extra effort. (This is remarkably similar to Marx's 'truly revolutionary' road from feudalism to capitalism.) There is the Oliver Twist model: cooption because of talent. There is the Horace Mann model: demonstration of potential via performance in formal education.

But the road to the diving board is minor. Most bourgeois become bourgeois by inheritance. The access to the swimming pool is unequal and sometimes capricious. But the crucial question is: can a given individual (or firm) swim? Being a bourgeois requires skills not everyone has: shrewdness, hardness, diligence. At any given time, a certain percentage of bourgeois fail in the market.

More importantly, however, there is a large group that succeed, many if not most of whom aspire to enjoy the rewards of their situation. One of the potential rewards is in fact not to have to compete as hard in the market. But since the market presumably originally provided the income, there is a structured pressure to find ways of maintaining income level without maintaining a corresponding level of work input. This is the effort – the social and political effort – to transform achievement into status. Status is nothing more than the fossilization of the rewards of past achievement.

The problem for the bourgeoisie is that the dynamic of capitalism is located in the economy and not in the political or cultural institutions. Therefore, there are always new bourgeois without status, laying claim to entry to status. And since high status is worthless if too many persons have it, the *nouveaux riches* (the new achievers) are always seeking to oust others to make room for themselves. The obvious target is that subsegment of the old achievers who are coasting on their acquired status but no longer perform in the market.

Ergo, at any one time, there are always three segments of the bourgeoisie: the 'nouveaux riches'; the 'coasters'; and the descendants of bourgeois who are still performing adequately in the market. To appreciate the relations of these three subgroups, we must bear in mind that almost always the third category is the largest one, and usually larger than the other two combined. This is the basic source of the relative stability and 'homogeneity' of the bourgeois class.

However, there are moments of time when the number of 'nouveaux riches' and 'coasters' as a percentage of the bourgeoisie rises. I think these are usually moments of economic contraction which see both rising bankruptcies and increasing concentration of capital.

At such moments, it has usually been the case that a political quarrel *internal to the bourgeoisie* becomes quite acute. It is often defined terminologically as the fight of 'progressive' elements versus 'reactionary' ones, in which the 'progressive' groups demand that institutional 'rights' and access be defined or redefined in terms of performance in the market ('equality of opportunity'), and 'reactionary' groups lay emphasis on the maintenance of previously acquired privilege (so-called 'tradition'). I think the English Revolution is a very clear instance of this kind of intrabourgeois conflict.

What makes the analysis of such political struggles so open to contention and the real outcome so often ambiguous (and essentially 'conservative') is the fact that the largest segment of the bourgeoisie (even during the conflict) have claims to privilege both in 'class' terms and in 'status' terms. That is, as individuals and subgroups they do not stand to lose automatically, whichever of the two definitions prevail. Typically, therefore, they are politically indecisive or oscillating and seek after 'compromises'. And if they cannot immediately achieve these compromises because of the passions of the other sub-groups, they bide their time until the moment is ripe. (Hence 1688–9 in the case of England.)

While an analysis of such intrabourgeois conflicts in terms of the rhetoric of the contending groups would be misleading, I am not suggesting that such conflicts are unimportant or irrelevant to the ongoing processes of the capitalist world-economy.

Such intrabourgeois conflicts are precisely part of the recurring 'shake-downs' of the system which economic contractions force, part of the mechanism of renewing and revitalizing the essential motor of the system, the accumulation of capital. Such conflicts purge the system of a certain number of useless parasites, bring socio-political structures into closer consonance with the changing economic networks of activity, and provide an ideological veneer to ongoing structural change. If one wants to call this 'progress', one may. I myself would prefer to reserve the term for more basic kinds of social transformations.

These other social transformations of which I speak are not the consequence of the evolving character of the bourgeoisie but of the evolving character of the proletariat. If we have defined the bourgeoisie as those who receive surplus value they do not themselves create and use some of it to accumulate capital, it follows that the proletariat are those who yield part of the value they have created to others. In this sense there exists in the capitalist mode of production only bourgeois and proletarians. The polarity is structural.

Let us be quite clear what this approach to the concept of proletarian does. It eliminates as a *defining* characteristic of the proletarian the payment of *wages* to the producer. It starts instead from another perspective. The producer creates value. What happens to this value? There are three logical possibilities. He 'owns' (and therefore keeps) *all* of it, *part* of it, or *none* of it. If he does not keep all of it, but therefore 'transfers' some or all of it to someone else (or to some 'firm'), he receives in return either nothing, goods, money, or goods plus money.

If the producer truly keeps *all* the value produced by him over his life-time, he is not participating in the capitalist system. But such a producer is a far rarer phenomenon within the boundaries of the capitalist world-economy than we commonly admit. The so-called 'subsistence farmer' quite frequently turns out on closer inspection in fact to be transferring surplus value to someone by some means.

If we eliminate this group, the other logical possibilities form a matrix of eight varieties of proletarians, only one of which meets the classic model: the worker who transfers all the value he has created to the 'owner' and receives in return money (i.e., wages). In other boxes of the matrix, we can place such familiar types as petty producer (or 'middle peasant'), tenant farmer, share-cropper, peon, slave.

Of course there is another dimension which is part of the definition of each of the 'types'. There is the question of the degree to which performing the role in a particular fashion is accepted by the worker under the pressures of the market (which we cynically call 'free' labor) or because of the exigencies of some political machinery (which we more frankly call 'forced' or 'coerced' labor). A further issue is the length of the contract – by the day, the week, the year, or for life. A third issue is whether the producer's relationship to a given owner could be transferred to another owner without the producer's assent.

The degree of constraint and the length of contract cross-cut the mode of payment. For example, the *mita* in seventeenth-century Peru was wage labor that was forced but of specified duration. Indentured labor was a form of labor in which the producer transferred all the value created, receiving in return largely goods. It was of limited duration. The peon transferred all value, received in theory money but in practice goods, and the contract was in theory annual but in practice lifetime. The difference between a peon and a slave was in the 'theory' to be sure, but in two respects in the practice. First, a landlord could 'sell' a slave but not usually a peon. Secondly, if an outsider gave money to a peon, he was legally able to terminate his 'contract'. This was not true for a slave.

I have not constructed a morphology for its own sake but to clarify some *processes* of the capitalist world-economy. There are great *differences* between the various forms of labor in terms of their economic *and* political implications.

Economically, I think it can be said that for all labor processes that can be simply supervised (that is, at minimal cost), wage labor is probably the most highly paid of the forms of labor. And therefore wherever possible, the receiver of surplus value would prefer not to relate to the producer as a wage earner but as something else. To be sure, labor processes that require more costly supervision are less costly if *some* of the surplus that would otherwise be spent on supervisory costs is turned back to the producer. The easiest way to do this is via wages and this is the historic (and ongoing) source of the wage system.

Since wages are a relatively *costly* mode of labor from the point of view of the bourgeoisie, it is easy to understand why wage labor has *never* been the exclusive, and until relatively recently not even the principal, form of labor in the capitalist world-economy.

However, capitalism has its contradictions. One basic one is that what is profitable in the short run is not necessarily what is profitable in the long run. The ability of the system as a whole to expand (necessary to maintain the rate of profit) regularly runs into the bottleneck of inadequate world demand. One of the ways this is overcome is by the social transformation of some productive processes from non-wage labor to wage labor processes. This tends to increase the portion of produced value the producer keeps and thereby to increase world demand. As a result, the overall world-wide *percentage* of wage labor as a form of labor has been steadily increasing throughout the history of the capitalist world-economy. This is what is referred to usually as 'proletarianization'.

The form of labor also makes a great difference politically. For it can be argued that as real income of the producer rises, and as formal legal rights expand, it follows consequently *up to a point* that proletarian class consciousness expands. I say up to a point, because at a certain level of expansion of income and 'rights', the 'proletarian' becomes in reality a 'bourgeois', *living off the surplus value of others*, and the most immediate effect of this is on class consciousness. The twentieth-century bureaucrat/professional is a clear instance of this qualitative shift, which is in fact sometimes visible in the life patterns of particular cohorts.

Even if this way of approaching the categories 'bourgeois' and 'proletarian' speaks clearly to the role of 'peasants' or 'petty bourgeois' or 'new working class', what, one may ask, is its relevance for the 'national' question and for the concepts of 'core' and 'periphery'.

To speak to this, we have to look at a currently popular question, the role of the state in capitalism. The fundamental role of the state as an institution in the capitalist world-economy is to augment the advantage of some against others in the market – that is, to *reduce* the 'freedom' of the market. Everyone is in favor of this, as long as one is the beneficiary of the 'distortion', and everyone opposed to the extent that one loses. It is all a matter of whose ox is being gored.

The modes of augmenting advantage are many. The state can transfer income by taking it from some and giving it to others. The state can restrict access to the market (of commodities or of labor) which favor those who thereby share in the oligopoly or oligopsony. The state can restrain persons from organizing to change the actions of the state. And, of course, the state can act not only within its jurisdiction but beyond it. This may be licit (the rules concerning transit over boundaries) or illicit (interference in the internal affairs of another state). Warfare is of course one of the mechanisms used.

What is crucial to perceive is that the state is a special kind of organization. Its 'sovereignty', a notion of the modern world, is the claim to the monopolization (regulation) of the legitimate use of force within its boundaries, and it is in a relatively strong position to interfere effectively with the flow of factors of production. Obviously also it is possible for particular social groups to alter advantage by altering state boundaries; hence both movements for secession (or autonomy) and movements for annexation (or federation).

It is this realistic ability of states to interfere with the flow of factors of production that provides the political underpinnings of the structural division of labor in the capitalist world-economy as a whole. Normal market considerations may account for recurring initial thrusts to specialization (natural or socio-historical advantages in the production of one or another commodity), but it is the state system which encrusts, enforces, and exaggerates the patterns, and it has regularly required the use of state machinery to revise the pattern of the world-wide division of labor.

Furthermore, the ability of states to interfere with flows becomes differentiated. That is, core states become *stronger* than peripheral states, and use this differential power to maintain a differential degree of interstate freedom of flow. Specifically, core states have historically arranged that world-wide and over time, money and goods have flowed more 'freely' than labor. The reason for doing this is that core states have thereby received the advantages of 'unequal exchange'.

In effect, unequal exchange is simply a part of the world-wide process of the appropriation of surplus. We analyze falsely if we try to take literally the model of *one* proletarian relating to *one* bourgeois. In fact, the surplus value that the producer creates passes through a series of persons and firms. It is therefore the case that *many* bourgeois *share* the surplus value of *one* proletarian. The exact share of different groups in the chain (property owner, merchants, intermediate consumers) is subject to much historical change and is itself a principal analytical variable in the functioning of the capitalist world-economy.

This chain of the transfer of surplus value frequently (often? almost always?) traverses national boundaries and, when it does, state operations intervene to tilt the sharing among bourgeois towards those bourgeois located in core states. This is unequal exchange, a mechanism in the overall process of the appropriation of surplus value.

One of the socio-geographic consequences of this system is the uneven distribution of the bourgeoisie and proletariat in different states, core states containing a higher percentage nationally of bourgeois than peripheral states. In addition, there are systematic differences in *kinds* of bourgeois and proletarians located in the two zones. For example, the percentage of wage-earning proletarians is systematically higher in core states.

Since states are the primary arena of political conflict in a capitalist world-economy, and since the functioning of the world-economy is such that national class composition varies widely, it is easy to perceive why the politics of states differentially located in relation to the world-economy should be so dissimilar. It is also then easy to perceive that using the political machinery of a given state to change the social composition and world-economic function of national production does not *per se* change the capitalist world-system as such.

Obviously, however, these various national thrusts to a change in structural position (which we misleadingly often call 'development') do in fact affect, indeed over the long run do in fact transform, the world-system. But they do so via the intervening variable of their impact on world-wide class consciousness of the proletariat.

Core and periphery then are simply phrases to locate one crucial part of the system of surplus appropriation by the bourgeoisie. To oversimplify, capitalism is a system in which the surplus value of the proletarian is appropriated by the bourgeois. When this proletarian is located in a different country from this bourgeois, one of the mechanisms that has affected the process of appropriation is the manipulation of controlling flows over state boundaries. This results in patterns of 'uneven development' which are *summarized* in the concepts of core, semiperiphery, and periphery. This is an intellectual tool to help analyze the multiple forms of class conflict in the capitalist world-economy.

Index

Abdel-Malek, A., 89–90
Abrams, P., 7n
administrators, in world-empires, 156–7, 158–9
Africa: absorbed into periphery of world-economy (19th cent.), 27–8, with abolition of slave trade, 28–9, 216; class and status groups in, 177–9, 193–5, 199–200; decolonization of, 31–2; 'hard core' poor countries in, 75; in present economic contraction, 67; 'scramble' for, 30; social groups in, 166–7, (precolonial) 167–8, (colonial period) 168, (after independence) 168–73
African Unity, Organization of, 117
agriculture: capitalist, in 16th cent., (core countries) 38, 45–6, 85–6, 197, (peripheral countries) 38, 40, 41, 197, (semiperipheral countries) 38; continuing world-wide capitalization of, 62; mechanized, 187
Akiwowo, A. A., 173
Algeria, 106, 174, 250; as semiperipheral country, 100, 247; war of national liberation in, 64, 154, 260
Allen, V. L., 176
Amin, Samir, 53, 71n, 74n, 80–1, 83, 87n, 142n, 148, 195n
Amsterdam, 40, 43, 48
Anderson, Perry, 146n
Angola, war of national liberation in, 64, 263
anti-trust legislation, 80
Antwerp, merchants of (16th cent.), 45
Argentina, 107, 228n–229n; as semiperipheral country, 100
aristocracy, a social group but not a class, 198
Aron, R., 15
Arrighi, G., 176n
Asia: absorbed into periphery of world-economy (19th cent.), 27; decolonization of southern, 31–2
Australia, 86, 128; as semiperipheral country, 100
autarky, 74n; during reordering of socialist countries, 108

Balandier, G., 168n
Baran, P., 78n, 146
Barbé, R., 193n
barter trading, by socialist countries, 108, 113
Bauer, P. T., 144n
Belgium, 83
Bettelheim, C., 19
Boahen, A. A., 28n
Bodenheimer, S., 66n
Bolivia, 9n
bourgeoisie: class consciousness of, 226; conflicts within, 287–8; contradictions in, 277; in core countries, 30, 38, 293; definition of, 285–6; Fanon's use of term, 258–9; labor aristocracy in alliance with, 266; methods of joining (often by inheritance), 286–7; not a static phenomenon, 286; in peripheral countries, 21, 40, 41, 78, 197, 198–9; petty-, 255, 266; v. proletariat, 162; redistribution of surplus value within, 279; in semiperipheral countries, 102, 103–5
Braudel, F., 2–3, 37, 72, 148, 269–70
Brazil, 33, 74n, 77, 79, 81; as semiperipheral country, 75, 87, 100, 247; slave trade of, 216
Brenner, T. S., 143n
bureaucracies: in core countries, 20, 26, 38–9; in independent African countries, 178; in socialist countries, 112n; see also state machineries
bureaucratization (expansion of state machinery, rise of state capitalism), 63, 274; never at level of political decision-making of a state structure, 226–7
Burma, 57
Burundi, 167n, 171
Busia, K. A., 168n

Cabral, A., 200, 229n
Cameroun, 171, 172
Canada, 84, 86, 117; Quebec separatists in, 59, 188, 230; as semiperipheral country, 100, 247; other references, 56, 76, 128
capital: accumulation of, under capitalism, 134, 276, 285; flows to high profit areas,